HARRIET BEECHER STOWE

Books by Edward Wagenknecht
Published by Oxford University Press

NATHANIEL HAWTHORNE: Man and Writer (1961)
WASHINGTON IRVING: Moderation Displayed (1962)
EDGAR ALLAN POE: The Man Behind the Legend (1963)
HARRIET BEECHER STOWE: The Known and the Unknown (1965)

CHAUCER: Modern Essays in Criticism (1959)
edited by Edward Wagenknecht

HARRIET BEECHER STOWE

The Known and the Unknown

EDWARD WAGENKNECHT

It is difficult for a poet not to paint himself while
he thinks he is describing only the creatures of
his imagination.... We rise from *Don Quixote*
as well acquainted with Cervantes as with the
knight of the rueful countenance. This is particularly the case with Mrs. Stowe.
    Nassau W. Senior, *Essays on Fiction* (1864)

NEW YORK OXFORD UNIVERSITY PRESS 1965

For NORAH LOFTS
whose novels have given me great pleasure,
and in whose friendship is true appreciation
and understanding

CONTENTS

HARRIET BEECHER STOWE

INTRODUCTION

I

Sometime in the 1930's I suggested to a distinguished publisher of limited editions that he bring out an *Uncle Tom's Cabin*. "If you will do so," I said, "I will write you an introduction in which I will call it the greatest American novel." Horrified by the idea of adding such a cheap book to his exclusive list, my friend replied that if I were willing to make such a statement, he would be willing to publish the book. This gave me an opportunity I could not resist, whereupon I took up the position that his letter had constituted a contract and that he was legally obligated to proceed with the work, and I think he had some uncomfortable moments before he discovered that I was joking. Some years later he did bring out an edition of *Uncle Tom's Cabin*, though not with an introduction by me. When I asked him how this could have come about, his attitude toward the book being what it was, he replied, "I just wanted you to know that there are still some people in the world who are capable of learning something."

This seems to me typical of the improvement in Uncle Tom's— and Mrs. Stowe's—literary reputation during our time. In 1933 it was still safe for Stark Young to speak of *Uncle Tom's Cabin* as "mere period trash." [1] Today, after Van Wyck Brooks, Edmund Wilson, Charles H. Foster, John R. Adams, Kenneth S. Lynn, and others, such a judgment would be laughed at.

Not, of course, that nobody ever appreciated *Uncle Tom's Cabin* until recent years. Anticipating some of its recent admirers, *The Nation* nominated it as the great American novel as far back as 1868—"a picture of American life, national in scope, recognizable and valid." In the 'eighties, J. W. DeForest, who, neglected as he has always been, was still surely a writer of whose praise any other writer might be proud, put Mrs. Stowe "at the head of all living novelists, especially in the characteristics of power and sincerity, both of feeling and style." In 1910 John Erskine included a generous and perceptive evaluation of her work in general in his *Leading American Novelists*. And in 1935 Lennox Bouton Grey, in a magnificent University of Chicago dissertation, "Chicago and 'The Great American Novel,'" spoke of *Uncle Tom's Cabin* as

the book which, in spite of conventional condescension of latter day critics, not only amply defines Southern, Border States, and Yankee morality, but offers the most comprehensive serious view of America and types of Americans before Mark Twain, and most clearly measures the relative maturity of American literary perception at the middle of the century.

Moreover, if there was appreciation in those days, there is also still, unfortunately, condescension in ours, even if it does not now generally proceed from very disinterested or well-informed persons. In 1956 we had a somewhat shrill book called *Goodbye to Uncle Tom*,[2] in which Mr. J. C. Furnas never did quite get round to explaining what he was angry about. His principal complaint seemed to be that in 1852 Mrs. Stowe did not have quite all the information about race that was available a hundred years later, and that consequently she unwittingly helped to perpetuate certain racial stereotypes. "The devil could have forged no shrewder weapon for the Negro's worst enemy." But Mr. Furnas also seemed disturbed because Harriet believed

that the "African race" had a special, glorious talent for Christianity. Tom survives each ordeal with his loving charity intact. His and Eva's comradeship in devoutness, which is usually taken to be mere Victorian lacework, actually symbolizes the intimacy of fellowship in Christ that, on the other side of the grave, assuages such mundane trials as innate racial differences.

Why that should be insulting I have no idea, especially since Mr. Furnas admits that racial differences do exist, that "present-day Negro distaste for . . . [Uncle Tom] means only current lack of sympathy with Christian values," and that Mrs. Stowe's Christianity "is the best thing about *Uncle Tom*" because "this field was really familiar to her."

Actually, an astonishing range of Negro life and character is portrayed in *Uncle Tom's Cabin*, as both Kenneth Lynn and Leslie Fiedler [3] have shown, and though, among its Negroes, there are some stereotypes, many embody the results of effects of slave life with a merciless realism which gives the lie to those who take up the position that Harriet did not know enough about slavery to be able to write about it. She knew just enough for a creative writer and not too much, which is to say that her knowledge set her imagination and intuition to work but did not inhibit their operation.

The best and most intelligent opinion of today concerning *Uncle Tom's Cabin* may be savored in Professor Lynn's introduction to the "John Harvard Library" reprint published in 1962 by the Belknap Press of Harvard University Press.

Those critics who label *Uncle Tom's Cabin* good propaganda but bad art simply cannot have given sufficient time to the novel to meet its inhabitants. If they should ever linger over it long enough to take in the shrewdness, the energy, the truly Balzacian variousness of Mrs. Stowe's characterizations, they would surely cease to perpetuate one of the most injust clichés in all of American criticism.

Lynn even dares to say that "for all its insight into the slave's emotions, Melville's 'Benito Cereno' (1856) spins a far less complex psychological web than does *Uncle Tom's Cabin*" and to find Topsy, "the diabolically amusing child of slavery, whose every perversity incarnates the guilty conscience of her adult owners, . . . a veritable black Pearl," worthy of the author of *The Scarlet Letter*. As of 1962, these are brave words.

Quite as interesting as the words themselves is the reception they were accorded. Reviewing Professor Lynn's edition of *Uncle Tom's Cabin* in the *New Statesman*,[4] Don Jacobson was "not sure whether we can learn more from the book's faults than from its merits," but he was sure "that we can learn something from our own misguided insistence, over these last many years, that the book has no merit at all." Even Mrs. Stowe's disregard of everything now currently fashionable in fiction—"points of view," "unity of action," "impersonality," etc.—made him realize "just how much our idea of what a novel is capable of doing has dwindled over the last century." Finally, that no concession whatever might be made to the "moderns," Mr. Jacobson concludes that "Mrs. Stowe's rhetoric does not seem ... really very much more objectionable than William Faulkner's, say; and it has the advantage over much of Faulkner's in being comprehensible." Meanwhile, Rosalie Packard was writing in the *Spectator* [5] that "the trouble with *Uncle Tom's Cabin* is that it's a good book." She wanted to give it to children at sixteen or eighteen.

Let them wonder at the energy and goodness of Mrs. Stowe. Let them discover that Uncle Tom was not the cringing hypocrite that his name has come in the realms of cliché to personify. ... Let them admire the extraordinary fair-mindedness and clear vision of Mrs. Stowe, who saw so well all sides of the question.

Jacobson's mention of Faulkner is interesting, the more so since it recurs in virtually every critic who has written about Mrs. Stowe during recent years. Of course she was not only the author of *Uncle Tom's Cabin*. No one has ever questioned her pre-eminence among fictional authorities on New England Puritanism, and her importance as a local colorist was gratefully acknowledged by such distinguished successors as Sarah Orne Jewett and Mary E. Wilkins Freeman. But though the passing of the Fugitive Slave Law triggered the forces that produced it, even *Uncle Tom's Cabin* is not exactly a "slavery novel." Harriet herself declared: "This story is to show how Jesus Christ, who liveth and was dead, and now is alive forevermore, has still a mother's love for the poor and lowly, and that no man can sink so low but that Jesus Christ will stoop to take his hand." She also recorded that she never realized what slave mothers feel when their children are torn away from them until after she herself had lost a child. In other words, the "peculiar institution" is not the essential theme of the novel but merely provides a theater for the working out of subjects of universal interest. Without this it would be difficult to understand why, though the "peculiar institution" is gone, the novel which helped to destroy it lives on. Of course there are elements of sentimentalism in *Uncle Tom's Cabin,* and of course I never seriously intended to call it the greatest of American novels. It came out of a sentimental age. But the real sentimentalists were the writers like Thomas Nelson Page and his school who later looked back upon the old South through a nostalgic haze. Harriet Beecher Stowe's affinity was never with them. Among her younger contemporaries she foreshadowed George W. Cable and Mark Twain; her later descendants are the realistic Southern writers of today, many of whose specific attitudes she would, no doubt, have abhorred.

II

Uncle Tom's Cabin was her passport to immortality, but, like all highly controversial works, it obscured as much as it illuminated. This book of mine is not about *Uncle Tom's Cabin;* it is a psychograph, or "portrait," or character study of its author. But the misapprehensions which have existed concerning her have easily equaled those which have clouded the fame of her book.

If Harriet Beecher Stowe appears a somewhat different—and certainly a vastly more complicated—figure in these pages than the familiar stereotype, the reason is not that the present writer claims to be a better biographer than all of his predecessors. But he has had access to a vastly wider and more varied array of unpublished letters than any of them ever saw.

My greatest obligation, by far, is to the incomparable collection of Stowe papers which the late Lyman Beecher Stowe presented to the Women's Archives at Radcliffe College. I am indebted to the director of the Archives, Dr. Barbara M. (Mrs. Peter H.) Solomon and her helpful staff for their courtesy in making these materials available to me, and I owe more than I can say to Mrs. Stowe's great-grandson, David B. Stowe, who, in behalf of his family, gave me unlimited permission to quote from any and all Stowe family papers which I should anywhere find relevant, without reading or seeking to read a line that I had written.

I have also drawn upon the resources of, or received courtesies from, the American Philosophical Society, Amherst College, Boston Public Library, Bowdoin College Library, Brown University, Buffalo and Erie County Public Library, University of California at Berkeley and at Los Angeles, Chicago Historical Society, the Cincinnati Historical Society, the College of William and Mary, the Colorado College, Columbia University, the Connecticut Historical Society, the Connecticut State Library, Cornell University Library, Dartmouth College, the Edward Laurence Doheny Memorial Library at St. John's Seminary, Duke University Library, Friends Historical Library at Swarthmore College, Georgetown University Libraries, Haverford College Library, the Rutherford B. Hayes Library, the Historical Society of Pennsylvania, the Houghton Library at Harvard University, Houghton Mifflin Company, Illinois College Library, Illinois State Historical Library, University of Kentucky Libraries, the Library of Congress, Massachusetts Historical Society, Mills College, the Pierpont Morgan Library, the New York Public Library (both the Henry W. and Albert A. Berg Collection and the Manuscript Division), Northwestern University, the Pennsylvania State University, Phillips Academy, Princeton University, the Rosenberg Library of Galveston, the State Historical Society of Wisconsin, the Stockbridge Library Association, the University of Minnesota, University of Pennsylvania, the University of the State of New York, University of Virginia Library, Vassar College, and Yale University Library.

Some of these institutions (such as the Rutherford B. Hayes Library, the New York Public Library, and the Library of Congress) have large and important collections, while others have only a few, or even single, letters; but I am grateful to all.

Institutions outside the Boston area have co-operated by sending microfilms and photostats, and some of these have been secured for me by the Boston University Libraries, whose director, Dr. G. A. Harrer, and reference librarian, Dr. Howard B. Gotlieb, have taken great pains in my behalf.

Where so many have been kind there is a certain awkwardness in singling out a particular institution for special praise, but I cannot fail to express my appreciation of the special service I received at the University of Virginia, where the extensive Stowe holdings in the Clifton Waller Barrett Library are a recent acquisition and had not yet been catalogued when I inquired about them; in listing them and making them available for my use, Miss Anne Freudenberg and Miss Elizabeth Ryall went far beyond the call of duty and manifested the kind of generosity whose discovery is one of the high rewards of scholarly work. Mr. Barrett, too, has been generosity itself in extending permission to quote.

I also desire to express my thanks for courtesy and hospitality to that scholar's paradise, the American Antiquarian Society, whose marvelous holdings in the older American printed matter must make every worker in the field feel that he has not lived until he has visited them.

My friend Professor John R. Adams, of San Diego State College, author of the *Harriet Beecher Stowe* volume in Twayne's "United States Authors Series," has kindly given my pages a critical reading.

The proverbial dog in the manger I encountered, oddly enough, only at the Stowe, Beecher, Hooker, Seymour, Day Foundation in Hartford, where I was refused permission to quote from unpublished letters on the ground that the Foundation might someday wish to publish them. Since the Foundation obviously has the right to make its own rules concerning the use of Foundation holdings, this fact is recorded without comment; by the same token, my right is clear to explain why I might otherwise seem to have overlooked an important collection.

It is not required of an author to summarize or anticipate the conclusions of his book in an introduction, but I might perhaps say that my view of Harriet Beecher Stowe differs from the popular image in at least one important respect. I regard her first of all as a daughter, a sister, a wife, and a mother. The familial relationships came first in her life, and the next most important thing was her art. Keen as her social consciousness was, her services as public servant and reformer come in a bad third. She was a natural-born storyteller; she could no more have avoided writing fiction than she could have stopped her breath. If she did much for the antislavery cause, the antislavery cause did much more for her, and she was never in the slightest danger of sacrificing her career to it. Her interest in "causes" she always kept in due proportion to life as a whole; despite her occasional extreme statements, she had a deep-seated bias in the direction of meliorism.

Where, it may be asked, does this leave Harriet as a religionist? Did not Forrest Wilson speak of her as "one of the most consistently Christ-minded women America ever produced"? It is true that Mrs. Stowe lived more steadily in the light of Eternity than most people do, but she never ceased to be aware of the difficulties involved in the attempt to embrace another world while we inhabit this one. In many ways she was a charmingly worldly woman. And she thought of God and of man's relation to God so consistently in terms of family relationships that however the importance of her religion be assessed, I can hardly think of it as upsetting the general evaluation of her interests which I have tried to state.

I do not mean, of course, that she will never strike the reader as "quaint"; that could be said of few nineteenth-century figures. Nobody should begrudge us the pleasure we derive from contemplating the eccentricities of our ancestors; our own will amuse our descendants soon enough. Harriet Beecher Stowe had plenty of faults and foibles. But I think the attentive reader will be more impressed by the depth of her understanding and the breadth of her sympathies than he can possibly be amused by her idiosyncrasies, and it may even be that the knowledge of her faults will bring her closer to him, and endear her, and strengthen his fellow feeling for her. Surely her courageous rejection of the barbarous theology on which she was reared, her amazing lack of prudery, her ability to face the human condition without blinking, and her unwavering fidelity to the crushing obligations that were laid upon her during her long lifetime are still worthy of appreciation.

A great many of Mrs. Stowe's words included in this volume have never appeared in print before, and I must add a word as to how I have handled them. Her carelessness as a writer has been much exaggerated. She was a good speller, and she had a sound feeling for the English sentence. But she was, as we say, allergic to all marks of punctuation except the dash. I have accordingly supplied missing periods, and I have supplied commas and, very occasionally, other marks of punctuation also where I thought they would assist the reader. I have also replaced her innumerable ampersands by the word "and."

Throughout the book I have italicized all titles of books, even in quoted matter in which they were not italicized.

Finally, there are my references to Mrs. Stowe herself. When one is writing of a man one can call him "Hawthorne" or "Poe" and be done with it. Women, as is their way in the world, at least where men are concerned, create problems. I cannot write "Stowe." "Harriet Beecher Stowe" is too cumbersome to repeat on every page, and "Mrs. Stowe" would, on the same basis, strike me as a little stuffy. I have employed both these forms on occasion, but I generally call my heroine "Harriet." This is purely a matter of convenience, and I intend no condescension.

BIOGRAPHY

Harriet Beecher Stowe lived the first forty-one years of her life in poverty and obscurity, then, suddenly, through the publication of *Uncle Tom's Cabin*, became the most famous woman in America, and, shortly, a world celebrity. Born in Litchfield, Connecticut, June 13, 1811, she was the seventh of the nine children (they had lost one) of one of the leading clergymen of the time, Lyman Beecher, and his first wife, the remarkable Roxana Foote. The Beechers had been in America since 1637. Lyman's mother was of Scottish descent. His father, grandfather, and great-grandfather were all blacksmiths, and his father, David, was locally celebrated for his learning.

Roxana died in 1816, and the next year Lyman married Harriet Porter, of Portland, by whom he had four more children. She died in 1835. Lyman had no children by his third wife, Lydia Jackson, whom he married in 1836.

Except for the shock of her mother's death, Harriet in her own writings gives the impression of a generally happy childhood, though it is clear that, like her fictional image, Dolly of *Poganuc People*, she was dominated in the family circle by her older brothers and sisters. When she was five, she went, hand-in-hand with her adored little brother, Henry Ward, to a dame school. At ten or eleven she was sent to Litchfield Academy. In 1824 she moved to Hartford, where she studied, and assisted her sister Catharine as student-teacher, at Hartford Female Seminary, on whose staff she became a full-time teacher in 1829.

The teaching continued at Cincinnati, whither the Beechers removed in 1832, when Lyman became president of the new Lane Theological Seminary. Here she remained until 1850, and the years, which were full of paradoxes and surprises, were crucial in her development. The seminary fell upon evil days when Lyman found himself unable to take up so advanced a stand upon the slavery issue as some of his students demanded, and a large group of them withdrew, under the troublesome and dynamic leadership of Theodore Weld, to become the nucleus of Oberlin. If this was a strange approach to the great moral-religious conflict of the time for the girl who was to become the author of the greatest and most influential of all anti-slavery manifestoes, the matter at least had been emphatically thrust upon her attention, and she had accumulated materials of which she was to make good use.

She felt herself worked to death in Cincinnati, as indeed she was. She was never to be anything else, though in later years celebrity and large rewards and the stimulus of appreciation and achievement relieved the strain. She began writing for the *Western Monthly Magazine,* the *New-York Evangelist,* and other media, and she contributed to a *First Geography for Children* (1833), produced in collaboration with her sister Catharine, which was a success from the first. In 1843 she published her first book of fiction—*The Mayflower: Sketches and Scenes and Characters among the Descendants of the Puritans.*

The way was no easier for her after, on January 6, 1836, she became the second wife of a young widower, Calvin E. Stowe, a professor in the seminary and ultimately a distinguished Biblical scholar, for Calvin, as she was later to remark, was rich in learning but in nothing else; he was also almost fantastically unequipped in all mechanical and domestic competencies. The marriage produced seven children, of whom all except the last were born in Cincinnati. Before Harriet got out of the place she was to live through race riots and a cholera epidemic and bury one of the children all by herself, her husband being away from home at the time.

Return to New England was achieved in 1850, when Bowdoin College called Calvin to a professorship. It was at Brunswick that Harriet wrote *Uncle Tom's Cabin* and made herself famous, but the Stowes lived there only two years, after which Calvin joined the faculty of the Theological Seminary at Andover, their home until he retired in 1864 and they moved to Hartford. Between 1868 and 1884 they spent their winters at Mandarin, Florida; after that Calvin was no longer well enough to make the trip. His wife nursed him devotedly until his death, at Hartford, on August 6, 1886, and she herself remained a Hartford fixture for the rest of her life.

She had toured Europe triumphantly in 1853, 1856, and 1859, and she lost, besides her husband, her son Henry, drowned while a student at Dartmouth in 1857, her son Frederick, who, after a valiant but vain attempt to rehabilitate himself following his Civil War experiences, went to San Francisco in 1870 and disappeared there, and, much later, when she was too old to feel the full force of her loss, her daughter Georgiana. But the accusation of adultery brought against her favorite brother Henry Ward, "the greatest preacher since St. Paul," in the 'seventies, probably hurt her as deeply as any of these losses, for the result was one of the most sensational of all American scandals, involving both ecclesiastical and civil trials and entailing incalculable strain and grief.

In the 'seventies too came the most amazing adventure of Harriet's later years, her career as a public reader from her own works. Though she had never engaged in any form of public speaking before, she took to this enterprise with an ease which suggests native powers that might well have been further developed.

As a reader [reported the Pittsburgh *Gazette*], Mrs. Stowe displayed no special elocutionary powers. Her performance could hardly be called a reading—it was recitative and she seldom glanced at the book.

Her voice betrayed decidedly the veritable Yankee twang, which made her rendition of the Yankee character much more effective than were the descriptions and dialogues from Uncle Tom. Her voice is low, just tinged in the slightest with huskiness, but is quite musical. In manner she was vivacious and gave life to many of the passages, more by suggestive action than by utterances. . . . She seemed perfectly possessed on the stage, and read with an easy grace that indicated either careful training or a thorough appreciation of what she read.

What was more, she bloomed under a regime that might well have been expected to kill her.

So far [she wrote her daughters, on November 9, 1872], my health has been better than any autumn for several years. The fatigue of speaking is nothing—the general fatigue of excitement &c lessens as I get accustomed to it and the fatigue of railroad travel seems to do me good. I never sleep better than after a long day's ride.

At the beginning she had been harassed by her "usual fall cough" and was "putting on mustard pastes all the time to get it quiet enough to sleep." Now, however, there was nothing of this. "I don't use any trochees or mustard pastes, am never tired so far as my lungs are concerned." She had used up "nearly four bottles of cod liver oil and phosphate of lime," and that was all.[1]

From 1852 on, however, Mrs. Stowe lived two lives—one in the world and the other in her books. We live in days when records are easily established, quickly broken, and still more quickly forgotten. Exact sales figures on *Uncle Tom's Cabin* are not available —in 1947 Frank Luther Mott conjectured 3,000,000 copies in the United States alone—but neither are they particularly important.[2] That the book caused the Civil War, as Lincoln is said once humorously to have suggested, is rather more than doubtful, but it certainly exercised a great influence on world opinion concerning slavery. "How she is shaking the world with UTC," wrote Longfellow in his journal, February 24, 1853. "At one step she has reached the top of the stair-case up which the rest of us climb on our knees year after year. Never was there such a literary *coup-de-main* as this." And Henry James reported retrospectively in *A Small Boy and Others:*

We lived and moved . . . with great intensity in Mrs. Stowe's novel. . . . There was, however, I think, for that triumphant work no classified condition; it was for no sort of reader as distinct from any other sort, save indeed for Northern as differing from Southern; it knew the large felicity of gathering in alike the small and the simple and the big and the wise, and had above all the extraordinary fortune of finding itself for an immense number of people, much less a book than a state of vision, of feeling and of consciousness, in which they didn't sit and read and appraise and pass the time, but walked and talked and laughed and cried and, in a manner of which Mrs. Stowe was the irresistible cause, generally conducted themselves.

Charles E. Stowe tells us that within a year *Uncle Tom's Cabin* existed in forty different editions. It seems to have been translated into every conceivable language, and Mary H. Eastman's *Aunt Phillis's Cabin; or, Southern Life As It Is* was only one of a whole raft of fictional "replies," none of them, unfortunately for the cause to which they were dedicated, written by a writer who came within hailing distance of Mrs. Stowe's genius. Macaulay called *Uncle Tom's Cabin* "the most valuable addition that America had made to English literature." George Sand found its author a saint. Tolstoy was to place it with *Les Misérables* and *A Tale of Two Cities* as exemplifying what high moral art ought to be, but Heine compared it to the Bible, whose sale it is said to have stim-u-lated in Paris.[3]

Fred Lewis Pattee stresses the influence of *Uncle Tom's Cabin* in breaking down the nineteenth-century Puritan prejudice against fiction. This is probably correct, but the influence of the play, for which Mrs. Stowe was not responsible and from which she derived no profit, must have rendered much greater service in an area where it was far more desperately needed, that of undercutting the opposition to the theater among religious people generally. The dramatic version of *Uncle Tom's Cabin*—"bloodhounds," duplicate casts, apotheosis of Eva, and all—was the closest approach to folk drama that America ever made, and it is said that from 1853 to 1930 it was never off the boards. Just as there were actors who appeared, in the whole course of their careers, in no other play—"Uncle Tomming," like the circus, was a recognized branch of the theatrical profession—so there must have been many Americans in the hinterlands who saw no other play but saw this one again and again. There were, as a matter of fact, a number of dramatizations, but it was the one by George L. Aiken which made history. Even when, in 1930, it was announced in the press that the last Uncle Tom company had disbanded, denials at once came pouring in.[4]

Her accuracy challenged, Mrs. Stowe wrote *A Key to "Uncle Tom's Cabin"* (1853), crammed with an accumulation of "real" slavery horrors whose force was somewhat weakened by the fact that much of her material had been accumulated after the publication of her novel. (She herself wrote Lord Denman that the material she found was worse than she had "supposed or dreamed.")[5] She continued her attack on the "peculiar institution" in *Dred: A Tale of the Great Dismal Swamp* (1856), after which she returned to the old New England life which she knew better than any other writer of her type and capacity had hitherto known it.

The most ambitious of the New England novels was *The Minister's Wooing* (1859), a love story with grim theological overtones, which Lowell considered its author's masterpiece. *The Pearl of Orr's Island* (1862) is an idyll of Yankee sailor life, fresh and charming in the first portion, which deals with its characters as children, but much less impressive in the latter portion, written after its publication in *The Independent* had been interrupted. In 1870 with *Oldtown Folks* (supplemented in 1871 with *Oldtown Fireside Stories*), and again in 1878 with her last novel, *Poganuc People*, she went back to the beginning, the first preserving her husband's memories of his boyhood in Natick, the latter her own remembrances of Litchfield. Oddly enough, *Oldtown Folks* is much the more elaborate and definitive, but perhaps this does not mean anything except that by the time she got to *Poganuc People* Harriet was considerably older and more tired. The fictional motifs of *Oldtown Folks* are conventional enough,

and the book suffers today from the manner in which they have
been worked to death by popular New England fictionists since,
but Harriet's picture of the life of a people is incomparable.[6]
Oldtown Folks does not have the passion and vitality of *Uncle
Tom's Cabin*, but in the usual sense of the term it has much more
authenticity.

Agnes of Sorrento (1862), the only novel in which Mrs. Stowe
lays her scene outside America, is a pastiche of conventionalized
nineteenth-century romances. She also produced three New York
"society" novels—*Pink and White Tyranny* (1871) and the much
superior *My Wife and I* (1871) and its sequel, *We and Our
Neighbors* (1875), both of which are written from the point of
view of their journalist hero, Harry Henderson. These books in-
volve a picture of contemporary New York journalism, with all
its time-serving and moral humbug, and of the vagaries of the
suffrage movement, with side glances toward virtually every snare
which metropolitan living throws out in the direction of the good
life. It is not surprising that Charles H. Foster should find that
"she here opened a new literary frontier, blazing the way hur-
riedly and sometimes crudely for later writers such as Howells,
Henry James, and John P. Marquand." [7]

She published one volume of *Religious Poems* (1867) and a
number of books for children, including *Queer Little People*
(1867), *Little Pussy Willow* (1870), and *Betty's Bright Idea*
(1876). *Sunny Memories of Foreign Lands* (1854) preserved
a detailed record of her first trip to Europe. She expressed her
religious convictions directly in *Footsteps of the Master* (1877)
and *Bible Heroines* (1878). She came perilously close to hack
work in her sketches of *Men of Our Times* (1868), which was
sold by subscription out of Hartford at enormous profits. Out of
a sense of loyalty to a dead friend, she opened herself up to scorn
as a scandalmonger in *Lady Byron Vindicated* (1870). Her *Palmetto Leaves* (1873) virtually began the Florida boom. Even the
pieces on domestic science through which she almost turned *The
Atlantic Monthly* into an anticipation of *The Ladies' Home Journal* were collected in the *House and Home Papers* (1864) and

The Chimney Corner (1868), both of them ultimately included in her collected works.

On top of all this—and intertwined with it—she had always been an indefatigable magazinist, as John R. Adams has pointed out:

... after 1857, she had become a regular contributor to the new *Atlantic Monthly*, selling it serial stories, articles, and short stories for years. After 1865 *Our Young Folks* used her sketches for children, and after 1870 the *Christian Union* absorbed most of her energy, with several serials and numerous miscellaneous essays. In addition, she served one year as associate editor of *Hearth and Home*. To the New York *Ledger* she sold a series of twelve travel sketches, "A Winter in Italy," which appeared between August 12 and October 28, 1865. Her name was also connected, as contributor or editorial associate, with such diversified publications as *Western Home, Old and New, Youth's Companion*, the *Continent*, and *Revolution*—this last devoted to woman's rights.

All in all, it may well be doubted whether any American woman up to her time had said her say so publicly upon so wide a variety of personal and public questions, and I doubt that any other has matched her in kind since.

With *Poganuc People* her work was about done. During the 'eighties her critical reputation declined, and though her anniversaries were duly noted in the public press, the references were often slighting. In 1890 her nephew-physician, E. B. Hooker, found it advisable to issue a statement concerning her:

She is neither insane nor an imbecile, but has reached the stage which we familiarly term "second childhood." She is pleased with trifles, with innocent amusements, just as a child would be. She will meet you and chat and laugh, or even call you by name if some one mentions it to her. Otherwise she recognizes by name her more intimate friends alone.

Perhaps her daughter Hattie did not help much when, that same year, she wrote a correspondent seeking an interview that her mother was "not now above a child of two or three years."

But Harriet did not really need anybody to speak for her, for she could still, on occasion, command such eloquence as nobody about her had ever been able to touch. On February 5, 1893, when she was eighty-two, she penned a moving letter to her beloved friend Oliver Wendell Holmes:

I make no mental effort of any sort; my brain is tired out. It was a woman's brain and not a man's, and finally from sheer fatigue and exhaustion in the march and strife of life it gave out before the end was reached. And now I rest me, like a moored boat, rising and falling on the water, with loosened cordage and flapping sail.

And, more elaborately:

My mental condition might be called nomadic. I have no fixed thoughts or objects. I wander at will from one subject to another. In pleasant summer weather I am out of doors most of my time, rambling about the neighborhood and calling upon my friends. I do not read much. Now and then I dip into a book much as a humming-bird, poised in air on whirring wing, darts into the heart of a flower, now here, now there, and away. Pictures delight me and afford me infinite diversion and interest. I pass many pleasant hours looking over books of pictures.

She roamed all over Hartford, through the streets and the adjoining fields, and into and out of her neighbors' houses, where she was allowed to do as she liked and made to feel as much at home as in her own dwelling. One day a boy named Edward W. Bok, who was to become the future great editor of *The Ladies' Home Journal,* came across her on Forest Street "shambling along ...unconscious, apparently, of people or surroundings." But when he had passed her, she called to tell him he had been leaning against something white and brushed him off with her switch. When he addressed her by her name, she acknowledged it and asked, "Are you going to have me arrested for stopping you?" Then "she gathered up her skirts and quickly ran away, looking furtively over her shoulder."

It was almost midnight on July 1, 1896, when her own call came. Her nurse had come in to give her her medicine, and she opened her eyes, spoke kindly, and quickly and easily died. The newspapers said that the cause of her death was brain congestion complicated by partial paralysis.

CHAPTER I

THE DAUGHTER

I

William James once remarked of his brother Henry that he was never really a native of anything except the James family. Harriet seems to have felt that it was difficult for her to express her feelings toward her family, but the Beecher sense of solidarity was certainly quite as close as that of the Jameses. "I have so long lived with them," she wrote Charles Kingsley, "that I can scarcely think of a separate mental history." Because her mother died while Harriet was still so young that she could barely remember her, her function was that of an ideal rather than a presence, but the father made up for this by being several sizes larger than life.

The classical tribute to Roxana's memory was paid, at the great birthday celebration which her publishers gave Mrs. Stowe at "The Old Elms," Governor Claflin's residence in Newtonville, Massachusetts, in 1882, by Henry Ward Beecher, who, since he was not born until 1813, was only three when she died: "My mother is to me what the Virgin Mary is to a devout Catholic." On another occasion he told an audience, "I do not see your faces more clearly than I see those of my father and mother." Harriet always felt the same way. In 1858 she wrote a friend of her daughter's who had just lost her mother, "Accept my sincere sympathy for a loss, which *I* have felt from my earliest childhood every year deeper—the one friend whom God never replaces—whom I never knew personally but yet have always deplored the want of." In her contribution to her father's autobiography she wrote that her recollections of her mother were "but few" and added that "the deep interest and veneration she inspired in all who knew her was such that during all my childhood, I was constantly hearing her spoken of, and from one friend to another, some incident or anecdote of her life was constantly being impressed on me." She particularized two specific memories, one of which at least seems significant. Roxana was "an enthusiastic horticulturalist," and one day her children, left alone in the house, ate up all her fine bulbs, under the delusion that they were onions. "My dear children," said Roxana quietly, "what you have done makes mamma very sorry. Those were not onions but roots of beautiful flowers, and if you had let them alone we should have next summer in the garden great beautiful red and yellow flowers such as you never saw."

Such a story goes far to indicate the sweetness of Roxana's spirit and to justify Harriet's idealization of her in *The Minister's Wooing, Uncle Tom's Cabin,* and elsewhere. We have the author's word for it that "the passage in *Uncle Tom,* where Augustine St. Clare describes his mother's influence, is a simple reproduction of this mother's influence as it has always been in our family." Catharine Beecher, who was sixteen when Roxana died, and who therefore knew her better than the younger children, wrote,

Mother was of that easy and gentle temperament that could never very strictly enforce any rules; while father, you know, was never celebrated for his habits of system and order. Of course there was a free and easy way of living, more congenial to liberty and sociality than to conventional rules. As I look back to those days, there is an impression of sunshine, love, and busy activity, without any memory of jar or cloud.

Roxana was one of the brilliant Foote girls of Nutplains, of a Tory, Episcopal family, and brought up, after their father's death, in the Guilford home of their legislator grandfather, General

Andrew Ward. Her acceptance of Calvinism, when she married Lyman, seems to have been somewhat qualified. She was not willing to be damned for the glory of God, since if she were to be damned she must be wicked, and she could not see how that could redound to God's glory. ("Oh, Roxana," exclaimed Lyman, "what a fool I've been!") Certainly the Anglican spirit lived on in her family, where Harriet encountered it as a child, in her grandmother and her Aunt Harriet.

When I broke my needles, tore my clothes, lost my thimble, slipped out of the house and sauntered by the river when I should have been sewing, grandmother was always an accessory after the fact; and when she could not save me from condign punishment, would comfort me with the private assurance that "I was a poor child, and that Harriet needed punishing a great deal more than I did."

Both these ladies held the same creed; thus early Harriet must have begun to understand that temperament exercises a larger influence over conduct than theoretical belief. She preserved the differences between her grandmother and her Aunt Harriet, though turning them both into Calvinists, in *Oldtown Folks*.

Roxana was disinclined to talk in company; too shy to perform the usual functions of a minister's wife, she knew that she could not lead a prayer meeting, and she did not try. But she prayed that all her sons should devote themselves to the ministry, and their religious lives all derived nourishment directly from hers. She was also a pacifist, a point of view which she did not, unfortunately, pass on to her descendants. "She was of a temperament peculiarly restful and peace-giving," wrote Harriet. "Her union of spirit with God, unruffled and unbroken even from very early childhood, seemed to impart to her an equilibrium and healthful placidity that no earthly reverses ever disturbed." Mentally and aesthetically she was quite as remarkable. She was passionately interested in philosophy, literature, and science. When Fanny Burney's *Evelina* was published, a friend rode out on horseback to get a copy for her. She was devoted to Richardson's Sir Charles Grandison and had made up her mind never to marry until she found his match. "I presume she thought she had," said Lyman dryly. She both read and spoke French. She was fond of music and played the guitar. She sketched, used both water colors and oils, and produced ivory miniatures of members of the family. She made such a beautiful carpet to cover the bare boards of the parsonage that one of the deacons was not only afraid to step on it but seriously questioned whether the parson could have "all this and heaven too."

When Roxana's time came, she went as quietly as she had lived. Like Edgar Lee Masters's Lucinda Matlock, though much younger, she "had lived enough, that is all." On the way home from visiting a parishioner she told her startled husband calmly, "I do not think I shall be with you long." When he asked why, she replied, "I have had a vision of heaven and its blessedness." She then spoke of "her habitual peace, her joy in Christ, and her *more* than willingness to leave him and her children." Nor was her calmness thereafter disturbed. But she left Lyman helpless and terror-stricken, crying, "*I am alone; Roxana is not here!*" He afterwards said that not a single sermon he wrote during the year that followed her death was any good, and he was never able to use any of them again.

II

The stepmother, Harriet Porter, is a rather mysterious figure in the Beecher family saga, and I think a very sad one. If there were nothing else, our suspicions would still be awakened by the curious obituary signed "C" which appeared in the Cincinnati papers after her death. Affirming Mrs. Beecher's virtue almost as if it had been impugned, but also proclaiming her sadness and her dislike for the West, the writer declares,

When approaching the presence of a perfect and holy Being, the retrospection of the deficiencies of the past brought such anxiety and dismay that her spirit died within her, and it was not until after the most contrite acknowledgment of all she deemed her failings in duty to others . . . that her spirit found peace.

If this was the work of a friend, the poor lady had no need of enemies.

Yet the beginning was happy enough. The children were in bed when Lyman unexpectedly brought her—and himself—home, and when they cried, "Why, here's pa!" her "cheerful voice called out from behind him, 'And here's ma!' " But the voice was soon to grow less cheerful.

The children were greatly taken by her beauty, but Harriet adds a chilling qualification—"she seemed to us so fair, so elegant, so delicate, that we were afraid to go near her"—and Henry Ward, who thought her serene, self-possessed, polished, and ladylike, and who admits that she "performed to the uttermost her duties, according to her abilities," declares also that she was cold and unapproachable and failed to call forth the affection he was eager to give her. When he fell asleep during his father's long sermons, she would wake him up by rapping on his skull with her knuckles, and once when they heard the death bell tolled while driving together, she asked him what his thoughts were on such an occasion: "*I* think was that soul prepared?" Yet her religious convictions (possibly as distinct from her temperament) were not unduly austere for the time, and once when Lyman was reading her a typical piece of Calvinistic rhetoric, she swept out of the room, declaring it a libel on the character of her Heavenly Father. Perhaps the coldness was not all on her side. I can find no overwhelming warmth in Harriet's reaction to her first sight of her half-brother James, Harriet Porter's last child: "he has nothing to distinguish him from forty other babies, except a very large pair of blue eyes and an uncommonly fair complexion, a thing which is of no sort of use to a man or boy." But when she wrote the sketch of her sister Catharine in *Our Famous Women* Harriet declared that there was a warm friendship between Catharine and her stepmother "which continued through life."

The second Mrs. Beecher wrote her own impressions of her new situation to her sister, the year after her marriage:

I am delighted with the great familiarity and great respect subsisting between parent and children. It is a home of great cheerfulness and comfort, and I am beginning to feel at home. I expect in this situation a great increase of happiness; but God knows what is best for me, and I am willing the government should be in His hands.

The calm and guarded character of this communication chills the blood. When a bride looks forward hopefully to an "increase" of happiness and submits herself to the will of God, one can only shudder for her, and sadly echo Dame Quickly's words to the dying Falstaff: "Now I, to comfort him, bade him a' should not think of God. I hoped there was no need to trouble himself with any such thoughts yet."

Lyman was greatly impressed by his wife's power in prayer, which "exceeded almost anything" he had heard in the way of supplication. It may be that her need was great. Her habit of prayer is confirmed by Henry Ward, who attributed almost mythical power to it and acknowledged the "sympathetic hold" it had on him but still "always felt when I went to prayer, as though I were going into a crypt, where the sun was not allowed to come; and I shrunk from it." Harriet, too, gave her stepmother credit for "a most unfaltering Christ-worship," but even here she enters an ungracious qualification. "Had it not been that Dr. Payson had set up and kept before her a tender, human loving Christ, she would have been only a conscientious bigot."

Poor Harriet Porter! Apparently she could do nothing right in the eyes of the Beecher children. "Mamma is well and don't laugh any more than she did." I hardly wonder. She was depressed by the cholera epidemic in Cincinnati and by the death of Calvin Stowe's first wife. She seems to have lacked the resiliency which enabled the Beechers to bear up against such things. But perhaps the real difficulty was that she lacked the resiliency necessary to bear up against the Beechers, and that between the doctor and his children she found the whole phenomenon of Beecherism somewhat overwhelming. Henry Ward himself suggests as much:

Her nature and habits were too refined and exacting for the bringing up of children of great animal force and vigor, under the strain and pressure of straitened circumstances. The absurdities and crudeness incident to the early days of such children appeared to her as serious faults, and weighed heavily on her conscience.

Yet when she was gone, it was Lyman's turn to be depressed:

Your mother's death sits heavily on my spirits. I feel her absence and am solitary. My affection for her was sincere and unfailing. But her mental sufferings, the result of constitution, habit, and disease, during her decline, which I could not possibly alleviate, connect sadness with every reminiscence.

"Which I could not possibly alleviate." It was easy to say, and Lyman being Lyman, Beechers Beechers, and Harriet Harriet, I am sure it was true. But none of this made it any easier for her.

By the time Lyman married his third wife, Lydia Jackson, all Roxana's children were far enough along so that they could afford to be indifferent to her, and she seems to have been quite unimportant to them except when, in Lyman's dependent old age, she tried to get as much money as possible out of Harriet and Henry and thus occasioned some unpleasant correspondence. In 1862, when Lyman was irrational, his physician declared that he could not hope to recover unless he should be "entirely separated from his wife for an indefinite period, that cannot now be determined. He ought not to see her nor know that he has a wife." In these words Calvin communicated the doctor's ukase to Lydia, who accepted it, and on this basis Lyman's children took on responsibility for him in his old age.

III

But that was Lyman only at the end. In his prime he was the "Pa-man," in Katherine Mansfield's phrase, if ever a father was, and the dominating influence in his children's lives. Professor Adams takes a dim view of him, obviously horrified not only by his Calvinism but by such pranks as his ducking Catharine's head into the washtub just for fun, or swinging her by her hands out the attic window to see if she would be frightened (she wasn't), or repeating a monotonous tune on his fiddle until he drove everybody mad, and then, when he launched into a lively tune and they attempted to dance to it, deliberately destroying the rhythm. I must admit that I share his horror over these things, yet I am inclined to question his conclusion.

As for the Calvinism, it is of course true that our ancestors went on reproducing themselves heroically in the sincere conviction that the odds were all in favor of running up the population figures of hell. But is it not also true that we ourselves continue to bring children into a world brooded over by the fear of nuclear destruction without having made any really adequate effort to remove that appalling menace? The critic, though not the crusader, must see these things in their proper perspective, and Lyman was, in his time, so far from being an extremist that the Calvinists themselves accused him of heresy. Lyman Beecher did not revolt against Calvinism; he simply undercut it by entertaining ideas not logically reconcilable with it. Theoretically, as Harriet pointed out, he believed in total depravity, "yet practically he never seemed to realize that people were unbelievers for any other reason than want of light, and that clear and able arguments would not at once put an end to scepticism." It was clearly of her father that she was thinking, too, when she wrote of a cleric in *Oldtown Folks* who was forever exerting himself "in favor of some original-minded sheep who can't be got into the sheep-fold without some alteration in the paling. In these cases I have generally noticed that he will loosen a rail or tear off a picket, and let the sheep in, it being his impression, after all, that the sheep are worth more than the sheepfold." So Lyman yearned over Napoleon, yearned over Byron, with whom he longed to converse, that he might win him and his "harp" for Christ, and burst into tears over the sufferings of Milton's Satan. The virtual founder of the American temperance movement, he could still say of a drunkard, "I indulge the hope that God saw it was a constitutional infirmity, like any other disease." (*Per contra*, the liberal Transcendentalist Thoreau could only suggest to a man who came to see him under the influence that he had better go home and cut his throat and do it quickly.) Lyman Beecher was no mossback in non-religious matters either.

During the War of 1812 he was keenly alive to the danger of suppressing free speech and the peril of military despotism. He was grieved when religious disestablishment came to Connecticut, but he soon came to see that this was the best thing that could have happened for religion. All in all, I am sure Henry Ward was right when he declared of his father that "though he thought he was great by his theology, everybody else knew he was great by his religion." And Harriet speaks, with pardonable hyperbole, of "my blessed father, for many years so true an image of the Heavenly Father."

Of course this does not mean that Lyman was necessarily a comfortable man to live with. There was too much of him for that, and he had the kind of vitality that often expresses itself overwhelmingly without at all intending to do so. He could vault over a rail fence when he was eighty, and when other exertions failed him he would go down cellar and shovel a load of sand from one corner to another. The same kind of energy went into his hunting, fishing, and nutting expeditions. Catharine records his having gone fishing for eels with two sons and come home with nearly a cartload. One Sunday he caught a fish on the way to church and slipped it into the pocket of his ministerial coat, where Roxana found it the next Sunday. He was a notoriously disorderly man in all things, always sprinting up the church aisle at the latest possible moment, often in a state of considerable disorder, and when preparing to take the children nutting, he thought nothing of emptying out the contents of all his wife's stocking-baskets, patch-baskets, linen-baskets, yarn-baskets, and thread-baskets, leaving their assorted contents in a state of confusion worse confounded.

Once he woke up to find a burglar pulling his clothes out through a broken pane in the bedroom window. He ran after him.

The fellow dropped his booty, and fled down one street and up another, doubling and turning, till at last I caught him. I took him by the collar; he attempted to strike; I warded off, and pushed him over and sprung on him, and choked him till he begged; then I let him up; saw he was fumbling in his pocket for a knife; took it away, and marched him back to my room, and made him lie on my floor by my bed till morning. If he stirred, I said, "Lie still, sir!" In the morning I had him before the justice, Squire Daggett, who discharged him because I lost sight of him once round a corner. I met the fellow afterward, but he would never look me in the eye.

A man with such energy could hardly have been expected to behave lethargically when his convictions were at stake. In 1826 he heard that his son Edward was in danger of turning Baptist.

I have no doubt of what is true on the subject, and do not expect that you will have any when you shall have had time calmly to examine it. But to me it seems as if you had better come home and be with me, and supply by exchanges, and attend the inquiry meeting, and a few such things, and be ordained when you are ready, especially if your mind is veering to the Baptist side of the question. I should be sorry to have it acquire any considerable momentum that way till I see you.

Freedom of thought has its difficulties in the presence of such a father, but we should not forget that none of his children finally accepted Lyman's theology, yet he remained on good terms with all of them. He once remarked that he had thought he knew how to preach until he heard Henry Ward.

He was much the same, it seems, in his relations with his wives. In 1810 he wrote a Mrs. Tomlinson:

As for my wife, if she is not so obedient to her husband as you are to yours, she is still obedient enough for me. I could never know the sweets of power if she never rebelled a little, just to try my strength, and manifest the predominance of her conscience over her will.

Once he beat some hogs which had vexed him, and Roxana came to the door and cried, "Lyman, don't, don't!"

I said something sharply, and she turned to go in. But oh, I had not time enough to get to the door and to say "I am ashamed, I am sorry," when one of the sweetest smiles shone out on her face, and that smile has never died and never will.

In a sense, he was a man who was peculiarly dependent upon his family, and he always needed advice and reassurance, even about his writing. "First he would read it to mother, and then he would say, 'I think now I'll go over and read it to Esther.' "[1]

So, though there can never have been any doubt in anybody's mind that Lyman was in the picture, domination is by no means the only prominent note in the symphony. A chronic dyspeptic, he was subject to the "hypo," and he played this piece with the same full orchestration he gave everything else, so that when he had a pain in his belly it could never be anything less serious than "cancer internal." But every morning the baby of the family had the job of waking him up by taking him by the nose and kissing him many times.

Oftentimes he would lie in bed after his little monitor had called him [writes Harriet], professing fears that there was a lion under the bed that would catch his foot if he put it out, and requiring repeated and earnest assurances from the curly head that he should be defended from being eaten up if he rose; and often and earnestly the breakfast-bell would ring before he could be induced to launch forth. Great would be the pride of the little monitor, who led him at last gravely into the breakfast-room, and related in baby phrase the labors of getting him up.

Habitually after the Sunday night service, he would have to "run down" by playing with his children.

Often his old faithful friend the violin was called into requisition, and he would play a few antiquated contra dances and Scotch airs out of a venerable yellow music-book which had come down the vale of years with him from East Hampton. Auld Lang Syne, Bonnie Doon and Mary's Dream were among the inevitables; and a contra dance which bore the unclerical title of "Go to the devil and shake yourself" was a great favorite with the youngsters.

His children were well aware that he had his limitations. Harriet portrayed him lovingly but humorously as Parson Cushing in *Poganuc People*. Cushing is powerless to comfort Zeph Higgins, or bring him to a better frame of mind, after his wife's death; in fact he does not try, thinking that only God can speak to Zeph. But Dolly speaks to him, after his bitter denunciation of himself in meeting, and tells him, as Eva told Topsy, that God loves him, thus not only transforming Zeph but setting off a genuine revival of religion.[2]

Nevertheless Lyman's children loved him. "You know how happy it makes us to be with father," Catharine wrote to Edward in 1825. "His society seems always to give a new impulse to the affection of the heart, and to every intellectual power." And though Harriet with her girls went on a shopping spree in Boston, on the way home from his funeral, I am sure she would have agreed. Once, when he was an old man, she was combing his hair one day as he lay on a couch before her. "Do you know," she asked, "that you are a very handsome old gentleman?" And Lyman replied, "Tell me something new." Even after his mind had failed, she loved to be with him and remember what he had been.

I am going this afternoon to sit with my dear blessed Father [she wrote her daughters in 1862]. He is always delighted to see me tho he knows not who I am. God bless his precious white head—it is white as silver snows and his poor trembling hands once so strong! I remember when the very touch of his hand seemed to put strength into me and his brisk joyful footstep at the door made me feel as if I had some one coming on whom I could lean all my cares.

CHAPTER II

THE SISTER

I

Harriet Beecher Stowe had two older sisters, besides three older and two younger brothers. Her father's second marriage provided her with two additional half-brothers and one half-sister. Of all these the most important to her were her oldest sister Catharine and her brother Henry Ward, who was two years younger than herself. So far as I know, there was only one among all these with whom she was ever on bad terms, but I have very little information on her relations with some of them.

She herself outlived all Roxana's children except Mary Perkins and Charles, both of whom died in 1900, Mary passing away in Hartford on the same day that closed the life of her half-brother Thomas in Elmira. The only child of the second marriage who predeceased Harriet was the youngest, James, who committed suicide, after a breakdown, in 1886. Her older brother George, too, had died of a self-inflicted wound as far back as 1842, but this was apparently an accident, and it seems a heavy price to pay for trying to clear robins out of a cherry tree. None of this takes account of the two children lost early—Roxana's daughter, the first Harriet, and Harriet Porter's first child, Frederick.

All the Beecher males, even the adventurous James, became clergymen, though some had to squeeze considerably to get into the fold, and several were accused of heresy, including Edward,

33

who believed in pre-existence. Charles was passionately interested in music. Henry Ward was the greatest preacher. Among the others, the one who lives most vividly in the modern imagination is probably Thomas K., who preferred being called teacher rather than minister. For many years he served the church in Elmira, often called the first institutional church in America, of which the Jervis Langdons were pillars, and was thus the pastor, during her formative years, of Olivia Langdon, who became the wife of Mark Twain. "I have always been struck with a curious similarity between your Uncle Tom's character and that of Thomas the doubter," wrote Harriet, in an undated letter to her son Charley, "a sad hearted-easily discouraged one is he, yet the dear Master has led him on, made him a place and cleared him a way and given him an uncommonly useful and fruitful ministry." [1] Though we hear little of her relations with her brother Charles, we get a glimpse of how warmly she felt toward him in a letter she wrote Mrs. Claflin in 1878: "So it seems you never saw my brother Charlie before. He is just the loveliest sweetest most perfect old gentleman you ever saw and I wish you could hear him play on the violin and sing. He has passed through bitter sorrows and come out purified like gold." When he was in danger of being branded a heretic by "moles and bats" she swung into a letter-writing campaign among the New England clergy with whom she thought she had influence and exerted it to good purpose. "Shall my father's son, by all allowed to have been a faithful, conscientious minister, be cast from the ministry by such a course as this?"

The half-sister with whom Harriet broke was Harriet Porter's only daughter, Isabella Beecher Hooker, but the kindest thing to say about Isabella is that she must have been a little mad. The issue was the integrity of Henry Ward Beecher, under accusation as an adulterer. A passionate suffragist, Isabella, like Elizabeth Cady Stanton and others, had swallowed whole that pathological liar, the disreputable Victoria Woodhull (who once sued the British Museum for having on its shelves materials containing derogatory references to her), and it was Victoria Woodhull who first made the accusations against Beecher public. Isabella wished to take charge of a service at Plymouth Church "as one commissioned from on high" and declare the truth about its pastor, and poor Harriet, who could always overawe her, had to sit in a front pew at every public meeting until it became clear that the danger had passed over and Isabella would not appear. In Isabella's mind, the commission from on high was no figure of speech. She expected, like "my adorable brother Jesus," herself to "grow into the hearts of men and women and children by the power of God our common Father" and looked forward to being "called to the presidency of a matriarchal government, which would spread from the United States across the whole world and under her leadership be merged with the kingdom of Christ in a great millennial period." [2] All the Beechers except Catharine, who, at seventy-five, did not wish to quarrel with anybody, turned against Isabella, and so did many other prominent Hartfordians including Mark Twain. Frank Moulton, that strange intermediary in the Beecher-Tilton case, claimed finally to have quashed her by charging *her* with adultery, but she never changed her mind about Henry Ward. When he was dying she tried to gain admittance to his house, to give him one last chance to admit that he was wrong and that she was right, but his wife Eunice slammed the door in her face, and she joined the reporters and sightseers on the sidewalk. In 1896 she attended Harriet's funeral, but she and Eunice did not speak to each other.

II

Though posterity has not chosen to remember her as often as Mary Lyon and Emma Willard, Catharine Beecher was as important as they in the pioneering of higher education for women in this country, and Milwaukee-Downer is only one of her monuments. Perhaps, as her biographer, Mae Elizabeth Harveson, suggests, she might have been better remembered if she had not been a Beecher, overshadowed by Harriet and Henry Ward. Judged by modern standards, she did not, at the outset, know very much, coaching for two weeks in Latin before she began to teach it, but she was industrious, and she learned, and she was a born teacher. Her photographs do not give the impression of any such charm or softness as Harriet possessed, yet she was noted for her humor, and she was attractive enough in her youth to win the heart of one of the phenomenal young men of the time, Yale's Alexander Fisher. There was no question in those days of her being overshadowed by Harriet; it was quite the other way around, and when she found Harriet, as a young teacher under her, wasting her time trying to write a poetic drama, she quickly put an end to such nonsense and set her to work studying Butler's *Analogy* instead. One is sure that in their collaborations Catharine must have been the dominant party. But even in later days she knew how to take care of herself, and there is an undated letter to Mrs. Fields in which Harriet complains that Catharine has undertaken a series of papers on domestic science in *Harper's* while her own are running in the *Atlantic* without bothering to check with her. In her youth, however, Catharine did give Harriet opportunity and valuable training, and doubtless a measure of confidence, thus becoming an important supplementing factor to Lyman himself in her development.

There was one thing more: Catharine set Harriet the example of rebelling against the John Calvin–Jonathan Edwards theology and moving toward a more humane conception of God. In 1822 on a Yale College commission to England, Alexander Fisher was shipwrecked and drowned off the Irish coast. A man of spotless life and noble aspiration, he had been a lifelong seeker who had never achieved the Calvinistic conviction of sin and assurance of salvation, and neither Lyman nor any Calvinist could assure Catharine that his soul would not burn in hell forever. To us this may seem like shadow-boxing; to a sensitive girl of 1822 the agony could not have been more real. It would not have been strange if her reason had collapsed under the strain. It did not; neither did she curse God and die. She visited Fisher's parents in pathetic search of positive evidence of her lover's conviction; when she did not find it she put her hand to the work there was for it to do, and then she set to work to refute the theologians.[3] "The ablest refutation of Edwards on *The Will* which was ever written," said a distinguished American theologian to a German colleague, "is the work of a woman, the daughter of Dr. Lyman Beecher." The German threw up his hands. "You have a woman that can write an able refutation of Edwards on *The Will?* God forgive Christopher Columbus for discovering America!"

Many years afterwards, when she herself had gone through a watered-down version of Catharine's agony in connection with the loss of her own son Henry, Harriet used both events obliquely in *The Minister's Wooing*. She suffered less than her sister in religious doubt, though not in human sorrow, because by that time the theological climate was changing, and she herself was farther out of the wilderness than Catharine had been in 1822. But it was Catharine's magnificent courage that had helped to deliver her, to slay a Monster-God and raise one intolerable burden from the hearts of men. If Catharine Beecher had never done anything else for her sister she would still have served her nobly.

III

What Henry Ward gave her is less certain, though there is no question about what he received. In a sense she recognized all his shortcomings, recalling that in early life his studies

were mostly with gun on shoulder, roving the depths of these forests, guiltless of hitting anything, because the time was lost in dreamy contemplation. Thence returning unprepared for school, he would be driven to the expedient of writing out his Latin verb and surreptitiously reading it out of the crown of his hat, an exercise whence he reaped small profit, mentally or morally.

In a sense she even foresaw his ordeal. "One would think you were a *prima donna*," she said to him when he stood at the crest. "What does make people go on so about you?" And, in a mood more complimentary to her brother, she wrote John T. Howard of *The Christian Union*, some years before the storm broke:

I feel, the more I think of it, sure that the world that hates Christ is just as real in our times as it was in his. . . . I have pondered that question in relation to Henry's popularity; but I feel that the world really does *hate* him to a degree that makes it safe to hope that he is about right. Such demonstrations as now and then occur show that they are only waiting for him to be down to spring on him, . . . in proportion as he makes Christianity aggressive on sin they are malignant and will spring joyfully on him when their time comes.

In retrospect she was even to feel that, in a sense, Henry had asked for it and that, rising to his ordeal, he had made the wrath of man to praise the Lord.

Your uncle [she wrote her son Charley, May 23, 1875] has had a degree of worldly success, he has had power and wealth and worldly strength, so that a rabble were following him for loaves and fishes using his name to sell quack medicines and him as a speculation. The Lord has lopped away all this worldly growth—none cling to him now but the really good. As to him he was in danger of over self confidence and of wandering into a sort of naturalistic philosophy. The trial has *driven* him to the Bible and Christ as a child clings to its mother. Best of all, I *do* believe that this severe affliction which has been to him a crucifixion has so entirely subdued his will to God's that he is now in that blessed state of rest which comes from having given up self altogether. He has so entirely placed himself in God's hands and God's will has so become his own that he has no care.

Nevertheless she thought of him as "the noblest and most Christlike human being I know" and as "he who is to me another self." In her family letters she summarized his sermons. In 1862 she wrote Hattie from Brooklyn:

I went to church Sunday morning and heard Henry in one of his happiest moods. Not one of the tearing excited ones, but calm clear bright elevated. The prayer seemed to open a wide and solemn path up into Heaven and to isolate one from earth. I could feel with my eyes shut as if there were such a great upward current as Titian represents in the Assumption of the Madonna. This is just the way the church service always affects me, but how few men—single men—there are with the power of being at the moment more than a whole liturgy.

Some times a thought would seem so beautiful so comforting so
tenderly and nobly expressed I would say, I will remember that, and
write it to the girls but it was just as it was on the sea beaches; one long
bright wave effaced the last and so one after another, each bright and
making room for another.

When the blow fell, she was with him all the way through the
severest, most protracted ordeal by scandal that any American
clergyman has ever been called upon to undergo. "Somehow we
feel that *we* can bear things in our body, that we cannot endure
to see laid on those we love."

The quality and character of *his* suffering depends upon
whether he was innocent or guilty, but there can be no question
about hers.

This has drawn on my life [she wrote George Eliot]—my heart's
blood. He is myself; I know you are the kind of woman to understand
me when I say that I felt a blow at him more than at myself. I, who
know his purity, honor, delicacy, know that he has been from childhood of an ideal purity,—who reverenced his conscience as his king,
whose glory was redressing human wrong, who spake no slander, no,
nor listened to it.

George Eliot and Mrs. Claflin were the people to whom she
expressed herself most freely.

It seems now but a little time [she wrote the novelist further] since
my brother Henry and I were two young people together. . . . I taught
him drawing and heard his Latin lessons, for you know a girl becomes
mature and womanly long before a boy. I saw him through college,
and helped him through the difficult love affair that gave him his wife;
and then he and my husband had a real German, enthusiastic love for
each other, which ended in making me a wife. Ah! in those days we
never dreamed that he, or I, or any of us, were to be known in the
world. All he seemed then was a boy full of fun, full of love, full of
enthusiasm for protecting abused and righting wronged people, which
made him in those early days write editorials, and wear arms and swear
himself a special policeman to protect the poor negroes in Cincinnati,
where we then lived, when there were mobs instigated by the slave-
holders of Kentucky.

Certainly they were close in those days, though there may be some doubt that he stayed very close to her after she became famous, for while Forrest Wilson's suspicion that he was jealous of her seems greatly overdone, he does not appear to have had much time for her or to have cared much about writing to her. When she told him she had begun work on *Uncle Tom's Cabin*, he urged her to finish it and promised "to scatter it as thick as the leaves of Vallambroso." It turned out not to need him, but he does not seem to have made much effort.[4] It may be that modern commentators are somewhat too subtle about this, however, and if Harriet ever was hurt, she gave no sign.[5]

This is not the place to tell the story of "The Great Henry Ward Beecher Scandal," as contemporaries called it, which is a subject for a book in itself, and which, incidentally, has never been adequately covered. Lyman Abbott, who had the qualifications for the job, evidently found the subject so distasteful that he disposed of it as briefly as possible in his biography of Beecher. Paxton Hibben merely did a hatchet job, now significant only as a monument of the "debunking" biography to which the 'twenties were so fatally addicted;[6] and Robert Shaplen's *Free Love and Heavenly Sinners*,[7] though extremely entertaining, is so hopelessly uncritical as to be absurd; even if Beecher was guilty, that does not make Theodore Tilton a demigod or Mrs. Tilton a wronged angel, wandering bewildered in a world wholly strange to a denizen of Paradise. One does not investigate a problem of this kind—and the complexity of the charges and countercharges, recriminations and denials is something unbelievable—by the simple expedient of believing everything that has been charged to the discredit of one party and refusing to credit anything against the other one, and Mr. Shaplen treats even Victoria Woodhull as if she were a cross between Flora MacDonald and Joan of Arc.

To state the facts of the case as briefly as possible, Theodore Tilton, who was a member of Plymouth Church and who had been associated with Beecher on *The Independent*, accused his pastor of having established an adulterous relationship with Tilton's wife, and the charges were whispered about for an astonishing length of time and repeated "in confidence" to an astonishing number of persons before Victoria Woodhull, broker, spiritualist, journalist, free lover, and adventuress, publicly branded Beecher an adulterer in an address at Boston in September 1872, and finding no respectable newspaper that would print the story, spread it, in November, over an issue of her own *Woodhull and Claflin's Weekly*.[8] Tilton's suit against Beecher for alienation of his wife's affections resulted in a disagreement which, since there were nine jurors in Beecher's favor and only three against him, was regarded as a defeat for Tilton. The ecclesiastical investigators all found for Beecher, and there was never any question about the loyalty of Plymouth Church.

If the story cannot be told in detail here, I certainly need not feel called to decide the question of Beecher's guilt or innocence. I suspect that no such verdict could be worth much except as it proceeded from a trained legal mind which had read and pondered with care the 3000-page record of the civil trial. But one need not do that to reject the cavalier assumption of some modern writers that Beecher *must* have been guilty because he was an extraordinarily emotional man, or because his wife was a "Gorgon," or because his style as a preacher was more florid than we happen now to admire. That Beecher showed poor judgment is undeniable. That he handled his own case ineptly is likewise undeniable, though it is only fair to add that he did not commit himself to his long and puzzling silence entirely without advices.[9] But all these ineptitudes are quite as reconcilable with Harriet's hypothesis of his extraordinary naïveté as with the hypothesis of guilt. "I never knew a person who knew man so well and men so ill as Henry Ward Beecher," said Edward Eggleston, and if there was any great man of his time who was quite capable of signing an incriminating document without reading it, as Beecher claimed he had done, nobody who has studied him at all can doubt that he was just such a man. Moreover, it is not true that he never talked freely of the matter. He spoke thus to Harriet. He opened his heart to the great Chicago preacher, David Swing, who visited him at the time (himself under accusation of heresy), and Swing left him absolutely convinced of his innocence. Years later, he even talked to Edward Bok. On any hypothesis, Tilton's behavior was erratic in the extreme. Mrs. Tilton accused, withdrew her accusation, reaccused, and withdrew again until one loses count and the head swims. Mrs. Woodhull, obviously, could be trusted with nothing, and in any case she had no independent knowledge and was only repeating what she had been told. In later years, in London, where she was trying to live down her past and become respectable, she even denied that she had ever accused Beecher at all. What it all adds up to is that Beecher's guilt—or innocence—never has been proved and probably never can be.

Beecher lacked calm, cool, critical judgment, and there were a great many things he did not know. Like most men who talk much, he said many foolish things. But one does not have to go through many of the sermons which poured out of him, as it were inexhaustibly, through the years before one becomes convinced that to match him modern preachers would have to begin by organizing a syndicate, and when one compares those who trusted and believed in him with those who hated him and tried to drag him down, it is difficult not to be prejudiced in his favor. "I found him to be an unostentatious, evidently able, straightforward, and agreeable man," wrote Charles Dickens in 1868; "extremely well informed, and with a good knowledge of art." Mark Twain thought it a pity "that so insignificant a matter as the chastity or unchastity of an Elizabeth Tilton could clip the locks of this Samson and make him as other men, in the estimation of a nation of Lilliputians creeping and climbing about his shoe-soles." Tilton's own chief of counsel, who believed Beecher guilty at the outset, was converted to a belief in his innocence as the trial progressed, and the presiding judge later presided over the public dinner that was given him on his seventieth birthday. Temperamentally, Lyman Abbott was about as different from Beecher as a man can be, with none of the dangers of Beecher's own exuberance about him, but there was never even a passing doubt in Abbott's mind concerning either Beecher's greatness as a preacher or his integrity

as a man.[10] But perhaps the final word had better go to Whittier—
and whose loyalty would any man value more?—"I love Beecher
and believe in him. He has done good to thousands. If he has fallen
into temptation I shall feel grieved, but would be ashamed of
myself were I less his friend."

This much must be said to avoid evasiveness and to tie our discussion to the facts of the case, but of course our only real concern
here is with the effect the whole thing had on Harriet. What hurt
her most was "to think that Henry, who never would listen to an
indelicate word, who has kept all this nauseous thing out of his
mind," must now "sit in open court and have this foulness dribbled
out before him!" She seems never to have lost her charity for
Elizabeth Tilton, whom she regarded as a pawn in her husband's
hands, almost the victim of an evil enchantment, but any charity
she may have felt for Tilton himself at the outset cracked and
wavered as time went on, and she frankly loathed Mrs. Woodhull
not only for what she had done to Henry Ward but also for the
"incredible infatuation" she had awakened in my "poor sister,"
and hoped yet to see "this Witch" in the penitentiary; there is
even one reference to "Mrs. Stanton and the free love roost of
harpies generally." In 1874 Harriet wrote George Eliot that for
ten years she and her friends had been calling Tilton "Tito," after
Romola's faithless husband, and described him as "an artful plau-
sible accomplished traitor," playing upon Beecher's "unusually
generous and susceptible nature and using him for his own advancement," and Lyman Abbott supports this to the extent of
recording that before any sexual scandal was whispered, he personally had tried to warn Beecher that Tilton was treacherous.
In 1875, in a letter to Charley, Harriet also tried to dispose of her
brother's other accuser, Henry C. Bowen.[11] "For years," she declared, he had "been regarded as a consummate villain and hypocrite in the commercial circles of New York, and his connection
with Plymouth Church has been a standing disgrace to them."
But they could not get the testimony they needed to expel him
"because Bowen is rich and powerful and a dangerous man to
offend."

It *is* a horrible pity that there should be such a man in Plymouth Church, but there was a Judas in the family of Christ himself and Christ bore with him and did not turn him out and took and gave the kiss of daily affection to the man whom he knew would betray him.

Whether all this was true or not, there can be no doubt that Harriet believed it, and through all her suffering she had one source of comfort: her faith never wavered.

I think I never knew any one so cruelly treated as my brother has been. If he had not the sweetest kindest most patient magnanimous nature to begin with, I don't think even Divine Grace could have led a man to bear what he has borne.

He is peculiar, in a sort of extreme delicacy of feeling, and an entire and utter inability to talk of what pains him. In the great sorrows of life, the loss of his brother and his little children, he has always shut himself up and been dumb—there is a terrible inward intensity. The trial of this vile story came on him three years ago when first with amazement and disgust and horror he learned that such a thought could enter a human soul with regard to him. Since then he has been busy forgiving—healing restoring returning good for evil and blessing for cursing, and God helping he will carry it through, notwithstanding this vile woman's attempt to tear open old wounds. I who know all and have seen all from the first feel as if I could give my life's blood for him.

Surely there never was a more faithful sister. And if Henry Ward Beecher did not deserve it, let us be glad that she never knew.

CHAPTER III

THE WIFE

I

"Calvin Stowe as a romantic figure," writes Forrest Wilson, "is a tough morsel for our cultivated taste in heroes. That the thick-shouldered, baldish, bearded scholar, gluttonous, neurasthenic, timid and lazy, a scatter-brain in emergencies, and quite devoid of that talent for getting things done which Harriet called 'faculty,' could have inspired any strong passion in a deep nature, taxes the modern credulity." This is true enough, and Harriet herself once wrote George Eliot that she considered her husband "as of Goblin origin decidedly—probably he pre existed in Germany and certainly it was a great mistake that he was born in America." But this was in 1869, and we must remember that it took Calvin a long time to eat himself into the astonishing rotundity of his final phase, when, according to Mark Twain, he was also disfigured by a cauliflower nose, and little Susy Clemens, having encountered him in the streets of Hartford, came flying home to her mother to report that "Santa Claus has got loose." [1]

Calvin was nine years older than Harriet and had been married to her friend Eliza Tyler, daughter of the Reverend Dr. Bennett Tyler of Andover, a leader of the "Old School" Presbyterians. As has been stated, he was a professor at Lane when Lyman Beecher was president there, and it was their common grief for Eliza that drew him and Harriet together. When their twin daughters were born in 1836, during Calvin's absence abroad, Harriet named one Eliza and the other Isabella, but Calvin, returning, changed Isabella to Harriet, thus having one daughter named for each of his wives. Every year on Eliza's birthday, Harriet and Calvin sat together before his first wife's portrait recalling and celebrating her virtues.

Despite his eccentricities and his tendency to melancholy, Calvin was a lovable man with a keen sense of humor. A graduate of Bowdoin, where neither his strict principles nor his piety had kept him from being admired in a free-living set, he had taught at both Andover and Dartmouth before coming to Lane. In the year of his marriage to Harriet, the State of Ohio sent him to Europe to study the public school system, especially of Prussia. His report was widely circulated and influential; he also had an important role in founding a teachers college in Cincinnati. Primarily, however, he was a Biblical scholar, and there was nothing cold or formal about his scholarship. Said Henry Ward Beecher:

He led me to an examination of the Bible and to an analysis of its several portions, not as parts of a machine, formal and dead, but as a body of truth instinct with God, warm with divine and human sympathies, clothed with language adapted to their fit expression and to be understood as similar language used for similar ends in every-day life.

The most curious aspect of Calvin's personality was his natural mediumism. From childhood he was haunted by immaterial beings, which came to him spontaneously, so early in his life that he never thought of questioning their reality. Nor did he ever get over this. He once held a psychic conversation with Goethe, and late in life, when Charley was studying in Germany, the devil came to him night after night, telling him that his son was dead and trying to destroy his faith. But, as he told a friend,

I was ready for him last night. I had fortified myself with passages of Scripture. I found some things in Ephesians which were just what I wanted, and when he came last night, I *hurled* them at him. I tell you, it made him bark like a dog, and he took himself off. He won't trouble me again.

Like many mediums, he was admirably undogmatic in his interpretation of his own experiences, having "serious doubts," he wrote George Eliot, "as to the objectivity of the scenes exhibited." He could even be materially-minded enough to seek physical (or semi-physical) explanations of the manifestations:

Is it absurd to suppose that some peculiarity in the nervous system, in the connecting link between soul and body, may bring some more than others, into an almost abnormal contact with the spirit-World (for example, Jacob Boehme and Swedenborg), and that, too, without correcting their faults, or making them morally better than others?

Harriet described Calvin's visions through Horace Holyoke in *Oldtown Folks*, but Calvin also left us his own factual account. There were several different sets of phantoms. The principal set were "rational" and "generally harmless," though "their countenances expressed pleasure or pain, complaisance or anger" according to his own mood, and "their appearance was always attended with considerable effort and fatigue"; the more distinct and vivid they were, the more they tended to take out of him. Though they favored dusk and solitude, they might appear at any time, passing with ease through floors, walls, and ceilings. Sometimes he heard as well as saw them, but he was never able to touch them.

They exhibited all possible combinations of size, shape, proportion, and color, but their most usual appearance was with the human form and proportion, but under a shadowy outline that seemed just ready to melt into the invisible air, and sometimes liable to the most sudden and grotesque changes, and with a uniform darkly bluish color spotted with brown, or brownish white.

Different apartments owned different sets of phantoms. Night after night he was visited by a very large Indian woman and a very small Indian man with a huge bass-viol between them. Once at least, six-inch fairies gambolled on the window-sill. An especial favorite was a vision which, like the imaginary rabbit in Mary Chase's play, was named Harvey, after "a boy older than myself whom I feared and hated." In a certain bedroom of Calvin's youth, Harvey appeared every night, "a very pleasant-looking human face," popping up out of the hallway which faced the foot of his bed, in an empty space between the ceiling and some boards which did not quite reach it, first peering over the top of the boards, then gradually pressing forward "his neck, shoulders, and finally his whole body as far as the waist."

But there was another set of spirits "which never varied in their form or qualities, and were always mischievous and terrible," whose appearance generally occurred when he was sick or depressed. "These were a sort of heavy clouds floating about overhead, of a black color, spotted with brown, in the shape of a very flaring inverted tunnel without a nozzle, and from ten to thirty or forty feet in diameter." Once he had a vision of hell, with four or five sky-blue, very gentlemanly-looking devils carrying off a dissipated man of the neighborhood named Brown, and once he found an ashy-blue skeleton in bed with him.

These psychic experiences of Calvin Stowe's seem curiously detached from his general personality. They do not appear to have induced a visionary outlook in general or to have affected his attitude toward life in other aspects.

II

A month before her marriage Harriet wrote her friend Elizabeth Lyman, "I feel that I am in for it, and must go through if I die for it." On her wedding morn she recorded that she felt "nothing at all" and, much later, that she could speak well of her marriage "after all." Consequently it has sometimes been inferred that she did not care greatly for Calvin, but this is a mistake. The premarital reactions were due to the overstrain of girlish nerves, being comparable in their way to the coldness toward God of which the saints complain. "Well," she says, "it is really a mercy to have this entire stupidity come over one at such a time."

Harriet herself later wrote Calvin that "I did love you with an almost insane love before I married you," then added, somewhat inconsistently, "for I loved you as I now love God." Eleven years after marriage she told her husband that "were I now free I should again love just as I did and again feel that I could give up all to and for you, and if I do not love and never can love again with the blind unwise love with which I married I love quite as truly though far more wisely."

Their letters are full of touching expressions of affection for each other. "If you could only come home today," he wrote her when she was away, "how happy I should be; I am daily finding out more and more (what I knew very well before) that you are the most intelligent and agreeable woman in the whole circle of my acquaintance." And she replied, "If you were not already my dearly loved husband, I should certainly fall in love with you." More fully he writes her:

Who else has so much talent with so little self-conceit; so much reputation with so little affectation; so much literature with so little nonsense; so much enterprise with so little extravagance; so much tongue with so little scold; so much sweetness with so little softness; so much of so many things and so little of so many other things?

She knew too that success could never lessen her need for him: "It is not fame nor praise that contents me. I seem never to have needed love so much as now. I long to hear you say how much you love me." Even when they were old and his health wrecked, she could write that she and Calvin had never "enjoyed each other's society more than this winter."

Yet it is only in a qualified sense that the marriage of Calvin and Harriet Beecher Stowe can be called a happy one. Their difficulties cannot be wholly understood by reference to previously published biographies, but they grow clear in the light of their letters to each other, now preserved at Radcliffe College.[2]

How much Calvin and Harriet remonstrated with each other about their shortcomings when they were together I have no idea, but they certainly had a passion for exploring the subject in letters when they were separated. Most of the letters were written in 1844 and 1847, but I do not believe that the sources of disagreement were wholly removed during later years.

It was not altogether a matter of their relationship *to each other*. Part of the difficulty was the soul-searing, heart-destroying Puritan self-searching which always demanded so much more of human nature, in oneself and in others, than human nature can give. Thus, though Calvin is a clergyman, Harriet often writes to him as if he were an ignorant young heathen whom she was striving to introduce to Christ:

My love, *you* must know the wonderful knowledge of Jesus which so subdues and transforms. You seek knowledge with a burning thirst. Even so you must seek Christ, that you may *know* him, as Paul says.

If the love of Christ fills your whole soul there will not be room for any thing else.... If he were daily and personally present with you and you in a habit of holy friendship and endeared communion would not many things that now vex you lose their power to annoy? All that is wanting is that you put personal holiness in the *first place*. If you had studied Christ with half the energy that you have studied Luther—if you were as eager for daily intercourse with him as to devour the daily newspaper—if you were drawn towards him and loved him as much as you loved your study and your books, then would he be formed in you, the hope of glory.

You do not sufficiently control your own mind on this subject—all your carefulness, prudence, caution and honesty I admire and commend, but when you become nervous anxious fretful and apprehensive of poverty then you have taken matters out of Christ's hands into your own, and are doing what he is very sorry to see you do.

Did Calvin resent such exhortations? On the contrary, he loved them and missed them when they were not forthcoming. In 1844 he was so dissatisfied concerning his spiritual condition that he wondered whether he ought not give up the ministry altogether:

I try to be spiritually minded, and find in myself a most exquisite relish and deadly longing for all kinds of sensual gratification. I think of the revival ministers who have lived long in licentiousness with good reputation, and then been detected, and ask myself, who knows whether there be any real piety on earth?

Indeed the only thought that gave him any "great comfort amid all the terrible sorrow" of his life was the thought that his wife was "growing in grace and the knowledge of Christ." He complains that her last five letters have not been so religious as their predecessors; he cannot read them to his friends. (Poor Harriet, who had to screw herself up to a pitch of religious ecstasy sufficient not only to save her clergyman husband but also to uplift and astonish his friends!)

Have you left off to pray and enjoy communion with Christ? Is the high state of spirituality which you seemed to enjoy all gone? It was my chief hope in the darkness and despondency of my own mind, that you were continuously approaching nearer and nearer to Christ. . . . that you could be continually a guide and support to my feeble and tottering steps in the way of life.

The unsympathetic modern mind may be excused if it admits a touch of comedy here; if not, it must surely enter with this sad but ludicrous letter of 1844, in which Harriet sees her husband already committed to the primrose path, with her whole family tripping along beside him! [3]

Yesterday Henry came from Crawfordsville uncommonly depressed and sober and spoke in church meeting of unexpected falls among high places in the church and the need of prayer for Christians. He seemed so depressed that a horrible presentiment crept over me. I thought of all my brothers and of you—and could it be, that the great Enemy has prevailed against any of you, and as I am gifted with a most horribly vivid imagination, in a moment I imagined—nay saw as in a vision all the distress and despair that would follow a fall on your part. I felt weak and sick—I took a book and lay down on the bed, but it pursued me like a nightmare, and something seemed to ask Is your husband any better seeming than so and so! I looked in the glass and my face which since spring has been something of the palest was so haggard that it frightened me. The illusion lasted a whole forenoon and then evaporated like a poisonous mist, but God knows how I pity those heart wrung women—wives worse than widows, who are called to lament that the grave has not covered their husband, the father of their children! Good and merciful God—why are such agonies reserved for the children of men! I can conceive now of misery which in one night would change the hair to gray and shrivel the whole frame to premature decrepitude! misery to which all other agony is as a mocking sound! What terrible temptations lie in the way of your sex—till now I never realised it.... I have no jealousy—the most beautiful woman in the world would not make me jealous so long as she only *dazzled the senses*, but still my dear, you must not wonder if I want to warn you not to look or *think* too freely on womankind. If your sex would guard the outworks of *thought*, you would *never* fall, and when so dizzying so astounding are the advantages which Satan takes it scarce is implying a doubt to say "be cautious."

Was there ever a letter of such mingled sophistication and naïveté? How astonishing is the suggestion that she would not be jealous of a woman who could only inflame men's senses! And what, on the other hand, are we to make of her wonderful prescription for ensuring fidelity in husbands—that a man should neither look at other women nor think of them?

But there were other difficulties with Calvin himself that were not fantastic at all but terribly real. In a long letter of September 23, 1844, he summed up his indictment of her. He loved her "as much as I am capable of loving a fellow creature," and she was the wife of his choice "if the whole world were open before me now to choose from." Nevertheless,

there are certain points in which we are so exactly unlike that our peculiarities impinge against each other and sometimes produce painful collisions when neither party is conscious of any intention to disoblige the other.

1) I am naturally anxious, to the extent of needlessly taking much thought beforehand. You are hopeful, to the extent of being heedless of the future, thinking only of the present. It requires as much grace to make you thoughtful of the future, as it does to make me content with the present and trust God for the future. The Lord grant us both the grace and all the grace we need.

2) I am naturally very methodical as to time and place for everything, and anything out of time or out of place is excessively annoying

to me. This is a feeling to which you are a stranger. You have no idea
of either time or place. I want prayer and meals at the particular time,
and every piece of furniture in its own place. You can have morning
prayer any time ... and as to place, it seems to be your special delight
to keep everything in the house on the move, and your special torment
to allow anything to retain the same position a week together. Per-
manency is my delight, yours everlasting change.

3) I am naturally particular, you are naturally slack—and you often
give me inexpressible torment without knowing it. You and Anne
[a servant] have vexed me beyond endurance often by taking up my
newspapers, and then instead of folding them properly and putting
them in their place, either dropping them all sprawling on the floor,
or wabbling them all up into one wabble, and sprawling them on the
table like an old hen with her guts and gizzard squashed out.

4) I am naturally very irritable, take offence easily, utter my vexa-
tion in a moment, and then it is gone—you are naturally more forbearing, take offence less easily, and are silent and retain the wound.

Five days later he added that he had not done her justice, not
acknowledging

your earnest and successful endeavor for self improvement. In all
respects in which both nature and an exceedingly defective and one-
sided education have made you imperfect, I recognize and admire in
you an earnest and Christian-like purpose to amend. Nature and bad
education have done me great injury, and I know by my own experience how hard it is to get the better of such defects; and you have
succeeded on your part far better than I have on mine.

He complains further that when she had (for example) raising
flowers on her mind, she would be diligent in caring for the
flowers but neglect everything else.

Again, you seldom hesitate to make a promise, whether you have
ability to perform it or not, like your father and like Kate, only not
quite as bad; and promises so easily made are very easily broken. On
this point Kate has no conscience at all, your father very little; and
you have enough to keep you from making such promises if you
would only think beforehand whether you could fulfil them or not.

This is painful reading. But Harriet had been brought up on New England logic too, and she was quite capable of managing an over-all indictment of her own. Writing on July 20, 1847, she recalls Calvin's tenderness in the early days of their marriage and marvels how he could have

become so altered as to say and to feel somethings such as you have since then expressed. I am satisfied that it is a *morbid disease*. I am certain when and under what influences it arose and now see by what causes it has been increased and to what results it has grown and what faults in me have increased it.

The root of the difficulty she finds in that not unfamiliar complaint—mother-in-law trouble. When the elder Mrs. Stowe lived with her daughter-in-law, she complained "that I was extravagant in expenses, that I needed much waiting on, that I inclined to keep too much help, &c &c." She kept up a "perpetual state of complaint" and continually pointed out Harriet's faults, so that Calvin became predisposed to view her "in a wrong light" and even to wonder whether she got more than her share of attention.

Your letters contain full admissions of my laborious conscientious self denying life as a wife and mother. You are at times fully sensible of all that I have done and suffered, of the difficulties I have had to meet and the undaunted firmness with which I have met them. If I should lay the things in your last letter side by side with many others you have written one would see how exactly contradictory they are.

Now with regard to myself I freely confess that I am constitutionally careless and too impetuous and impulsive easily to maintain that consistency and order which is necessary in a family—that I often undertake more than I can well perform and so come to mortifying failures. I also see *now* plainer than I ever did before that I have felt too little the necessity of conceding to such of your peculiarities as seemed to me unreasonable, and have too often pushed my own purposes without reference to them.

She complains of her husband's neglect of letter-writing:

It is very trying for me . . . to watch the mail day after day and not get any letter and when after long long delay one comes it is also trying to find so little in it—five minutes more or ten it does seem would be little while you are about it and would make *so much* difference with me.

There is also a more fundamental complaint:

One thing would make a great difference with me. If when you have said things hastily and unjustly you would only be willing to retract them in calmer moments. This is what you almost never do in any particular case.... You leave the poisoned arrow in the wound. Now my nature is such that I *cannot* forget such words—if they are only taken back I get over them directly but if not they remain for months. ... It does seem to me that with such a foundation for mutual respect and affection as there is in us—with such true and real and deep love, that we might exercise a correcting power over each other—that I might help you to be kind and considerate, you me to be systematic and regular.

And as late as 1860 she knows that "you try to do all right and that in your heart no one is more loving than you" but begs for "a word of encouragement."

My dear husband do write me one calm kind considerate letter in memory of all the love I have ever borne you for the earthly time for these things is running low.

III

Which was the dominant party in the Stowe menage? In *My Wife and I* Harry Henderson tells Eva Van Arsdale, who has some conscientious qualms about promising to "obey" him, that "there can be no obeying where there is no commanding, and as to commanding you I should as soon think of commanding the sun and moon." I do not believe that Calvin, for all his complaints, "commanded" Harriet. She knew very well that on the domestic front women are more than a match for men and always have been, that if a man loves a woman she has a hold over him which no legal privileges that he may hold can possibly counterbalance, and that if he does not wish to kill her or discard her, he *must* please her. Nor did she imagine any of this to be a modern development. The Old Testament sets up Sarah as "a model of conjugal behavior," but no woman need be frightened by the pattern, for Sarah herself was

too wise to dispute the title when she possessed the reality of sway; and while she called Abraham "lord," it is quite apparent from certain little dramatic incidents that she expected him to use his authority in the line of her wishes.

Even under slavery a woman like Cassy could do pretty well in managing a man like Simon Legree.

From the beginning of their married life Harriet realized that Calvin needed her to manage all his domestic affairs. Her own gifts as a homemaker have been warmly described by Elizabeth Stuart Phelps [4] and others, and though she did think that Calvin developed somewhat as a family man in the course of time, his ineptitude in all household matters (some of which she memorialized in "A Scholar's Adventures in the Country") [5] was always very great; he was indeed so much a cipher in this aspect that at least one fellow-townsman thought of her as "Widow Stowe." It is significant that when he was away from Cincinnati during the cholera epidemic, she insisted that he stay away until it was over, realizing that the only thing he could possibly do for her, should he return, would be to give her another child to look after. As long as he lived, she justified her care for her own health on the ground that the very existence of her family depended on it. "For your Father depends so on me for his very life and all the affairs are so in my hands that if my health gives out there will be a general break up." And during his last years she used to pray to "my dear Lord with all submission not to take me . . . till my dear husband is gone, for nobody else *can* do for him what I can."

When fame came to her Calvin was perforce thrust into the position which so few men have the character to endure with dignity—that of being the husband of a celebrity. As early as 1844 he was offended when "a *young gentleman*" asked him if

"*Mrs. H. B. Stowe* was any connexion of mine," and he told Lyman he was determined that from now on Harriet "shall call herself Mrs. C. E. Stowe," but he soon got over such nonsense. After *Uncle Tom's Cabin* he feared for a time that she might be spoiled. He should have known her better. Even if she had been corruptible, she was too dreamy and introverted to be importantly affected by anything so external as worldly success. "If the Dutch beat the D——l, she beats the Dutch." When they were in Europe, he acted as her spokesman at public banquets and elsewhere, and once at least he showed what was in him when, stung by what seemed to him offensive British assumptions of superiority toward America, he bluntly told a distinguished audience that without British purchase of Southern cotton, slavery would wither away. In Florida too he could assert himself nobly in repelling intruders upon the Stowe privacy, as when he told the lady who remarked that she was glad to see him but would rather have seen Mrs. Stowe that he quite agreed with her.

But Harriet was not really dependent upon him for such services. Though he undertook to conduct her battle with the Reverend Joel Parker, when she was threatened with a libel suit for blasting him as an apologist for slavery in *Uncle Tom's Cabin*, she never hesitated to address her opponent directly when she felt she had something to say. Neither in Europe nor later in Florida does she ever seem to have held back from anything she wished to participate in because Calvin refused to join her, and when he had to return to Andover for the beginning of the new term, she simply continued her travels without him. When she needed financial advice, she turned not to him but to her brother-in-law, Thomas C. Perkins, and when she built that white elephant, her first Hartford house, she seems to have paid no attention to anybody. This time all Calvin's dire prognostications of disaster were justified, but about all the satisfaction he got came when he started up out of bed in the middle of the night, with the water pipes bursting over his head, and bellowed, "Oh, yes, all the modern conveniences! Shower baths while you sleep!"

Harriet recognized his dependence upon her and, when it appeared, his rebellion also; it was not without reference to her own experience that she believed every wife must be a mother to her husband. In 1879 she wrote Charley:

Your father is quite well. The sea had its usual exhilarating effect upon him. Before we left New York he was quite meek, and exhibited such signs of grace and submission that I had great hopes of him. He promised to do exactly as I told him, and stated that he had entire confidence in my guidance. What woman wouldn't call such a spirit evidence of being prepared for speedy translation? I was almost afraid he could not be long for this world. But on the second day at sea his spirits rose, and his appetite reasserted itself. He declared in loud tones how well he felt, and quite resented my efforts to take care of him. I reminded him of his gracious vows and promises in the days of his low spirits, but to no effect. The fact is, his self-will has not left him yet, and I have no fear of his immediate translation.

But I do not think we need waste too much sympathy upon Calvin in this aspect. He accepted the situation, as so many men do, because he knew he would be quite helpless without his wife. One day a visitor made a complimentary remark about his children. "Yes," he exclaimed proudly, "Beechers, every one of them!"

IV

There remains one specialized subject in connection with the relations between Harriet and Calvin Stowe, and this is his relationship to her writing. He encouraged her at the very beginning of her career:

My dear, you must be a literary woman. It is so written in the book of fate. Make all your calculations accordingly. Get a good stock of health and brush up your mind. Drop the E. out of your name. It only incumbers it and interferes with the flow and euphony. Write yourself fully and always Harriet Beecher Stowe, which is a name euphonious, flowing, and full of meaning. Then my word for it, your husband will lift up his head in the gate, and your children will rise up and call you blessed.

It was her own view that she could always speak with him more freely than with anyone else and that she could have written nothing without him. There was never any question as to the information he placed at her disposal. In addition to his great supply of general knowledge, he was adept in theology and New England local color, and if she made a mistake he could always be counted upon to correct her.

The interesting thing is that he should have professed to have no aesthetic capacities whatever. "I cannot discover that I possess either taste or talent for fiction or poetry." Yet he was an excellent mimic and storyteller, and his son says that Sam Lawson's *Fireside Stories* "are told as they came from Mr. Stowe's lips, with little or no alteration." However that may be, it is not fantastic to suggest that his limitations may have been as valuable to her as his more positive qualities, as she herself suggests when she says that "though one may think a husband a partial judge, yet mine is so nervous and so afraid of being bored that I feel as if it were something to hold him." Held he was in the most generous way possible, and we see him "with his long gray beard, white hair, and piercing black eyes, . . . with his pocket handkerchief spread out upon his knees, alternately shaking with laughter, or heaving with sobs." And so they went on to the end: "My old rabbi and I here set up our tent, he with German, and Greek, and Hebrew, devouring all sorts of black-letter books, and I spinning ideal webs out of bits that he lets fall here and there."

A postscript to the foregoing might concern Harriet's relationship to Calvin's writing—what there was of it. He read and studied incessantly, but he hated to write—Harriet called his handwriting "Arabic quail tracks"—and she was ever scheming to remedy this situation. Once he planned a book on Luther and Charles V and once a book on Goethe, but neither ever got itself written.

In regard to Mr. Stowe [she once wrote James T. Fields], you must not scare him off by grimly declaring that you must have the *whole manuscript complete* before you set the printer to work. You must take the three-quarters he brings you and at least make believe begin printing, and he will immediately go to work and finish up the whole; otherwise, what with lectures and the original sin of laziness, it will be indefinitely postponed.

But in the end it was not Fields but the Hartford Publishing Company that got a big book on the Bible out of Calvin, which was sold by subscription and earned large profits.

Chapter IV

THE MOTHER

I

"Childhood nowadays is unceasingly fêted and caressed, the principal difficulty of the grown people seeming to be to discover what the little dears want,—a thing not always clear to the little dears themselves." These words from *The Pearl of Orr's Island* (1862) may perhaps serve to indicate that if children are not what they used to be, they never were. Though Harriet Beecher Stowe did not believe in overindulging children, her writings afford abundant evidence that she sympathized with them even when they were naughty, as, for example, with "Little Edward," [1] who could not learn how to keep the Sabbath. She kills Edward off prematurely, but this was not by way of punishment, for she treats far too many of her saintly children the same way. Like Dickens, she was convinced that the ability to look at the world from the child's point of view was a rare achievement in adults. She disliked confining "little animals" in kindergarten, and she wanted boys left free to make a lot of noise. "The male element sometimes pours into a boy like the tides in the Bay of Fundy, with tumult and tossing." The overcareful mother, who is more interested in rugs and furniture than in children, is very unsympathetically handled in *Little Foxes*, and there was not much of a case left for the strict disciplinarians after Miss Lois and her mother had fought the issue out between them in *Oldtown Folks*.[2]

When her own children came, she was just the kind and loving mother that anybody who had known anything about her would have expected her to be. Not that it was "roses, roses all the way," or even, as St. Francis of Assisi described the service of God, "sweet and easy." Harriet said frankly that, while the first child was always a poem, those that followed were quite unsentimental prose. When they were small, they were, "like other little sons and daughters of Adam, full of all kinds of absurdity and folly," and growing up did not seem to cure them of their faults. She felt very keenly both the all-importance and the impossibility of training them adequately, and they made her feel old at thirty-seven.

Her love for her children was shared by Calvin, but he lacked her ability to express it. There are letters to Hatty and Eliza, written in 1859, in which she admits a barrier between them and their father and tries to break it down:

He is like both of you, proud and sensitive, and waits for advances from others. . . . I can't think why open as he is to me he is so reserved to others. But I hope you will learn to know him and then you must appreciate what is in him.

Papa likes to be loved and wants to be told so and you must say all you feel—you *feel* enough and must *let all out*. Georgy once said that there was a *wall* between him and her, but now it seems quite down.

Calvin was much attached to Henry and much saddened, perhaps permanently, by his death. He went traveling alone with Fred, which was no small price for a man of his temperament to pay even for a son's rehabilitation. In his last years he was much attached to Charley, "the very light of his eyes," Harriet says.

Being the kind of woman she was, it was inevitable that Harriet Beecher Stowe should yearn over her children from the point of view of their spiritual welfare more than in any other aspect. Once she had been emancipated from the theological horrors of her youth, the threat of eternal damnation no longer hung over their heads with the same urgency as of yore, but this did not lessen her zeal to bring them into the fold. There is a suggestive memorandum among her papers in the Women's Archives:

In thinking how all my life and strength and almost my separate consciousness passed away from me into my children and how they seem to depend on me from day to day for sympathy, I seemed to understand what Christ meant when he spoke of himself as being made bread and giving his flesh and blood as the vital food for his own.

And in Rome, in 1860, she composed a long intercessory prayer in their behalf:

I know my own faults and imperfections, and how far I have been from doing as I should by them, but Thou knowest there has not been any hour of my life when it has not been the first and most absorbing wish of my heart that they should truly know and fervently love Thee.

I know not what course to pursue and pray Thee to teach me. I have done and said everything I knew how. I do not know how to act and I pray Thee oh Lord Jesus to help me....

How reasonable Harriet's religious passion for her children is to be judged will of course depend upon the reader's own religious beliefs and attitudes. I find it unwholesome and masochistic only in one undated letter, written, apparently, not long after the death of the baby she lost in Cincinnati. Here she speaks of the living Henry as her "lovely dear little baby," then adds,

but my departed one is a purer source of joy to me—who knows that it is a blessing to have these dear ones live! I hold him fondly to my heart these lonely nights with a sort of sad satisfaction—poor child!— it is a hard thing to be born to such a lot as this life! and I could not find it in me to mourn if God should also resume him.

Fortunately there are also more wholesome expressions of religious zeal, oriented toward life. All her brothers had become clergymen, but she herself was able to dedicate only one son to the ministry, and the letters of exhortation and advice she wrote him are innumerable. One example must suffice here:

For a week past my heart has been yearning towards you with an unspeakable love, a love that seemed to bear my spirit to your spirit in prayer. Over and over I have been giving you up to Christ, to be His own and asking Him to come and take full possession of your heart and dwell in you that you may live to continue that lovely and beautiful work of blessing and saving men begun by your grandfather, continued by your father, bequeathed to you as a sacred trust by their prayers and consecrations.

II

Four children she lost—the first Charley as a baby; Henry in his college days by drowning; Fred, who disappeared; and the brilliant and charming Georgiana, wife of an Episcopal clergyman and mother of Dr. Freeman Allen, who succumbed after years of nervous illness. She had always felt so close to Henry that it seemed unnatural to her that he could not share her grief after he was gone. "I *do love you* Henry," she had written him, "and I know you do love me—but oh my darling I want you to choose my Redeemer—your Father's and mother's God for your own." The special elements of mental anguish involved in his death are considered elsewhere in this volume. "If ever I was conscious of an attack of the Devil trying to separate me from the love of Christ, it was for some days after the terrible news came." [3] There may have been elements of tragedy in Georgy's death also, for Forrest Wilson says that she had become a victim of morphine through unwise medication. We do not have any details of this disorder, and nothing more can be said about it here. Fred's ordeal, however, which lacerated his mother's heart for years, must be described at greater length, and fortunately the letters now in the Women's Archives make it possible to give a fuller and more sympathetic picture of him than has previously been drawn.

First, however, three other children must be mentioned: the twins—Hattie and Eliza—and the youngest child, Charles Edward. He was the only one she ever wrote a book about,[4] and he returned the compliment by becoming her biographer. Charley started out somewhat uncertainly, for in his youth he heard the call of the sea, and when he was fourteen his complaisant mother allowed him to go to the Mediterranean in a Boston sailing vessel! When he returned, "with hands so spread with hard work that they look twice too big for him," she seems to have been so pleased by the manliness the hard life had developed in him that she looked forward resignedly to further separations. "Unfortunate is the hen who hatches a duck, but she must make the best of it." Charley, however, recovered from his water mania and settled down, though not without some characteristic Beecher-Stowe struggles, to the life of a Congregational minister. During his mother's later years, he was located at Hartford, where she attended his church, though by that time her formal affiliation was with the Episcopalians. Apparently Charley had an attack of skepticism while studying in Germany;[5] later his mother went through another ordeal with him when she thought him in danger of becoming a Unitarian; this launched her into a theological letter-writing campaign which can rarely have been equaled, and which was quite successful.[6]

The twins never married; they kept her house; at the end of her life she was more their child than they hers. "My twin daughters," she wrote George Eliot in 1876, "relieve me from all domestic care; they are lively, vivacious, with a real genius for practical life." To the girls themselves she had written many years before, "You don't know how I love you—you never will till you love some one as I do you—you have educated me quite as much as I you—you have taught me the love of God, by awakening such love in me."

Unfortunately, in an imperfect world we cannot have quite untroubled relations even with those we love; on the contrary, they are the only ones who can really hurt us. So in 1861 we find Harriet writing her daughters:

I long to put the experience of fifty years at once into your young hearts to give you at once the key of that treasure chamber every gem of which has cost me tears and struggles and prayers, but you must work for these inward treasures yourself, but I hope I may save you some mistakes, some wearisome ill directed efforts and put you in shorter ways to the result. I hope so but Christ may see differently— I may not be the one to lead you into the promised land.

This seems general enough, but in 1863 there were definite grievances to be aired:

Now, when I think of appealing to you for help in various crises which arise I find you with your own plans all laid—your time divided and your wishes very strong. Tho you always beautifully assent to my wishes yet it is so evident that I break in on your plans and derange them that I often suffer any inconvenience and go far beyond my strength rather than ask one of you to help me.

She complains that when some one is ill, the whole burden of nursing falls on her, and that though she dislikes accounts as much as anybody could, she does them rather than ask the girls "to do what you say you so much dislike." Yet if they do not find some way to relieve her, it may be that they will have to look forward to "*another mother*" coming in!

No, my girls, while you have your mother you have it in your hands to keep her by taking from her the burdens which draw her life away but you cannot do it without being willing to take trouble and *work* as I do.

On November 20, 1865, she returns to these complaints and adds others:

Remember my children, nobody can help me who depresses my spirits. My courage, hope and animal spirits are the fund on which I, and you and all depend, and when I feel that all around me are gloomy and depressed, it is a *sorer drain on my vitality than any amount of hard work*. . . . I think my children do not often enough consider my nature, its wants and needs. I am very sensitive, very affectionate. A word spoken harshly by any one *to any other* grates on me—I bear the blame of all. . . . Then too I have so little society. Papa goes off by himself and reads—you and Eliza go by yourselves and talk—I have no companion unless one of my sisters.

But the sisters—or one of them—made her relations with the girls not less difficult but more:

Sister Katy is always good natured and sympathetic and ready to do any little thing for me. It grieves me that my children take so much to heart her little peculiarities and are made uncomfortable by her stay. ... I think for my sake you might be more willing to have her with us because it is a comfort to me.

There is another letter, conjecturally dated August 24, 1869, in which Harriet writes to Eliza: "You and Hattie have helped me always in taking charge of household matters and accounts." Let us hope that this records a permanent change.

III

The Civil War began in April 1861. On May 2, Harriet wrote as follows to her daughter Hattie:

Ever since war was declared which is now about two weeks—a little over—I have been like a person struggling in a nightmare dream. Fred immediately wanted to go, and I was willing he should if he could only get a situation where he could do any good. But as a mere soldier I felt he was not strong enough and might therefore only get sick and do no good. He applied to go as surgeon's aid but as he was only in his first year of study and so many graduated medical men applied he could not get any situation of that kind. At last Mrs. Fields' brother Dr. Adams ... said that if Fred would enlist with him as a private he would immediately choose him for Hospital Steward when the army got into action.

The worst of all, Hattie, is that which is not seen, the anxiety of heart. It is not that I would not give my son's life, but the temptations and dangers of the camp, and the fears that sometimes will obtrude, of his being prisoner among barbarians, or wounded and helpless—I put them out but they are there. Fred and I had a long talk Sunday night and he said he was willing to lay down his life for the cause and that if he died he felt he should go to the pure and good he had always longed for, and he and I kneeled down hand in hand and prayed for each other....

Frederick William Stowe is generally thought of as a victim of the Civil War. In a way he was also a victim of his mother's fame and of *Uncle Tom's Cabin*, for it is said that one reason he was so anxious to go to war was that "people shall never say, 'Harriet Beecher Stowe's son is a coward.' "

They never did. What they said instead was, "Harriet Beecher Stowe's son is a drunkard." He was wounded in the head at Gettysburg "by an iron splinter piercing so near the brain as to destroy hearing of one ear and shatter his whole nervous system." His father started out to go to him but, with his customary practical efficiency, got himself robbed in Springfield and was compelled to return home. Why Harriet did not go I have no idea. The wound remained open and painful for a long time.

The injury thus sustained is supposed to have been responsible for Fred's inability thereafter to control his appetite for liquor, and this may be true. But it seems clear that he was no teetotaler before the war, and it is certain that he was already the problem child of the family. On October 22, 1854, Harriet wrote to Mrs. D. H. Allen:

He is a smart bright lively boy—full of all manner of fun and mischief, fond of reading more than of hard study.... To say the truth, tho Fred gives me twice the uneasiness that Henry does, yet I have great hopes of him. He is the exact image of what his Uncle Henry was at his age, and I know he has the same warm affectionate heart so that tho he is always getting into some scrape and making me anxiety, I hope he will yet be as good a man.

She also speaks, ominously, of dashing Southern boys at school, with a taste for pistols and cigars,

and I have had great pains to combat various passions of Fred's inspired by such company, and we have to be very watchful but hope he will come out strait at last.

On December 18, 1859, Fred wrote his father from Florence about the latter's desire to have him study medicine. He would like this much, he says,

but the question is wheather [7] I can do it wheather I have strength
enough now or ever shall have—it has been nearly four years that I
have been able to do nothing I have tried every thing and instead of
getting better have rather got worse and now if this trip which I am on
makes me well is there not danger that the intence application that I
should have to give to the study before I could do anything for my
self would not break me down again and I would be helpless on your
hands a worse clog than before.

Moreover, he realizes that he is badly prepared, being now so
far behind in everything that medicine "would require the moast
intence and steady applycation." On March 31, 1860, he wrote
his father again, this time from Rome:

Father I have been a very troublesome thing to you for a long while
and I hope that when I come bac I will be able to be a comfort to you.
I feel that I have changed a great deal since I have been travelling and
I hope you will think so when you see me and think that I have
changed for the better. There was plenty of room for it when I left.

Since he did enter medical school, this resolve would seem to
have been kept, in part at least. In November 1862, when his
mother went to Washington, Fred got leave to be with her, and
his closeness to her is shown in his exclamation: "Oh, this pays
for a year and a half of fighting and hard work!" But earlier that
month she had been worried over a report that an army doctor
had given him whiskey for his ague. "What the temptations of
soldiers are in so cold and comfortless a life as theirs!" There is
also an undated letter from Fred's army days, full of pitiful good
resolutions, as he always was. He liked the army so well that he
even wanted Charley sent to West Point: "I think that it would
be a good plan to let the family have a good representation in the
army now as the Pulpit has had the monopoly all along." And
on March 23, 1863, he wrote his father: "I have made a solemn
vow not to touch or taste any kind of wine or liquor for I am
not going to loos all that I have gained and then I ment to save
my money and get married just as soon as I can for I think that
a wife is the best thing for me." The liquor problem, then, did

not begin with Gettysburg, however it may have been accentuated by what happened there.

By 1867 he is in an institution, feeling, as he writes his sisters, that he is better off there than he would be disgracing their name in the world: "I have but little hope of being able to restore the confidence you once had in me by anything I may say now for oft repeated promises of amendment have so often been broken until my presence home was a curse and not a pleasure." And four years later he writes Calvin from Mandarin of his desire to go to sea as a means of supporting himself and escaping from temptation:

I *can not* live on shore and did I only think of my own comfort I would kill myself and end it all but I know that you and all the family would feel the disgrace such an end would bring upon you and the talk and scandle it would give rise to and too it might drag poor Mays name before the public and she poor child has suffered too much from me now. . . . I am willing to serve seven ten or twenty years or even the rest of my life in the navy rather than to live on shore subject to the continual torment and fear of falling into a sin I hate and despise but before which I seem to be powerless. . . . I know that it will be said that I have not tried by some, but I do not care what they say I know that I have and do put forth all my strength and yet I fail. . . .

At Mandarin he managed—or rather mismanaged—his mother's orange grove, which she had purchased partly to give him a chance to rehabilitate himself. Of course he failed, and her financial loss was great, but this was nothing to her compared to the wreck of her son's life.

I do believe [she wrote her daughters touchingly, before the war was over] that *despising* another human being is in Christ's sight worse than all or any of those sins into which we are hurried by the infirmities of the flesh. If poor Fred fails in one respect, he is *exemplary* in others, where many find self control is difficult. He is gentle and patient, forbearing, unable to judge harshly or speak evil of others, and this is the more affecting as his brain and nerves are so shattered that it is difficult for him to steady himself at all.

Another, later letter shows how hard it was for her to give up hope:

Fred will not fall away so as finally to perish, and I have strong faith in his final recovery. He must go into an asylum and be under medical care for a year or so and your Aunt Catharine has gone to make inquiries and arrangements for this. God *will* hear my prayers and open some way of escape, I know.

Finally, Fred did take to the sea. He is known to have rounded the Horn and arrived in San Francisco, but at this point he disappeared forever from the knowledge of mankind. Perhaps he did kill himself, as he had thought of doing, but his faithful mother never thought so. If the dead live as long as they are remembered, then poor Fred died only with her. In the senility of her last years she embraced a stranger in Hartford and claimed him on the street as her long-lost son. And one can only think of the sad words of *John Inglesant:* "Nothing but the Infinite pity is sufficient for the infinite pathos of human life."

IV

The only daughter-in-law Harriet ever had was Susy Munroe, who married Charley, and I wince over a letter she wrote her on January 5, 1874, after Charley had written how much his wife had encouraged him to go into missionary work or wherever he might be called: "Dear brave little woman! . . . it is women like you that can help make men heroes, but unless a man loves something higher than any woman, he knows not how to love like a brave man." And she goes on to describe how St. Matthew responded immediately to the call of Christ, without waiting to consult his wife or anybody else! But Harriet was much more human in a later letter to Susy's mother in which she doubted whether the health of either of the children would justify a long stay at Presque Isle: "I am no advocate for sacrificing women to the mere physical necessities of life and I hold it perfectly proper that a minister who has formed an engagement should consider the ability of his wife as well as his own."

Her only complaint about Susy herself seems to be that she did not write enough letters:

You are an unfortunate little girl with one mother who can't give you up and another pulling to get you. Well, of course, if you write to your Cambridge mother every day, it is rather of a tax to write to your Stowe mother too. I quite feel for you, specially since you tell me you don't like letter writing. Well, having a great deal of it to do is just the way to make it come easier.

It is a pleasant letter enough, but I do not see much relinquishment in it.

Her first grandchild was Georgy's Freeman, and when he was born she became "first lady-in-waiting on his new majesty.... I am getting to be an old fool of a grandma, and to think there is no bliss under heaven to compare with a baby." She sent his picture to George Eliot, describing him as

one of those grave gentle angelic little ones that make one tremble lest they have hidden wings on which they will fly away some bright day and leave us alone. His little mamma says the picture does him but half justice because it does not give the golden hue of his curls nor his brilliant complexion—these must be imagined. He is one of those quaint dainty children all whose ways are peculiar and original.

Charley and Susy gave her two more grandsons—Lyman Beecher and Leslie, and if one may judge by his photograph as a child,[8] it must have been difficult for even Freeman Allen to be more beautiful than Lyman.

CHAPTER V

THE FRIEND

I

Harriet Beecher Stowe seems to have believed that socializing appealed more to women than to men, but her own enjoyment of it was limited. She often stresses her dislike of crowds, and she did not care for large parties, though she never condemned them. New York, she wrote Fanny Fern, "always half kills me—dazzles—dizzies—astonishes, confounds and overpowers poor little me." She believed in the human creature's right to privacy even in the family circle, and in the 'seventies she declared that "one evening company takes from me two or three working days."

Yet she was no hermit, nor was the hermit way of life her ideal. Even when declaring her comparative indifference to society, she admits the necessity of going into it to break her tendency toward too much introspection.

I am trying to cultivate a general spirit of kindliness toward everybody [she wrote in her youth]. Instead of shrinking into a corner to notice how other people behave, I am holding out my hand to the right and to the left, and forming casual or incidental acquaintances with all who will be acquainted with me. In this way I find society full of interest and pleasure—a pleasure which pleaseth me more because it is not old and worn out.

Being a girl, Harriet was generally left behind on her father's sporting expeditions, though she had some small part in them. But

73

though she had a certain understanding of hunting lust, she was not sympathetic toward English hunting customs, and in Florida she was an outspoken advocate of legislation to protect birds and animals against savages who could find nothing in the wilderness except a stimulus to slaughter.[1] She praised Luther for saying that his sympathies were always with the hunted, not the hunter, and even extended a certain charity to "those animals confessedly noxious and antagonistic to man, such as rats."

There are frequent references to bathing in the sea, which she felt revived her and relieved weakness and debility. She enjoyed coasting and snowballing with her children when they were small, and without them too when she was at the Brattleboro "water cure." "I wish you could be with me in Brattleboro'," she wrote Calvin, "and coast down hill on a sled, go sliding and snowballing by moonlight! I would snowball every bit of the *hypo* out of you!" There was horseback riding on occasion, and she was always a mighty pedestrian. Once, when she was an old woman, she tried to get a little girl whom she met on the street to teach her how to ride a bicycle.

Indoors there were charades, blindman's buff, and whist, but the only game about which she was really insane was croquet, which gets a whole chapter in *My Wife and I,* and to which there are many references in her letters to Mrs. Claflin. She seems obsessed with the desire to get a return match with the Governor, who had beaten her; in fact she feels "just as the French do about the Germans." And Mary Claflin has a really shocking story about how Harriet and Henry Ward would play croquet at "The Old Elms"

in a pouring rain, and when the darkness of night overtook them so that lanterns were necessary to enable them to see the wickets and the balls; often becoming so absorbed in their game that they were un-mindful of everything around them.

On one occasion they were summoned three times to greet an old friend of their father's who had called but failed to come until after the visitor had taken his departure to meet a train.

Soon after he left, the two culprits came slowly up the path to the piazza, wiping their faces, and arguing briskly about the position of the balls; each contending vigorously that he or she would have obtained the victory if the other had not hit the ball so-and-so.[2]

Harriet had the best of all possible motives for socializing in her interest in human beings; she could not, she says, be brought into contact with a person without wishing to find out about him. She showed considerable capacity for organizing parties and entertainments—at Andover, much later in Florida, and even, briefly, in Rome, where, in 1860, she held Wednesday evening receptions at which Browning, Charlotte Cushman, the Fieldses and others attended.

She says of herself that she would rather listen than talk. She liked intuitive people, for whom everything did not need to be spelled out, but this does not mean that she could not talk delightfully when she wanted to, especially with intimate friends. "Let me put my feet upon the fender," she said to Mrs. Fields, "and I can talk till all is blue."

Only she did not always want to. Says Mary Claflin:

I have known her to wander from room to room, humming softly to herself, seeming unconscious of everything about her, as if she were in a trance; and then, as though she had been communing with some spirit from another sphere, she would burst into eloquent language, a divine rhapsody, and entrance those around her with what she had seen and heard.

Mary Claflin knew. Once Harriet chose to go to bed instead of coming down to a reception which had been arranged in her honor, and when she was sent for she explained that she had a headache and it could not possibly make any difference to anybody whether she were there or not.

This is what Thomas Wentworth Higginson called "the mixture of *mauvaise honte* and indifference" which she displayed. She could go into a brown study almost any time, even if she were at the table. Obviously this was not all pose, but it is hard to believe that, after she had become a celebrity, she did not cultivate it somewhat as a means of saving her strength. When strangers called on her, she received them courteously but briefly, reserving to herself the privilege of terminating the interview. This she could do even with a celebrity like Frances Willard. As a young girl, Harriet Prescott Spofford was once left alone with her for forty-five minutes before a dinner, and when Higginson asked her what they had talked about, she replied, "Nothing, except that she once asked me what o'clock it was, and I told her I didn't know." She enchanted Agnes Park as a child by telling her a story, then invited her to return next day for another, but when the morrow came Agnes was told that Mrs. Stowe was too busy to see her. But I do not know anything more unconsciously self-revealing along this line than Harriet's own account of her first encounter with the Negro preacher and mystic Sojourner Truth. "Knowing nothing of her but her singular name, I went down, prepared to make the interview short, as the pressure of many other engagements demanded." Having conversed with her a short time, she "thought her manner so original that it might be worth while to call down my friends," which she accordingly did. Ten pages later in the account we read: "Sojourner stayed several days with us, a welcome guest." If she had not been, I am sure she would not have been invited.

II

If frankness is a social asset, Harriet was well qualified.

The utter failure of Christian, anti-slavery England [so she wrote the Duchess of Argyle during the Civil War] in those instincts of a right heart which can always see where the cause of liberty lies, has been as bitter a grief to me as was the similar prostration of all our American religious people in the day of the Fugitive Slave Law. Exeter Hall is a humbug, a pious humbug, like the rest.

She was quite as frank with Garrison and other colleagues in the antislavery fight when she disagreed with them: "I sympathize with you fully in many of your positions. Others I consider erroneous, hurtful to liberty and the progress of humanity." She was frank on literary matters also. She did not care for Annie Fields's poems. She told George Eliot that *Middlemarch* lacked humor —"You write and live on so high a plane!"—and that she had given up trying to read one of George Henry Lewes's books because, at her age, it was too much of a task to master his vocabulary. And though she did not try to force her own religious convictions on George Eliot, she certainly did not conceal them:

I seem to feel that you exhaust yourself with too constant giving of your life forces to others and that you need a more positive communion with Him who is immortal youth, health, strength and vitality.

She also writes:

You say of Dorothea [in *Middlemarch*], she no longer prays, not knowing what to ask for. But prayer is *not* merely asking—it is resting —it is renewing of vitality, hope, courage in our Father's arms—it is listening to his voice and feeling his life pass into us.

But her frankness was matched by her toleration—which *is* a social asset! Only political differences seem ever to have robbed her of her fundamental human charity. In *Men of Our Times* there are many severe judgments on Southerners and those who supported them. Stephen A. Douglas made "that very sparing use" of truth "which demagogues always do," and "that lost Archangel of New England," Daniel Webster, "moved over to the side of evil" when he supported the Fugitive Slave Law, and spoke with a "serpent voice." But the only one of her ideational comrades of whom she speaks critically in this volume is Wendell Phillips, "a teacher of the school of the law rather than that of the Gospel," who failed to "appreciate and make allowances for the necessary weaknesss and imperfections of human nature."

From Fénelon she took the principle that "perfection alone can bear with imperfection," from the slave woman Milly Edmundson, whose daughters were auctioned off by Henry Ward Beecher as an antislavery demonstration in Plymouth Church, the admonition that one must love the sinner while one hates the sin. In her Old Testament studies she found Aaron's appointment to the priestly office suitable because he was "a man peculiarly liable to the sins and errors of an excess of sympathy." Though painfully conscious of the extent to which worldliness had invaded the church and corrupted the professing Christian's way of life, she yet insisted that "there can be no definite rules laid down, and no Christian can venture to judge another by his standard." Zeph Higgins of *Poganuc People* is a hard man who conducts family worship mechanically, but it is something that he should wish to conduct it at all, and "such a human being has his place in the Creator's scheme." In her paper on Horace Greeley, published after his death, she cites the report of his having quoted "I know that my Redeemer liveth" on his death bed.

Is it needful that a man live the life of a saint, that he be spotless, perfect, and without fault, in order that he may say this in his dying hour? May not he who has often and many times failed, who has been tossed with passion, misled by ambition, and yet through all, kept a hand of the central desire of good, say at last, "I know that my Redeemer liveth"?

She was even willing, in what some would have regarded as a dangerously self-indulgent fashion, to extend the principle of toleration to one's own shortcomings. "Sometimes when I try to confess my sins, I feel that after all I am more to be pitied than blamed."

But Harriet's toleration did not stop with sins, nor even with faults; she also tolerated individual idiosyncrasy. How keen is her own relish of human eccentricity in her paper on "New England Ministers," [3] and how normal even the most erratic of the Beechers look beside them! In the novels, Sam Lawson is a monument to her appreciation of "the lubricating power of a decided do-nothing." She was always clear that the natural bent of a person's nature must be respected; you cannot force the best upon anybody, even a child. The chapter on "Repression" in *Little Foxes* is a moving study of the way a bride's natural gaiety is crushed in an over-austere family. The same principle is applied to servants also and even (oh, final test of female toleration!) to thoughtless and inconsiderate husbands, and she knew that an ordinary woman, if she is kind, may accomplish more with a man than a more high-minded sister who takes up a superior or over-critical attitude toward him.

III

A very interesting example of Harriet's toleration was provided by her contacts with Europe. "Beautiful Paris! What city in the world can compare with thee?" And again: "Rome is an astonishment! Papal Rome is an enchantress!"

Paris was the real test case. "Why Paris charms me so much more than other cities of similar recommendations, I cannot say, any more than a man can tell why he is fascinated by a lady love no fairer to his reason than a thousand others." She had to conquer prejudices before she could acknowledge this charm, and she never did conquer them altogether. She makes fun of anti-French feeling among the ignorant. "They say he reads and speaks French like a native," says Miss Debby of *Oldtown Folks*, "and that's all I want to know of anybody." Yet in *Pink and White Tyranny* even French décor seems associated with moral turpitude. "In France, the flirting is all done after marriage, and the young girl looks forward to it as her introduction to a career of conquest"; in France, indeed, "women are trained more systematically for the mere purposes of attraction than in any other country, and . . . the pursuit of admiration and the excitement of winning lovers are represented by its authors as constituting the main staple of woman's existence." French fashions are set by the demimonde, and French painting is smart, superficial, imitative, and heartless. All in all, France would seem to have lost her last chance for moral grandeur when she expelled the Huguenots.

In spite of all this, however, there was a great deal about France which appealed powerfully to Harriet Beecher Stowe. She perceived that the Puritanical attitude toward pleasure which prevailed in the United States prevented Americans from cultivating the art of enjoyment as Europeans did; consequently their play was coarse in comparison. Americans did not enjoy conversation either, and their only idea of entertaining was to feed people, though they did not do that very well. She admired French communal cooking, baking, and laundry establishments as lifting heavy burdens from the housewife; she admired the superior comfort of French railway coaches, the politeness and gallantry of the French police, the French freedom from color prejudices. All in all, the French were "kindlier mannered than the Anglo-Saxon, gentler and softer in all their addresses and the mode of their intercourse." No wonder life in Paris was "altogether more simple and natural than in England." No wonder French critics seemed to have "a finer appreciation of my subtle shades of meaning than English" (what a pleasant and modest way of discovering hitherto unsuspected subtleties in Harriet Becheer Stowe)! Having heard Monod preach, she even relinquished the idea that French was defective as a language of devotion. "The very sweetest and softest, as well as the most austere and rigid type of piety has been given by the French mind; witness Fénelon and John Calvin—Fénelon standing as the type of the mystic, and Calvin of the rationalistic style of religion." But I should say that Harriet passed the supreme test when she visited the Jardin Mabille. There was dancing; there was gambling; there were assignations. Young ladies residing in Paris never went there and matrons very seldom, "yet occasionally it is the case that some ladies of respectability look in." Yet it was "a scene perfectly unearthly, or rather perfectly Parisian, and just as earthly as possible; yet a scene where earthliness is worked up into a style of sublimation of the most exquisite conceivable." There was no "word, look, or gesture of immorality or impropriety. The dresses were all decent; and if there was vice, it was vice masked under the guise of polite propriety." She could not but reflect how different all this was from "the gin palaces of London," where there was "nothing artistic, nothing refined, nothing appealing to the imagination. . . . The end is the same—but by how different paths! Here, they dance along the path to ruin, with flowers and music; there, they cast themselves, bodily, as it were, into the lake of fire." If we must go to hell, let us at least take an elegant train, where everything is conducted with propriety and good taste.

I am sure Harriet's ancestors would have feared a certain weakening of fibre in her as she confronted the seductions of Paris; indeed they probably would have said the same of her capitulation to the softness of Florida and even to the ritualistic elegancies of the Episcopal Church. Leonard Bacon once remarked that America was inhabited by saints, sinners, and Beechers; George Sand, reviewing *Uncle Tom's Cabin*, had reservations about Harriet's literary art but canonized her without question. Yet if Harriet was a saint, she wore her halo at a slightly rakish angle. She had her worldly, luxury-loving side, and this may well have been a very valuable element in her character; without it she would have been in far greater danger of becoming a moral snob. In later years, Florida was in a sense her Paris, and though there was no Jardin Mabille there, she was far enough from Litchfield austerities when, in 1872, she wrote Mrs. Fields:

I love to have a day of mere existence. Life itself is a pleasure when the sun shines warm and the lizards dart from all the shingles of the roof and the birds sing in so many notes and tones the yard reverberates— and I sit and dream and am happy and never want to go back north.

IV

But general socializing is one thing, and the capacity for friendship is another. Harriet distinguished sharply between the two:

The greater part that I see cannot move me deeply. They are present, and I enjoy them; they pass and I forget them. But those that I love differently; those that I LOVE; and oh, how much that word means! I feel sadly about them. They may change; they must die; they are separated from me, and I ask myself why should I wish to love with all the pains and penalties of such conditions?

In *Agnes of Sorrento* she shows her awareness

that the discovery even of the existence of a soul capable of understanding our inner life often operates as a perfect charm; every thought, and feeling, and aspiration carries with it a new value, from the interwoven consciousness that attends it of the worth it would bear to that other mind; so that, while that person lives, our existence is doubled in value, even though oceans divide us.

To which we may add the moving exclamation out of *The Minister's Wooing:* "Oh, Mary, we never know how we love till we try to unlove."

Yet I should not say she was a person who made very many close friends—if anybody ever does that. Looking back over her life from old age, she wrote:

I was passionate in my attachments in those far back years, and as I have looked over the files of old letters, they have all gone (except one, C. van Renssalaer), Georgiana May, Delia Bacon,[4] Clarissa Treat, Elizabeth Lyman, Sarah Colt, Elisabeth Phenix, Frances Strong, Elisabeth Foster. I have letters from them all, but they have been long in spirit land, and know more about how it is there than I do. It gives me a sort of dizzy feeling of the shortness of life and nearness of eternity when I see how many that I have traveled with are gone within the veil.[5]

The letters to Elizabeth Lyman (addressed as "Dear Wife" and "My dear Wifie") in the Connecticut State Library and the letters to Mary Dutton at Yale display considerable emotional capacity, although one might add that at least one of the letters to Elizabeth indicates no very highly individualized type of emotion, as when she tells of how she kissed Henry Ward madly when he came to see her when she was ill:

Well you see Liz, it would have been all the same if you or anybody else having human kindness had come to me when I felt so sick and uncomfortable and every thing else—at such times I feel dreadfully as if I must love somebody and if any body speaks a kind word I go strait to crying forthwith.

An 1838 letter to Mary Dutton begins:

Confiteor Confiteor—Oh Mary—you precious good soul you dear friendly kindly cosy warm hearted little body without whom we

might all have died forty times over of the blues during the last winter
—I do most humbly and freely confess and acknowledge that I have
three letters from you at this present writing lying unanswered.

In another letter to Mary, she writes with reference to a mis-
understanding on the part of another friend: "I shall fix my affections no more on friends—they are all broken reeds—if we bear on
them they pierce—I am resolved henceforth to be happy." But
obviously this is the utterance of one who knows the pains of
friendship, not of one who is indifferent to it.

After she became a celebrity, Harriet came into contact with
many of the world's great and found some good friends among
them—Mrs. Browning, George Eliot, the Duchess of Sutherland,
and others. Oliver Wendell Holmes's first approach to her was
made gingerly, fearful that he might be too unorthodox for her
theologically, but she received him warmly, and he became one
of those she trusted most. She seems to have captivated even the
self-withdrawn Hawthorne on an Atlantic crossing; at least he
enjoyed the voyage so much that he wished it might never end.
"I don't like you one whit more for your rank and station," she
wrote Lady Amerley, "tho I do like you more for the use you
are making of it. I like you for being a whole hearted large souled
generous woman brave and courageous, gallant and chivalrous."
And when she found a person really congenial to her, like Ruskin
or Charles Kingsley, it seems that her shyness was thrown off very
easily, and intimacy developed quickly. As she herself put it after
visiting Kingsley: "How we did talk and go on for three days!
I guess he is tired. I'm sure we were." [6]

But the friend Harriet loved best and honored most was Lady
Byron, and it was this friendship which unleashed an even more
pitiless storm of obloquy upon her than the whole slave oligarchy
had been able to command. It was an astonishing thing that the
most sensational magazine article of the nineteenth century should
have been written by the same woman who wrote the century's
most sensational novel. Henry Adams ranked Harriet's defense of
Lady Byron at the top of her literary bent,[7] and both Oliver
Wendell Holmes and Henry James, Sr., defended her against her

critics, but this was not the majority view. True, the public reception of "The True Story of Lady Byron's Life" (*Atlantic Monthly*, September 1869) was less one-sided than it has often been represented; the clippings preserved in the Women's Archives at Radcliffe show a higher proportion of favorable comment than might have been supposed. Byron connections in England regretted the publication of the article but did not actually deny the central charge.[8] Yet the attacks made upon Harriet were savage and vulgar in the extreme, and it seems sad that even Lowell should have found her performance so incredible as to be driven to ignore all her obvious motives and dive below the surface in search of utterly fantastic ones: "I am afraid that Madame was quite as eager to proclaim her intimacy with Lady B. as to defend her memory."[9] The number of cancellations the *Atlantic* received after the article had appeared was frightening, and it says much for the integrity of Fields and Osgood that they should have stood by Harriet as they did and agreed to publish the book *Lady Byron Vindicated* in which she elaborated and sought to sustain her charges.

Byron's caricature of his wife as Donna Inez in *Don Juan* is well known. Ever since their separation he and his apologists had industriously circulated the legend of the cold, selfish woman whose self-righteous priggishness had driven him to all his later excesses. Harriet herself, in her Byron-enamored youth, may have believed this; if so, her disillusionment must certainly have strengthened her feeling that she had a duty to perform not only to Lady Byron but to her own sense of self-respect. It was in 1856, on her second visit to England, that Lady Byron confided to her the terrible secret that Byron had committed incest with his half-sister Augusta Leigh and had had a child by her, and requested her opinion as to whether, in justice to herself, she ought to make this fact known. Harriet's first impulse was to reply in the affirmative, but having talked the matter over with her sister Mary, she advised silence, on the ground that the unpleasant publicity which such a revelation would bring upon Lady Byron might well be more than she could bear. Lady Byron died in 1860 with her secret unrevealed. There the matter rested until 1868, when Byron's last mistress, Countess Guiccioli, published the recollections in which, once again, the virtuous wife was pilloried. It was this book and the favorable review thereof in *Blackwood's Magazine* that convinced Mrs. Stowe she had a duty to perform, and her article was the result.[10] And this time, whatever may have been true of *Uncle Tom's Cabin,* she knew exactly what she was doing and braced herself for the storm, for she consulted Oliver Wendell Holmes beforehand, telling him specifically that she was not asking his advice about whether or not she should publish, since she had made up her mind about that, but merely wished his help to make her article as effective as possible. She also consulted Charles Sumner on the legal aspects.

Harriet's great strategic weakness was that she had no proof; she knew only what Lady Byron had told her, and she had to ask the public to take her word for that. From her point of view this was not very important. She *believed* in her friend, and she had always put faith above knowledge. "Of course I did not listen to the story as one who was investigating its worth," she says. To Osgood she complained that

the wild and distracted calling on me for proof—entirely ignoring the only kind of proof that I have to give shows that the public is not yet in a proper state to weigh anything. Nobody ever called for proof from any of the numberless writers who reported their conversations with Lord Byron.

In time, she thought, the proofs would probably appear,[11] "but my belief is founded on Lady Byron's known character—a character remarkable for truthfulness, accuracy, self-control, patience." And she added, not unreasonably, that "reliable human testimony is the only proof of facts which we rest on, in anything."

When Henry Ward Beecher was accused of adultery, his sister's refusal to believe the charges against him was contrasted, to her discredit, with her readiness to believe scandal about Byron. But the two cases are not really parallel. Though it was Harriet who first put the Byron scandal into print, it was not exactly new when it reached her. Byron's own poems reeked of incest; if he did not commit it, he certainly had it on the brain, in the sense in which D. H. Lawrence speaks of "sex in the head." Beecher was accused, on the other hand, as a man whose reputation had hitherto been untouched. The charges against him did not emanate from his wife, and his sister had seen nothing in his life to cause her to accept them. Henry Ward Beecher was alive and denied the allegations. Byron and Lady Byron were both dead, and this made it possible for some of the poet's admirers to argue that Mrs. Stowe had misunderstood Lady Byron, who had never intended to accuse her husband of incest at all. Though some intelligent persons seem to have credited this, it is nonsense. "Mrs. Stowe, he was guilty of incest with his sister!" Harriet understood English, and she was not a lunatic, she did not understand this out of something else, and Dr. Holmes was quite justified when he wrote, "That Lady Byron believed, and told you, the story will not be questioned by any but fools and malignants." If Harriet is to be attacked at all, the attack must take quite a different line. It *might*, I think, be argued that Byron, out of sheer devilishness, could have told his wife that he had committed incest simply to torture her, and this would agree quite as well with the hypothesis of moral insanity which both Mrs. Stowe and Lady Byron postulated as did the assumption of guilt itself.[12]

There was no snobbism, then, and no self-vaunting in Harriet's defense of Lady Byron, "the severest act of self-sacrifice that one friend can perform for another," she calls it. But while this was true, it was not the whole truth. There *was* a good deal of feminist feeling present. Harriet herself says that she saw Lady Byron as an illustrious victim of immemorial male vice and brutality and that she rejoiced to defend her in this aspect. And though she does not tell us, I think we may be equally sure that she enjoyed slapping down the eternal wanton as represented by the Guiccioli, and that she must have welcomed the opportunity to enjoy with a clear conscience the sadistic pleasure which such an act gives to all "good" women.

Harriet's admiration for Lady Byron was boundless. "In you

I think I see 'an earnest of the purchased possession'—a soul in whom the redeeming work is done and only waiting for the frailest thread to break." With the individuality of the woman we can do little, for the response of one personality to another is always a mystery, even to the persons involved. But Lady Byron was the widow of the great idol of Harriet's youth, and she had lived through one of the great scandals of the century and emerged white as snow. Moreover, her attitude toward life was much like Harriet's own. She too was fighting her way out from an inherited Calvinism—which she regarded, with considerable justice, as in large measure responsible for having wrecked her husband as a spiritual being—and she had got farther along the road than Harriet had traveled by the time they met. Lady Byron regarded all creeds as chains, and she wanted all affirmations of belief to come spontaneously, even from children. She could not believe that the soul's probation ended at death. She favored a lay ministry. More significantly still, her temperament was such that Harriet was able to leave Byron's corner and come over into hers, for she was already in Byron's corner. She may have been, as her enemies insist, an unbearable prig, whose habit of being everlastingly right about everything was the one thing a man of Byron's temperament could not endure; but there can be no question that she loved him and never gave up hope for him. Moreover, she understood and forgave Augusta. In its time, *Lady Byron Vindicated* was resented because it was regarded as an attack on a dead man. It was not. It was a defense of a dead woman who loved a dead man who was presented in it not as a scoundrel but as a moral invalid (no wonder Oliver Wendell Holmes was one of the few persons who understood it). Real wickedness was comprehensible neither to Harriet Beecher Stowe nor to Lady Byron; it was simply beyond them that any man could deliberately pray, "Evil, be thou my good." When they encountered it, they could only postulate moral insanity.

It is just possible that they may both have been right. Of course Harriet's defense of Lady Byron was "unwise." Even her husband and her son did their best to dissuade her. But these were purely prudential considerations. On the very lowest reckoning, Lady Byron was entitled to her day in court, and that is what Harriet gave her. This, however, is not the most important consideration. Years later Harriet remarked of *Lady Byron Vindicated* to her unauthorized biographer Mrs. McCray that "the devil and all his angels could never make me sorry that I wrote it." When one you love is maligned, there is nothing any decent person can do except defend him, especially if he is no longer in a position to speak for himself. You may be ridiculed for this—you may be sneered at—you may even be ruined—but these things do not matter, especially if you have been brought up with the New England conscience and the New England habit of speaking out unpleasant truths when conscience commands. The pure in heart know these things. It is only worldlings with whom expediency has replaced principle for whom they need to be spelled out. Harriet Beecher Stowe could have done nothing in the Byron matter except exactly what she did. With Lady Byron she faced the ordeal by friendship and passed it triumphantly.

CHAPTER VI

THE WOMAN

I

Harriet Beecher Stowe's most famous description of herself was made in a letter to Mrs. Follen in 1853: "I am a little bit of a woman,—somewhat more than forty, about as thin and dry as a pinch of snuff; never very much to look at in my best days, and looking like a used-up article now." The impressions of others are not wholly out of line with this, yet she did not lack her admirers. Henry Drummond was not thinking of her beauty particularly when he described her, on his visit to Hartford, as "a wonderfully agile old lady, as fresh as a squirrel still, but with the face and air of a lion," but he adds, "I have not been so taken with any one on this side of the Atlantic." Mrs. Browning's first impression was less enthusiastic, for while she was pleased by Harriet's refinement and the absence of "rampant Americanisms," and thought her "nice looking, too," with "something strong, copious, and characteristic in her dusky, wavy hair," she also felt that "the brow has not very large capacity" and that "the mouth wants something both in frankness and sensitiveness."

Writing to Charles Kingsley before visiting him in England, Harriet deplored the build-up she had received:

The poor people seem to expect something quite angelic. I wish for their sakes I was rather more than I am. I am sorry to break up their innocent illusions by the vision of a little matter of fact commonplace

woman—neither good looking nor accomplished, not even learned...
and entirely ill adapted to any kind of speech making or show making
in any form.

But Kingsley did not agree with her, and she was pleased that
he did not: "as beauty has never been one of my strong points,"
she wrote her husband, "I am open to flattery upon it." She hated
the fantastic pictures of her that were circulated in England—
thought the Sphinx in the British Museum might have sat for most
of them, and that they had only the value of the Irishman's sign-
board which showed which way the road did *not* go—though she
admitted that they did have the happy effect of causing people
to remark, upon meeting her, that she was not so ill-looking as
they had expected. She took all this quite philosophically; once,
exhorting her girls not to ridicule people for their personal appearance, she asked them how they would have felt if the English
had called her "the little humpback" and Calvin "Old Stumpie."
Her admiration for pretty clothes being what it was, it seems
odd that she paid so little attention to her own,[1] though she did
wear curls and cultivated that most seductive of all forms of
feminine lure, bands in the hair. Once she wore a wreath on her
head at an *Atlantic* dinner, which Longfellow at least thought
very becoming.

Yet Harriet was not wholly indifferent either to her appearance
or her iconography. She knew that Richmond's crayon portrait [2]
flattered her, but this did not keep her from sending Garrison
some proof-engravings of it to sell for an antislavery benefit.
Mrs. Fields says she was often asked in effect, "Why did you not
tell me that Mrs. Stowe was beautiful?" The fact seems to be that,
though she had considerable charm and sweetness, such beauty
as she possessed was less of the flesh than of the spirit. When
she went "owling about," as Henry called it, she looked dull
and dumpy, but her face was always subject to sudden incursions
of light, the result of interest or strong feeling, by which it could
be transformed. "She is not a beautiful woman," wrote David
W. Bartlett in 1859, "and yet her eyes are not often surpassed in

beauty. They are dark and dreamy, and look as if some sorrowful scene ever haunted the brain."

She suffered from all the neuralgic and other complaints that were fashionable for nineteenth-century ladies; once she described herself to Lord Denman as "standing . . . between the living and the dead, feeble in health and often very sorrowful." In youth the note of morbid self-indulgence is sometimes sounded, as in 1827, when she wrote Catharine,

I don't know that I am fit for anything and I have thought that I could wish to die young, and let the remembrance of me and my faults perish in the grave rather than live, as I fear I do, a trouble to every one. You don't know how perfectly wretched I often feel; so useless, so weak, so destitute of all energy.

On "a dark, sloppy, rainy, muddy, disagreeable day in 1845," when she had been working in the kitchen discovering the deficiencies of a domestic who cleaned only the outside of the platter, she wrote her husband a letter which still gives the reader a sympathetic pang for her: "I am sick of the smell of sour milk, and sour meat, and sour everything, and then the clothes *will* not dry, and no wet thing does, and everything smells mouldy; and altogether I feel as if I never wanted to eat again." But she grows less winning as she proceeds:

As to my health, it gives me very little solicitude, though I am bad enough and daily growing worse. I feel no life, no energy, no appetite, or rather a growing distaste for food; in fact, I am becoming quite ethereal. Upon reflection I perceive that it pleases my Father to keep me in the fire, for my whole situation is excessively harassing and painful. I suffer with sensible distress in the brain, as I have done more or less since my sickness last winter, a distress which some days takes from me all power of planning or executing anything; and you know that, except this poor head, my unfortunate household has no mainspring, for nobody feels any kind of responsibility to do a thing in time, place, or manner, except as I oversee it.

This was not Harriet's usual note to Calvin; she could not afford to strike it often with such a hypochondriac. Constance

Rourke was not quite fair when she suggested that Harriet refused to tolerate the indulgences in Calvin which she permitted herself. "My dear Soul," she once wrote him, "I received your most melancholy effusion, and I am sorry to find that it is just so. I entirely agree and sympathize. Why didn't you engage two tombstones—one for you and one for me?" And she sent him a wicked little drawing. What Miss Rourke overlooked was that when Calvin had the "blues" he went to bed. Harriet blew off steam—and went on working.

The complaints, however, continued from time to time:

1863: Ever since the effort of writing those two stories at once I have not been what I was. The liability to this distressing headache and weakness in the back of my head—an indescribable languor and lassitude that attends it have often made me feel that perhaps my day for doing as I have done is over—but this is balanced in my mind by the great cheerfulness and power of quick recovery which God has given me.

1877?: I have made a step downward and shall never be as I have been. You know I wrote you last winter that I suffered with some strange and peculiar affection of the heart. They were so different from anything I ever felt before that I felt afraid. Not that I am afraid to die but as St. Paul says to abide in the flesh is needful to you and I am sure I can't think what your father could do without me.

1880: This winter I have been troubled with a sort of bilious affection which has troubled me principally in my head and eyes. As a consequence I have had to give up reading almost entirely—and have read only in the Bible—specially reading the Life of Christ.

There is also an undated letter in which she says, "My lungs are more tender and fidgety than I could wish—I keep taking cold— notwithstanding that I bathe in ice water every morning and go out freely." "Notwithstanding"!

She became interested in homeopathy—Howells once heard her argue the subject against Oliver Wendell Holmes all through a dinner at the Fieldses [3]—and she was a "sucker" for "galvanic batteries" and every other faddish form of health treatment she encountered. She seems to have had a weakness for rushing off from the family for health reasons, when she would write home that she would feel selfish to be enjoying herself so much except that she knew her health was as important to their welfare as to her own. Her most extended absence was at the water cure establishment in Brattleboro, Vermont, in 1846, where she went through a course of treatment that might have killed a horse:

For this week, I have gone before breakfast to the wave-bath and let all the waves and billows roll over me till every limb ached with cold and my hands would scarcely have feeling enough to dress me. After that I have walked till I was warm, and come home to breakfast with such an appetite! Brown bread and milk are luxuries indeed, and the only fear is that I may eat too much. At eleven comes my douche, to which I have walked in a driving rain for the last two days, and after it walked in the rain again till I was warm.... After dinner I roll ninepins or walk till four, then sitz-bath, and another walk till six.

She does not seem to have been much better after her return home, by which I, for one, am not surprised.

Though this is amusing to read about, I do not wish to indicate that I think it must have been amusing to experience. Nor does the fact that Harriet lived to be a very old woman really have much to do with the case, for one can experience very unpleasant maladies without dying of them. Yet I am sure that she was a very strong woman, and I think she recognized what we would now call a psychosomatic element in many of her illnesses. The Calvinistic orientation on which she was reared was not calculated to soothe the nerves of a sensitive girl, and she overworked all her life. "My brain is sore with the number of things I have been thinking of," she writes. And again: "But these feelings are I know caused by *nervous* obstruction of some kind." After the long strain of Calvin's final illness was over, she wrote a correspondent that she did not consider her health " 'shattered' but only enfeebled and requiring care—I am seeking restoration by daily open air exercise." "If I am not feeling well," she told Frances Willard in her old age, "I can usually walk it off, or if not, I sleep it off, going to bed by eight o'clock." But the perfect comment, and the most revealing of all, was made when she wrote, after a period of particular strain, "I have worked so hard that I am almost tired." And it was not the word of a weakling.

Health and temperament are closely connected. As a small child, Harriet seems to have been considered an odd little girl. "Harriet makes just as many wry faces, is just as odd, and loves to be laughed at as much as ever." And when she is staying with one of her Foote relatives, Catharine writes to her:

We all want you at home very much, but hope you are now where you will learn to stand and sit straight, and hear what people say to you, and sit still in your chair, and learn to sew and knit well, and be a good girl in every particular; and if you don't while you are with Aunt Harriet, I am afraid you never will.

Conventional-minded people thought all the Beechers eccentric, but I should not call Harriet so particularly except in her tendency to reverie. "I once knew a person who was wont to retire into the garden of revery whenever he wished to break the force of an unwelcome truth," said Lyman. "I told him that he must give up the habit or be damned!" If he was right, then all the Beechers were lost, including Lyman himself, who inherited his absentmindedness from his father David and passed it on to his descendants. He once remarked that he had spent half his life looking for his hat, and in his old age he made a habit of leaving his false teeth in the stage. With Harriet, as we have already seen, it took other forms, but its most amusing manifestation came in her old age, when she would wander in and out of her neighbors' houses, sometimes completely ignoring them, sometimes taking possession of the piano and "singing ancient and melancholy songs with infinitely touching effect," and sometimes, as Mark Twain relates, slipping "up behind a person who was deep in dreams and musings and fetch[ing] a war whoop that would jump that person out of his clothes." [4]

This anecdote conveniently calls attention to one of the most valuable aspects of her endowment—her unfailing energy. In one of her travel letters to *The National Era* she remarked incidentally, "Some of the party go to sleep. I go out to climb a neighboring peak." She was a good traveler because she soon felt at home anywhere, and when her husband urged her not to get too excited, as at her first encounter with the literary and storied past of Scotland, she shut him up in a hurry: "Mr. Stowe, this is a thing that comes only once in a lifetime; do let us have the comfort of it." She never panicked in the presence of danger, and though she did not deny fear when she sat on a donkey's back on the edge of a precipice in the Alps, she found "the thrill of this sensation . . . not without its pleasure." She speaks of herself as "bounding through bushes, leaping, and springing, and climbing over rocks"; she was even silly enough to take part in dislodging a two-ton rock and send it bounding down the slopes, and who knows where she might have gone from there if the guide had not feared that there were sheep and shepherds in the valleys below who might be injured?

Nobody who has ever read a book by Harriet Beecher Stowe needs to be told that she was a humorist. John R. Howard says that during her later years she gave the impression that she could not be "moved to agitation or profound emotion," but this must have been protective coloration.

We have the impression that a vast deal of genial humor is conscientiously strangled in religious people, which might illuminate and warm the way of life. Wit and gayety answer the same purpose that a fire does in a damp house, dispersing chills and drying up mold, and making all wholesome and cheerful.

Like Stevenson, who also had a Calvinistic background, she could view happiness as a duty: "To be happy is a duty we owe to ourselves and our friends and like other things is under the control of our will to some considerable extent." But I get the impression that her natural temper was gayer than his. Her humor could be what we call "corny," as when she ends a letter to Mrs. Fields with "Drop me a line, as the fish says." The Fieldses were "Mr. and Mrs. Meadows" too, and one letter was endorsed "To Sweet Fields beyond the swelling flood." It could also be tart, as when she warns the readers of *Oldtown Folks* to skip Chapter XXIX if they do not enjoy thinking—"and who knows what may happen to their brains, from so unusual an exercise?" It could even be grim, as when Calvin, in his final illness, complained that the Lord had forgotten him, and she snapped back, "Oh, no, He hasn't; cheer up! your turn will come soon." But characteristically it was none of these things; it was only gay.

My house with *eight* gables is growing wonderfully. I go over every day to see it. I am busy with drains, sewers, sinks, digging, trenching, and above all with manure! You should see the joy with which I gaze on manure heaps in which the eye of faith sees Delaware grapes and D'Angoulême pears, and all sorts of roses and posies, which at some future day I hope you will be able to enjoy.

And again: "Tell Eunice I don't feel proud because my baby has teeth before hers. I think just as much of her as if it hadn't happened." "P.P." was her private abbreviation for "Providence permitting," and one day, when "Pa" got "mad" because she had inadvertently cooked the eggs he intended for a brooding hen, she brought him into good spirits again by perching herself, all her children, and even the dog Rover on a beam in the barn, whence they greeted him by cackling like hens. If her Hartford neighbor Mark Twain was appropriately nicknamed "Youth," the label would seem to have fitted her quite as well. "Not for years," the invalid wrote home from Brattleboro, "have I enjoyed life as I have here—real keen enjoyment—everything agrees with me." She was not, I think, boasting when she wrote her easily discouraged husband, "I never doubt or despair."

II

Perhaps it was because Harriet had been brought up on New England logic that it was not enough for her to live a woman's life; she also had to ponder—and to the best of her ability solve—all the problems involved in it. If she was not an extremist on the subject of women's rights, this was partly because she feared the coarsening effect on women of their being taken out of the home and thrust into the market place and partly because she was realistic enough to understand Sojourner Truth's question: "Ef women want any rights more'n dey's got, why don't dey jes' *take 'em*, and not be talkin' about it?" But there was no question where she stood on the central issue. In her salutatory article in *Hearth and Home* she declared in 1868:

> We see nothing unfeminine or improper in a woman's exercising the right of suffrage; we see no impropriety in her pursuing an extended career of study, which shall fit her to be a physician, we think that women may become architects ... or they may become landscape-gardeners, and find abundant exercise for taste and skill, and healthy, remunerative employment; they may even be teachers of a naval school, and expound to disciples the mysteries of ocean navigation, as a woman at this day is successfully doing—in short, there is no earthly reason why they should not ... use every advantage which God and nature have put into their hands....
>
> In this view, we see no impropriety in a woman's becoming a public character, when constitution and genius evidently fit her peculiarly for such a course. No one ever listened to Mrs. Fanny Kemble's public interpretations of Shakespeare and had any doubts of the propriety of her giving them because she was a woman. Anna Dickinson's career has fully shown that the good sense of the community justifies even a young woman in being a public lecturer, who has a gift and genius for oratory. All such instances make their own laws, and the general good sense of mankind admits them.

But she goes on to stress the importance of women performing the functions for which they are peculiarly fitted, cultivating "the *art of living well*, of making life cheerful and charming," "the *art of being healthy*" and relieving the sick, "the doctrine and practice of economy," "household chemistry," education—"above all things, woman's profession"—and the care of dumb animals. The next year (May 25, 1869) she wrote George Eliot:

> We are busy now in the next great emancipation—that of woman. This session I trust Connecticut will repeal *the whole of the old unjust English marriage property laws as regards woman and set her free* and

then I shall be willing to claim Connecticut as my mother. Massachusetts has half done this work—New York *half*—but if the amendments
just drafted by my brother in law John Hooker and now before the
house pass, Connecticut will have the proud superiority of being the
first state since Louisiana to recognize the absolute equality of *woman
in the marriage relation.*

Harriet Beecher Stowe portrayed fribbles like Lillie Ellis, selfish
pious hypocrites like Nina Gordon's Aunt Nesbit, and managing
horrors like Maria Wouvermans. She acknowledged the cat element in women in their relations with men, and she could admit,
even of so noble a woman as Anne Clayton of *Dred,* that she
"had not a particle of ideality in her." Basically, however, she
thought women more spiritual than men, more loyal to their
principles, the normal, natural guides of their husbands, and more
essential to the survival of religion than even the theologians.
"Man's utter ignorance of woman's nature is a cause of a great
deal of unsuspected cruelty." The reader of *Sunny Memories of
Foreign Lands* is surprised when she takes up a comparatively
dim view of Anne Hathaway, but she makes up for this by assum-
ing that the perfections of Shakespeare's heroines were all derived
from his mother.

This glorification of the Christian home—"that appointed shrine
for woman, more holy than cloister, more saintly and pure than
church or altar"—becomes almost comic at times in Harriet's
writings and threatens to take on a touch of self-idolatry. Her
feminism comes out continually in her Old Testament studies.
She praises the law of Moses as indicating more care for women
than contemporary codes, perceives in Isaac "one of those delicate and tender natures that find repose first in the love of a
mother, and, when that stay is withdrawn, lean upon a beloved
wife," and hails Joel's "On your sons and daughters I will pour
out my spirit, and they shall prophesy" as testifying to the equality of the sexes in Israel. "So far as we know, there is not a
Jewish prophetess who is not also a wife, and the motherly character is put forward as constituting a claim to fitness in public
life." But, as John R. Adams has pointed out, when she comes

to write of Jesus and Mary, she cannot conceal her feminine satisfaction that "lacking mortal father, Jesus was absolutely his mother's boy," nor yet her disappointment that Mary should not have had a larger share in her son's ministry, and she insists that "there was in Jesus more of the pure feminine element than in any other man," a statement of which we may surely hope she did not catch all the implications.

The great evangelists in her fiction are all female—some of them little girls like Dolly in *Poganuc People* and Eva in *Uncle Tom's Cabin,* who saves Topsy by embodying the power of Jesus's love,[5] some young women like Mary Scudder,[6] Nina Gordon, or Angie Van Arsdel, who looks like a little ball of fluff and who makes her serious clerical lover Mr. St. John realize "how much there was of pastoral work which transcended the power of man, and required the finer intervention of woman." But the two really great preachers of the Christian Gospel in Mrs. Stowe's novels are two Negro women—Candace, who comforts Mrs. Marvyn in *The Minister's Wooing,* after the supposed loss of her son at sea, and the slave Milly in *Dred;* as a presentation of Gospel ethics, Milly's account of how she learned to forgive her selfish mistress stands beside the best of Tolstoy and Dostoevsky. Uncle Tom and Old Tiff of *Dred* live the Gospel quite as impressively as these women do, but neither expounds it with such power. And even so, a number of commentators have discerned a strong feminine element in Uncle Tom, even as Harriet thought she perceived it in Jesus.

But women did not have to be saints to hold Harriet's interest, especially if they were young. No male novelist was ever more enslaved to the charms of his girl heroines than she was. Her ideal girls are angels like Eva or Mara of *The Pearl of Orr's Island,* of whom Cap'n Kittredge says that "she's got the real New-Jerusalem look, she has—like them in the Revelations that wears the fine linen, clean and white." But sometimes one is inclined to believe that she gave even more of her heart to the fashionable, pretty girls, with a healthy interest in boys and pretty clothes, who have a thoroughly good time while they are young and then settle down to become the joy of their husbands' lives and the central heart and conscience of a good Christian home. In between the two moves, in various incarnations, a more down-to-earth type, like Cerinthy Ann of *The Minister's Wooing*, Sally Kittredge of *The Pearl of Orr's Island*, and Nabby of *Poganuc People*—all basically "good" girls, with a certain tendency toward snippiness and a mild fondness for the cat-and-mouse game, quite capable of being sobered by responsibility but perhaps never destined to have all the rough edges smoothed.[7]

"Of all the forms of fame," Richard LeGallienne once remarked, "that of Beauty is the greatest, for it is not the fame of achievement, of which one can trace the beginnings and follow the development, but it is the fame of a miracle." One gathers that Harriet would have agreed. She makes Horace Holyoke say as much when he discerns genius in beauty—"genius which does not declare itself in literature, but in social life, and which devotes itself to pleasing, as other artists devote themselves to painting or to poetry." When Lady Byron told her about Byron's entanglement with Mrs. Leigh, the first question Harriet asked was whether she was beautiful. It is the kind of question one would expect a man to ask. Perhaps what she wanted essentially was what Harry Henderson wanted: "a baptized, Christianized Greek face! A cross between Venus and the Virgin Mary!"

Nina Gordon of *Dred* is Mrs. Stowe's most elaborate study of the lively girl. The contemporary British writer Nassau Senior found Nina "a vulgar flirt" in her first phase, later transformed unconvincingly into a "glorious being."

It is possible that what to European readers appears the most offensive vulgarity of sentiment and expression may be a fair representation of an average American young lady. But if Mrs. Stowe is writing for posterity, if she wishes her works, after they have served their immediate purpose of anti-slavery pamphlets, to take a permanent place in English literature, she must devote to the task of adapting these to the taste of the best educated part of the English public far more labour than she has as yet bestowed on them.

Transatlantic condescension could hardly go further than this, which inclines one to feel that James was cutting even deeper in *Daisy Miller* than we have hitherto assumed, but surely posterity, both European and American, was more with Mrs. Stowe than with Senior.

There are difficulties in the portrait of Nina, but they are due essentially to Harriet's over-earnestness and to the limitations of her art. The girl herself is quite as adorable before her transformation as afterwards, and surely Harriet sympathized with her, and intended her readers to sympathize, in the amusing scene in Chapter IV in which she permits her to express some of her own favorite ideas ("I don't see that it is any better to think of black silk than it is of pink") in the course of demolishing the soul-crushing gloom which is all her shallow Aunt Nesbit knows as religion. Absurd as Senior was about Nina, however, he was right when he insisted that her transformation was unconvincing, but this was only because Harriet did not know where to stop. Nina's awakening to the serious responsibilities of life through her love for the wise and tolerant Edward Clayton is beautifully done, but to carry it on to the point of practically canonizing the girl was about as reasonable as not letting go of Topsy until she had become a missionary to Africa. Actually, Mrs. Stowe herself was Nina's worst enemy, for when she changed her mind about the kind of book she was writing, she heartlessly killed her off two-thirds of the way through the novel instead of permitting her to become the happy wife and mother she was obviously meant to be. It was a sad fate for what might have been one of the most delightful heroines in American literature.

There are other problems in connection with the lively Tina of *Oldtown Folks*, said to have been suggested by Georgiana Stowe, and Harriet goes skating over some pretty thin ice when Tina falls in love with the worthless Ellery Davenport. Fortunately he dies and lets her come to her true love Horace Holyoke in the end, but Horace takes her deviation so philosophically, and their final mating is so mildly and matter-of-factly handled that it hardly gives the reader the satisfaction he might have expected.

Perhaps, all in all, the most successful heroine is Angelique Van Arsdel of *We and Our Neighbors;* for once we have the pleasure of enjoying all the graces of a fashionable girl plus all the perfections of a quite unassuming little saint.

Angelique belonged to the corps of laughing saints—a department not always recognized by the straiter sort in the Church militant, but infinitely effective and to the purpose in the battle of life. Her heart was a tender but gay one—perhaps the lovingness of it kept it bright; for love is a happy divinity, and Angelique loved everybody, and saw the best side of everything; besides, just now she was barely seventeen, and thought the world a very nice place.

Angie has no particular faults to overcome; she has simply been brought up in a fashionable home; and she matures spiritually as well as physically, without ever becoming, even in the slightest degree, fanatical about it, until she falls in love with a man who is worthy of her, if any man could be, and embarks upon a useful way of life which gives every promise of being happy and successful for both of them. It is all exactly the way life should be —and seldom is.

But Harriet's sympathy for pretty girls was not dependent on their all turning out as well as Nina Gordon, Tina Percival, or Angie Van Arsdel. She knew the temptations of society life, and she could be sarcastic about the girls of Newport, but she had no patience with the traditional New England association of virtue and shabbiness, and it was never really in her heart to deprive her girls of anything. American girls are free in their behavior because they feel themselves equal to dealing with any situation that may confront them. Harriet admits that she came to Saratoga with prejudices against it, but she found it so bright, cheerful, varied, and independent that she capitulated almost at once.

Her toleration toward feminine foibles is one of her most endearing qualities; it is, of course, much rarer in women than the rather coarse toleration for male rakes.[8] Even when she creates so bad a girl as Lillie Ellis, she shows a tendency to blame the system more than the girl herself. Much in our present civilization is geared to the production of Lillie Ellises, and even the clergy, "when off duty," do not help them much.

Lillie was confessedly no saint; and yet, if much of a sinner, society has as much to answer for as she. She was the daughter and flower of Christian civilization of the nineteenth century, and the kind of woman that, on the whole, men of quite distinguished sense have been fond of choosing for wives, and will go on seeking to the end of the chapter.

Of course it was wicked of her to go to church to show her fine clothes and awaken admiration.

But is she so much worse than others?—than the clergyman who uses the pulpit and the sacred office to show off his talents?—than the singers who sing God's praises to show their voices,—who intone the agonies of their Redeemer, or the glories of the *Te Deum*, confident of the comments of the newspaper press on their performance the next week?

III

Underneath all these things was a force that nineteenth-century novelists did not talk about as such—and modern novelists, perhaps consequently, make up for this by talking about nothing else. This force was sex. But the nineteenth-century novelists who knew their business were aware of its presence nevertheless, and Harriet was not less aware than others.

Kenneth S. Lynn has remarked that both Harriet and Henry Ward Beecher

succeeded in satisfying the enormous, pent-up need of the English-speaking world for emotional release—and they accomplished this without ever having to admit (even to themselves!) that some of the thoughts they inspired in their admirers' minds were illicit. Like the patent medicines to which many temperance advocates were so curiously devoted, Henry Ward's "religion of love" and Harriet's phenomenal best-seller offered their audience a means of short-circuiting the moral strictures of the era which blocked the pathway to questionable pleasures. Yet at the same time that they short-circuited these strictures, they reaffirmed them—thereby eliminating the possibility of a guilty conscience.[9]

The ethical standing ground of this passage seems somewhat ambivalent. Did the author mean to praise or to blame? Perhaps he himself shared the vagueness he attributes to the Beechers. I am not prepared to say that "love" quite covers the religious problem, nor even that the religion of love, as the Beechers presented it, was quite free from all elements of self-delusion. At present it looks as though we might be the last generation ever to be haunted by the curious notion that sexual pleasure is displeasing to God; perhaps then we should only praise Harriet for having contributed to our relative emancipation. Had she been as squeamish about sex as many of her contemporaries were, she could hardly have written about slavery at all. The most hideous and unbelievable feature of the "peculiar institution" is that Southern planters could have brought themselves to sustain the most intimate of all human relationships with women whose basic humanity they virtually failed to recognize and that, having done so, they could sell the offspring of their own bodies as chattels. "Any lady," wrote Mary Boykin Chesnut, in her now famous *Diary from Dixie*,[10] "is ready to tell you who is the father of all the mulatto children in everybody's household but her own. These, she seems to think, drop from the clouds." [11] And even today *Uncle Tom's Cabin* cannot be understood unless it is recognized that it has very little to do with the political or ideological aspects of slavery. It is a woman's protest against a system that made chastity impossible for women and then deprived them of the children they might still love as deeply as any mother ever loved her children even though legally they had no right to have been born.

Miscegenation is the special subject not of *Uncle Tom's Cabin* but of *Dred*, where Harry, the slave son of his master, is the faithful, high-minded, efficient steward of his father's estate, and the protector of his beloved half-sister Nina, while the white son and heir, Tom, is utterly vicious and bad. But it appears in *Uncle Tom's Cabin* too, as nobody who remembers Cassy needs to be told—and who could ever forget her? "Lust, illicit love, suicide, murder, and sadistic cruelty"—these are all staple ingredients of the plot, as Jay Hubbell has observed. Harriet had always known about these things; was there not the family legend of Aunt Mary Hubbard, who had returned broken-hearted from Jamaica after making the discovery that her English planter-husband was not only the owner of slaves but their father? "You know, Mrs. Stowe, slave women cannot help themselves." Harriet accepted this explanation when it was offered to her, and directed her indignation where it belonged—against the perpetrators of the system, not its victims. Even in her letter to Lord Carlisle she spoke frankly of the sexual degradation inseparable from slavery. After the war she accepted calmly the still unlegalized unions of many of her black neighbors in Florida, and in *The Christian Union* she wrote admiringly of Aunt Kathy, an ex-slave woman who had had eleven children by her master.

Harriet's frankness on this point has always been recognized by friend and foe, and her pre-war enemies charged that she had been attracted to the anti-slavery theme by her libidinous imagination. The most extreme statement of this view was that of William J. Grayson, who, in *The Hireling and the Slave* (1856), said of Mrs. Stowe that she

> hunts up crimes as beagles hunt their prey;
> Gleans every dirty book—the felon's jail,
> And hangman's mem'ry, for detraction's tale,
> Snuffs up pollution with a pious air,
> Collects a rumor here, a slander there;
> With hatred's ardor gathers Newgate spoils,
> And trades for gold the garbage of her toils.

The Southern imagination, undismayed by the reality of the white man with the black woman, recoiled in shuddering horror from the vision of the white woman with the black man, and even if Fanny Wright had not advocated the amalgamation of races,

Southerners would still have seen the female abolitionist as a menace to more than the institution of slavery. So the editor of *The Southern Literary Messenger* ordered a review of *Uncle Tom's Cabin* "as hot as hell fire, blasting and searing the reputation of the vile wretch in petticoats who could write such a volume," and even a man of the stature of William Gilmore Simms could stoop to finding her so obsessed by the "personal beauty" of George Harris that he wished to condemn her to a "perpetual bed-fellowship" with him.

Harriet proved her lack of squeamishness again when she broke the Byron scandal, leaving many persons who had tolerated her improprieties on the subject of slavery for the sake of a great cause quite unable to grant that any decent woman could publicly admit that she knew there were such offenses in the world as incest and homosexuality. When she heard the *castrati* in Europe, she wrote her son that "the miserere sung by emasculated human beings is indeed a weird wonderful wail—but to me it speaks of the anguish of souls crushed under that unnatural system and crying in vain for an absent Lord." In *The Minister's Wooing* James Marvyn describes the temptations of men in a fairly frank and knowledgeable way; the story "The Minister's Watermelons" [12] deals with corruption in a boys' school; the *Chimney-Corner* paper, "How Shall We Be Amused?" considers pornography and sex education and the temptations of underprivileged girls. I think "The Minister's Watermelons" an overoptimistic story in its conclusions, but its tone is not snivelling, and there is an air about it which, if Harriet were a male writer, one could only call manly. In both *A Dog's Mission* and *Our Charley* her understanding of boys is really noteworthy; there are passages in the former of which Mark Twain would have no need to feel ashamed.

I suppose that in Harriet's time Miss Asphyxia's aversion to matrimony on the ground that "she knew t'much to put her nose into hot swill" may have been as shocking as some contemporary fictional improprieties are to us, though I have an idea we often exaggerate the prudery of our ancestors. After *Dred* Harriet herself wrote her publisher that "creating a story is like bearing a child, and it leaves me in as weak and helpless a state as when my baby was born." *The American Woman's Home* lays down the principle that "as a general rule, it is safe for a healthful child to wear as little clothing as is sufficient to keep it from complaining of the cold," and advocates exposing well-massaged infants "naked to sun and air in a well-ventilated room" for the benefit of their health.

Fifty years ago, it was not common for children to wear as much clothing as they now do. The writer well remembers how even girls, though not of strong constitutions, used to play for hours in the snow-drifts without the protection of drawers, kept warm by exercise and occasional runs to an open fire.

This does not sound much like the traditional caricature of the people who put pantalettes on piano legs.

What Harriet would have thought of the near-nakedness that women have achieved today I do not know, but she loathed corsets, and she emphatically rejected the idea that "there was something radically corrupt and wicked in the body and in the physical system" or that "physical beauty of every sort was a snare, a Circean enchantment, to be valiantly contended with and straitly eschewed." She admired the "glorious physiques" of Italian opera singers as exemplifying "a warmer, richer, and more abundant womanly life" than Americans in general could show, and she once wrote Sarah Josepha Hale, the editor of *Godey's,* that "the idea of presenting at one and the same time fashions and a healthful, well proportioned female figure, is a new and original one of which your magazine may be justly proud. I hope you will have the grace and strength to go through with it." [13] Woman's evening dress she seems first to have encountered when she went to England. She did not adopt it for herself, but she contemplated it with reasonable calmness.

As to the nude in art:

The human form is indeed divine, as M. Belloc insists, and rightly, sacredly drawn, cannot offend the purest eye....

If, then, the painter rightly and sacredly conceives the divine meaning, and creates upon the canvas, or in marble, forms of exalted ideal
loveliness, we cannot murmur even if, like Adam and Eve in Eden,
"they are naked, and are not ashamed."

In "the salacious images of mythological abomination" this was
not always achieved, however, and

The cheek that can forget to blush at the Venus and Cupid by Titian,
at Leda and her Swan, at Jupiter and Io, and others of equally evil
intent, ought never to pretend to blush at any thing. Such pictures are
a disgrace to the artists that painted, to the age that tolerates, and to the
gallery that contains them. They are fit for a bagnio rather than public
exhibition.

If this seems naïve, nobody doubts that there are unchaste nudes
as well as chaste ones; the distinctions between the two often require pondering and do not necessarily hold good for all observers.
Harriet pondered Dannecker's *Ariadne*—"a beautiful female riding
on a panther or a tiger"—with some care:

Two thoughts occurred to me: why, when we gaze upon this form so
perfect, so entirely revealed, does it not excite any of those emotions,
either of shame or of desire, which the living reality would excite?
And again: why does not the immediate contact of feminine helpless-
ness with the awful brute ferocity excite that horror which the sight
of the same in real life must awaken? Why, but because we behold
under a spell in the transfigured world of art where passion ceases, and
bestial instincts are felt to be bowed to the law of mind, and of ideal
truth?

These seem to me fairly sophisticated distinctions, and it is noteworthy that she puts the sexually objectionable in the same class
with that which is objectionable in other ways, which is something that neither prudes nor sexually obsessed persons ever
achieve. In *Footsteps of the Master* she praises Jesus for taking
the ground "that the sins of a fallen woman were like any other
sins, and that repentant love entitled to equal forgiveness." In this
connection it is interesting to remember Harriet's great admiration for George Eliot, who lived much of her mature life with

George Henry Lewes without benefit of clergy, and who was an unbeliever besides. "She is a noble, true woman; and if anybody doesn't see it, so much the worse for *them*, and not her." Calvin went right along. "I think you are a better Christian without church or theology," he wrote the novelist, "than most people are with both, though I am, and always have been in the main, a Calvinist of the Jonathan Edwards school. God bless you!" [14]

IV

There is a fascinating mixture of realism and idealism in Harriet's attitude toward marriage in general. "Love, to an idealist, comes not first from earth, but heaven. It comes as an exaltation of all the higher and nobler faculties, and is its own justification in the fuller nobleness, the translucent purity, the larger generosity, the warmer piety, it brings." Nor is this surprising since "GOD is the great maker of romance. HE, from whose hand came man and woman,—HE, who strung the great harp of existence with all its wild and wonderful and manifold chords, and attuned them to one another." In the great passage in *The Minister's Wooing* on the rungless ladder, from which Professor Foster has taken, in its theological aspects, the title of his penetrating study of her relationship to New England Puritanism, she makes human love a schoolmaster to bring mankind to the love of God:

There is a ladder to heaven, whose base God has placed in human affections, tender instincts, symbolic feelings, sacraments of love, through which the soul rises higher and higher, refining as she goes, till she outgrows the human, and changes, as she rises, into the image of the divine. At the very top of this ladder, at the threshold of Paradise, blazes dazzling and crystalline that celestial grade where the soul knows self no more, having learned, through a long experience of devotion, how blest it is to lose herself in that eternal Love and Beauty of which all earthly fairness and grandeur are but the dim types, the distant shadow.

On the other hand, she knew the insidious quality which exists in sexual attraction, and admitted frankly that we often fall in love not with another human being but with love itself, that, in a refined or idealistic nature, the emotion, when once thoroughly aroused, seldom stays very close to the object that has inspired it, and that all marriages are inevitably disappointing, for the simple reason that while courtship is romance, marriage is realism.

Disenchantment must come, of course, and in a love which terminates in a happy marriage, there is a tender and gracious process, by which, without shock or violence, the ideal is gradually sunk in the real, which, though found faulty and earthly, is still ever tenderly remembered as it seemed under the morning light of that enchantment.

That is the happiest ending that human beings can expect, but even when it does not occur, love is not to be rejected:

If ever you have so loved that all cold prudence, all selfish worldly considerations have gone down like driftwood before a river flooded with new rain from heaven, so that you ever forgot yourself, and were ready to cast your whole being into the chasm of existence, as an offering before the feet of another, and all for nothing—if you awoke bitterly betrayed and deceived, still give thanks to God that you have had one glimpse of heaven.

No matter how it comes? No, not quite. Harriet had enough sympathy for transgressors to rebel against Dante's consigning Paolo and Francesca to hell, as depicted in Ary Scheffer's painting—"a libel on my Father in heaven," she called it. "No. It is *not* God who eternally pursues undying, patient love with storms of vindictive wrath." She praises the Catholic Church for making marriage a sacrament and criticizes it for requiring continence of the clergy, and she permits Harry Henderson's uncle to suggest that Fénelon ought to have married Madame Guyon. Historically she was quite correct in separating Puritanism from asceticism— "our forefathers were, in many essential respects, Jews in their thoughts and feelings with regard to this life"—and Jim's rough ridicule of the Anglican rector Mr. St. John's "holy virginity" in *We and Our Neighbors* ("Holy grandmother!") is abundantly justified when St. John falls in love with Angie Van Arsdel. Cap'n

Kittredge of *The Pearl of Orr's Island* says that "sparkin'" is "the Christianest thing I knows on," and the persona of the *House and Home Papers* wants courting and flirting done in the open. Harriet understood the attraction of opposites also. "She is not at all the person I ever expected would obtain any power over me," says Clayton of Nina Gordon. "She has no culture, no reading, no habits of reflection; but she has, after all, a certain tone and quality to her, a certain *timbre*, as the French say of voices, which suits me." Harriet believed also that it was important for boys and girls to have an opportunity to get to know each other thoroughly before marriage, and she consistently favored co-education. In *My Wife and I* she even allowed Harry and Eva to begin with a "pick-up." [15]

In a letter to her daughters written in 1859, Mrs. Stowe tells of the engagement of a girl they know to a man she has loved for eight years but with whom her connection had been broken off by her parents because he was the father of an illegitimate child. "The fault was that of a boy of 18—and he has always supported both the woman and child. The parents feel dissatisfied but Agnes is *firm*. It is real love she marries for, *nothing else*." Love out of bounds enters her fiction importantly in connection with both Aaron Burr's affair with Madame du Frontignac in *The Minister's Wooing* and that of Ellery Davenport (who is also Burr) with Emily Rossiter in *Oldtown Folks*. In neither case is there any paltering on the author's part with "conventional" standards of morality,[16] but she does frankly recognize, in the first instance cited, the power of even an illicit love to produce beneficent results:

A new world awoke around her,—the world of literature and taste, of art and of sentiment; she felt somehow as if she had gained the growth of years in a few months. She felt within herself the stirring of dim aspiration, the uprising of new power of self-devotion and self-sacrifice, a trance of hero-worship, a cloud of high ideal images; the lighting up, in short, of all that God had laid, ready to be enkindled, in a woman's nature, when the time comes to sanctify her as the pure priestess of a domestic temple.

Emily is a rebel against Calvinism, subdued by the doctrines of Rousseau and Voltaire. But though she lives with Ellery Davenport out of wedlock and bears him a child, Harriet is quite clear that the two inhabited different worlds and that he finally left her because she was "a woman standing on too high a moral plane for Ellery Davenport to consort with her in comfort."

In her sketch of Delilah in *Bible Heroines* Harriet makes a distinction between "the frail sinner falling through too much love" ("the weak, downtrodden woman, the prey of man's superior force") and "the terrible creature, artful and powerful, who triumphs over man, and uses man's passions for her own ends, without an answering throb of passion." Her Delilah is of course the second type; [17] her Maggie of *We and Our Neighbors* is the first. But the emphasis here is not so much on whether or not the girl is culpable as on what can be done to redeem her. It is Eva Henderson who saves her through love—as another Eva saved Topsy—by taking her into her home and patiently nursing her back to self-respect, and who, even after Maggie has run away and entered a house of prostitution, goes after her, in the spirit of Jesus, to seek and to save that which was lost. Harriet clearly approves of Eva and disapproves of Maggie's stern Irish mother and uncle, whose harshness angers and antagonizes the girl and nearly destroys her, and she disapproves even more of that "virtuous" woman Maria Wouvermans, Eva's aunt, whose hardness of heart when Maggie worked for her contributed to her fall; in fact, Harriet even seems to prefer the "madame," Mother Moggs, with whom the girl takes refuge after having fled from Eva's home. "To say the truth, Mother Moggs was by no means all devil. She had large remains of that motherly nature which is common to warm-blooded women of easy virtue."

But the most interesting thing is Harriet's treatment of Maggie herself. The work of redeeming sinners would be much easier "if the sinner sought to be saved would step forthwith right across the line, and behave henceforth like a saint." Unfortunately this does not happen and cannot be expected to happen. Harriet sees Maggie's lover and her fall through Maggie's eyes. She understands how reasonable it was that the girl should fall, and how reasonable it was that she should feel "less repentance for sin than indignation at her own wrongs." Does the reader gag at this? Then

let us Christians who have never fallen, in the grosser sense, ask ourselves if, with regard to our own particular sins and failings, we hold the same strict line of reckoning. Do we come down upon ourselves for our ill temper, for our selfishness, for our pride, and other respectable sins, as we ask the poor girl to do who has been led astray from virtue?

Ill temper, selfishness, pride, and other "respectable sins"? Are they, then, really as bad as unchastity? The great moralists have always known it. But it was not quite the usual view with pious Protestant American novelists of the nineteenth century.

But even when Harriet functioned as advocate for sinners she was not starry-eyed. She thought Elizabeth Stuart Phelps was, and for this reason she was able to control her admiration for *Hedged In* (1870). In this novel a "fallen" woman is taken into a Christian home and rehabilitated. She becomes a teacher, after which she brings home and acknowledges her illegitimate son. The school officials consider asking for her resignation, and the author condemns them for it. Harriet fears that she has begged the question of probabilities.

It is not that Harriet has any doubts about the duty of Christian people to rescue the fallen. But she is not so sure that they should be brought into Christian homes and allowed to associate freely with the children. The reason, basically, is

the same as the reason why the insane have to be treated in the lunatic asylum, the drunkard in the inebriate asylum. It is not because they are sinners above all others, not because it would either dishonor or defile a Christian family to receive them, but because their recovery requires specific conditions and specific care, which cannot co-exist with the wants of common families.

As Harriet saw it, a "mush of concessions" would solve neither this nor any other moral problem. "Because persons who have sinned have repented and become changed characters, are they to be treated in society as precisely on a level with those who have not sinned at all?" She did not think so, though she did not explain where she would find those who had not sinned at all. When a correspondent of *The Christian Union* suggested fines and imprisonment for brothel keepers and their patrons, she replied that unfortunately such laws could not be enforced. "Legislation upon moral subjects, to be of any sort of use, must come from a convicted and converted community, and not have the task of forming such a community."

Only, Harriet Beecher Stowe was not completely consistent any more than other mortals. Despite all her bold insight and brave common sense, she did not always follow her reasoning through to its logical conclusion. In the last analysis, sexual irregularity *did* carry a unique taint of heinousness in her eyes; in the last analysis, therefore, she cannot refrain from prostrating herself before the cruel idol of indissoluble marriage.[18] In *Oldtown Folks* Jonathan Rossiter is made to argue that "hard as marriage bonds bear in individual cases, it is for woman's interest that they should be as stringently maintained as the Lord himself has left them." Quite unconvincingly, when we remember that we are reading a writer who was under no delusion as to nature serving as a reliable index of the mind of God, he continues: "What saints and innocents has the fire tortured, and what just men made perfect has water drowned, making *no* exceptions! But who doubts that this inflexibility in natural life is after all the best thing?" But if we are to model ourselves on fire and water, then will and consciousness—and conscience too—must abrogate. And if merciless, unthinking inflexibility—natural law—is to prevail in one area, why not elsewhere as well? In *Pink and White Tyranny* Mrs. Stowe presented the test case of the high-minded John Seymour married to the worthless Lillie Ellis and decided that, having chosen her, he must retain her to the end. Fortunately she remembered that she was novelist as well as moralist; consequently she persuaded Lillie to be accommodating about dying, to the accompaniment of considerable soft music, which was the usual fate of unworthy (and unwanted) mates in pre-divorce age fiction. Here, if anywhere in her work, Mrs. Stowe shows Dickensian influence, for Lillie's domestic ineptitude is straight out of *David Copperfield*. But her moral worthlessness is not derived from Dora, and her eleventh-hour redemption is completely unconvincing. What rings true in Dickens, consequently, becomes quite false and sentimental here.

CHAPTER VII

THE AESTHETE

I

"When the Pilgrims came to Plymouth in 1620," wrote Gamaliel
Bradford, "they brought with them the English conscience and
intellect and energy, but, roughly speaking, it may be said that
the English imagination stayed behind, with the children of Shakespeare." [1] Of this Harriet Beecher Stowe was well aware. It is
true that there were times when she herself was sufficiently within
the Puritan shadow so that she thought of beauty as a snare to
draw the soul away from God,[2] but these were her weaker moments. If the Wesleys saw no reason why the devil should have
all the good tunes, Lyman Beecher was with them in his conviction that "too long . . . has the devil held in his exclusive possession
the fine arts," and the day would come when his daughter would
remark boldly that the Negroes who gave up dancing when they
joined the church might well have found a better test of their
sincerity, and even that too much prayer meeting might be as
debilitating as too much amusement.

As she saw it, the appetite for beauty was as natural as the
appetite for food, and she could perceive no evidence that God
was a Puritan in the color and energy of the world that He had
made. The beauty-hating, image-smashing aspects of Puritanism
seem to have operated as strongly as any aspect of it to turn her
finally against it. True, some aspects of beauty made little appeal

to her; unlike Henry Ward, she cared nothing for gems. But she certainly opposed utilitarianism in women's attire (in *Oldtown Folks*, Miss Asphyxia's indifference to her toilet is used to make her even more hateful than she would otherwise be), and she is clear that saints injure the cause of goodness when they make themselves personally repulsive. Moreover, she wanted prettily-dressed women to inhabit prettily-furnished houses, and her household papers in the *Atlantic* and elsewhere gave as sensible advice toward achieving this end as anybody could have asked for. It was not luxury she wanted basically, and she knew that neatness and good taste and imagination are more important in the creation of an attractive home than a great deal of money, but she does not quite reject luxury either, whether she encounters it in the residence of her friend the Duchess of Sutherland or in such new luxury hotels as the Grand Pacific in Chicago.

Mrs. Marvyn's aesthetic hunger in *The Minister's Wooing* probably reflects Roxana even more than Harriet. Yet Harriet approached the Louvre as "one who has starved all a life, in vain imaginings of what art might be." She was fond of searching for an ideal unity underlying all art, and she speaks of going with Shakespeare "into an ideal world of men and women, or with Mozart into a dreamland of sound, or with Rubens into an ideality of color, or with the old Greeks into a labyrinth of beautiful forms." The architect who designed Melrose Abbey was a Mozart in architecture; there was a strong Gothic quality in Shakespeare; Cuyp's pictures suggested Longfellow's poems; Rubens was like Shakespeare, Rembrandt like Hawthorne, and Correggio like Tom Moore. And of course it was all beautiful because it reflected and expressed the character of God. "It is he you feel in music," she wrote one of her children—"it is His presence you feel in the enthusiasm of art." Without this, art itself is only pain:

Music, exquisite scenery used sometimes to almost wring my heart. Now all is joy. When these things wake up the deeper wants within, the answer is always near, the longing of my soul meets an instant answer, whenever I call he answers "I am here."

But even this cannot be taken in a narrow or pietistic sense. On the contrary, creative souls "have a beauty and a worth about them entirely independent of their moral character.... We may say ... that it has no moral excellence in it; but none the less do we admire it. God has made us so that we cannot help loving it; our souls go forth to it with an infinite longing, nor can that longing be condemned."

II

Pious people have generally been less suspicious of the beauties of nature than of those of art, and Harriet had the good fortune to be born in one of the loveliest parts of New England: "My earliest recollections of Litchfield are those of its beautiful scenery, which impressed and formed my mind long before I had words to give names to my emotions, or could analyze my mental processes." From "Uncle Lot" to *Poganuc People* her writings are full of close, delighted observation of all the fauna and flora that came within her range, and when she grew sophisticated enough to lament New England's aesthetic inferiority to Europe, she comforted herself with "the inspiring thought that Nature is ever the superior. No tree painting can compare with a splendid elm, in the plenitude of its majesty. There are colorings beyond that of Rubens poured forth around us in every autumn scene; there are Murillos smiling by our household firesides." In *Pink and White Tyranny* Lillie's indifference to nature is presented as one of the elements of her superficiality.

Later, at Niagara and again in the Alps, she came in contact with more spectacular elements of nature. Still later, there was "the glorious, bewildering impropriety" of Florida, "where Nature has raptures and frenzies of growth, and conducts herself like a crazy, drunken, but beautiful bacchante." At first the "ragged and untidy" appearance of the land displeased her. "We miss the sharp-edged frosts of the North which cut and shrivel and clear away the rubbish of the past. We need a definite dividing line in the seasons and to know just when one ends and the other begins." She also disliked the litter of the live oaks. But further reflection convinced her that such things served as a salutary reminder that man is not alone in the world. The great tree "was here rejoicing in the habitable parts of the earth long before you were born—he will be here long after your dust has gone back to the earth as it was." And she adds, "For our part, we are glad that there are trees so mighty that they humble the pride of man and laugh at the axe of the wood man."

Practically all New England's trees are described and praised somewhere in Harriet's writings. Trees were what she missed most in Rome; the land seemed stony and dead without them. She loved flowers too, had a green thumb for raising them and great skill in arranging them; in Florida she tired out her guests hunting exotic blooms through the swamps. "I am glad you are going to have a flower garden," she wrote Charley. "A minister's flower garden is a means of grace." She quite sympathized with the poor German who was reported to have killed himself in despair because his neighbor's hens scratched up his plants; she even granted the beauty of many weeds. She wrote a panegyric to Central Park, especially as a paradise for lovers! She also left her descendants a solemn warning (which they have chosen not to heed) on the importance of preserving trees, for she had no sympathy with

the arrogance of man, in his contempt of everything that cannot be pressed into his own bodily service. If he can neither eat a thing, drink it nor wear it, nor make it in any capacity his minister, then what right has it to be? Away with it from the earth!

She even looked forward with dread to the disappearance of sailing ships, which she foresaw as soon as Yankee ingenuity should be capable of effecting it. "That race will never rest till everything antique and poetic is drilled out of the world." She loved the coast, especially in Maine, where the shore is not bare, as in Massachusetts and Connecticut, but the sea "luxuriates, swells, and falls, in the very lap of the primeval forest." She thought the ocean "like God—a mysterious power, beneficent, strengthening, purifying." It was also "a moral teacher" and "a sanitary institution," and it gave "bodily health which is physical religion." But full enjoyment of the joys of sailing was denied her. "I wonder that people who wanted to break the souls of heroes and martyrs never thought of sending them to sea and keeping them a little seasick." [3]

Yet, much as she loved nature, she was too firmly grounded in Christian doctrine to fall into the pantheistic revery that confused so many nineteenth-century writers. Perhaps the harsh New England climate helped her here. "Litchfield was a mountain town, where the winter was a stern reality for six months of the year, where there were great winds, drifting snows of a sublime power and magnitude." The snow had its own beauties, and "Our Wood Lot in Winter" and "The Snow Siege" are worth reading along with Lowell's "A Good Word for Winter," [4] but it was hard to be sentimental about it. As we have seen, the sea can heal. Tina even finds healing in flowers on her way home from the terrible Miss Asphyxia, and Mary Scudder is comforted by barnyard fowl. There are times too when nature is to be preferred to man. "Ignorant boor that he is, and all incapable of appreciating the glorious works of Nature, it seems to be his glory to be able to destroy in a few hours what it was the work of ages to produce." But she will have nothing to say to the pathetic fallacy, for "sunshine never pales at human trouble."

When flies delight to assail nervous tissue at early daylight, and cause your angry passions to rise before you are fairly awake, we must admit that the enemy has you at disadvantage. Grace is apt to be asleep and nature rampant at that hour. We remember that Beelzebub was the god of flies, and the aptness of the designation is striking.

She could have echoed Tennyson's

> I found Him not in world or sun,
> Or eagle's wing, or insect's eye.

"Surely, without the revelation of God in Jesus, who could believe in the divine goodness?" With her it was never *Through Nature to God*, as John Fiske charted the way in his book of that title, but *Through Man to God* with George A. Gordon.

It seems hardly necessary to add that she loved birds and animals. From childhood on the Beechers lived with animals; in the early days the dogs even went to church, and Harriet wrote some very lively passages describing their behavior there. In *Bible Heroines* she praised the laws of Moses which enjoined consideration for dumb creatures. "Not the gentlest words of Jesus are more compassionate in their spirit than many of these laws of Moses." Harriet loved Scott more for his love of animals. She thought it quite unnecessary to apologize for the love lavished on pets, and in *My Wife and I* Bolton goes so far as to believe in their immortality. When she went away to visit, her letters home always mentioned the animals she encountered, along with their human companions.

In Hartford days, the press described the Stowe dogs as "resplendent and musical in their breast colors and ribbon bows and tinkling silver bells," and when Frances Willard called, she found "three well-to-do cats, one yellow, one tortoise, one black, and all handsome," in "dignified positions on the walk, the porch, and the rug before the door respectively." One letter to Hattie is written as from a dog, and one to the twins begins, "My darling little cats." In addition to the reasonably prominent part which animals play in Harriet's fiction, there are a number of papers, like "Our Dogs," "Dogs and Cats," and "Hum, the Son of Buz," which are composed of close, delighted observation of bird and animal behavior.[5] In "The History of Tip-Top" the cat is cruel and dangerous and serves as an image of temptation, but this must not be taken to indicate that Harriet did not like cats, for she cherished them all her life. She had "a special kindness for toads, partly because they have been so much abused, and partly because they are so honestly and patiently homely. They take no airs. They know they are not good-looking, but don't fret about it." Her passion for roses destroyed any sympathy she might have felt for slugs however.[6] When she was in Italy she was distressed over the treatment of animals there, especially donkeys, and she praises Parisians for their kindness to cats and dogs.

But she was not sentimental even about animals. It is true that when she got to Florida "unsavory" was the worst adjective she could find even for the moccasin, but it was not the moccasin she was being tender about but Florida itself. She saw both a large snake and an alligator killed and skinned, apparently without batting an eye. She faces the horrible brutality of nature—life feeding on life—as frankly as H. G. Wells did in *The Undying Fire*, and she was clear that unwanted animals must always be humanely killed. She says nothing anywhere about the inhumanity of wearing fur or feathers. Even her own dog Giglio is memorialized as morally worthless: "Giglio's singular beauty and grace were his only merits; he liked to be petted and kept warm, but it mattered nothing to him who did it."

III

Mrs. Stowe knew little about either art or architecture. She achieved some fine descriptions of New England meetinghouses, but these were endeared to her more by religious than aesthetic associations. The architecture of her heart, Gothic, she encountered first when she went to Europe.

In this Gothic architecture we see earnest northern races, whose nature was a composite of influences from pine forest, mountain, and storm, expressing, in vast proportions and gigantic masonry, those ideas of infinite duration and existence which Christianity opened before them. A barbaric wildness mingles itself with fanciful, ornate abundance; it is the blossoming of northern forests.

This was "Alpine architecture," expressing a state of mind "too earnest for mere polish," Hebrew in spirit, not Greek. It was "a tribute to religion such as Art never gave before and never can again,—as much before the Pantheon as the Alps, with their virgin snows and glittering pinnacles, are above the temples made with hands."

She knew that the Gothic tolerated absurdities which less romantic and irregular styles could not embrace:

If people will make such dismal hobgoblin saints, and such fat virgins and such roystering, blackguard angels, I would much rather have none. There was a crucifix high up in the nave, enough to make one sick to look at it; and on one side of it a virgin, with a gridiron on her head, and on the other a very fat saint, in yellow petticoats.

Yet she found it irresistible, even in such a wild example as Scott's Abbotsford:

There are gables, and pinnacles, and spires, and balconies, and buttresses any where and every where, without rhyme or reason; for wherever the poet wanted a balcony, he had it; or wherever he had a fragment of carved stone, or a bit of historic tracery to put in, he made a shrine for it forthwith, without asking leave of any rules.

Whatever architects might say of it, it was a valuable expression of Scott's mind, an externalization of the "development of his inner life," a poem in wood and stone "as irregular, perhaps, and as contrary to any established rule, as his *Lay of the Last Minstrel,* but still wild and poetic."

Her romanticism attracted her to Moorish architecture too, but she was cold to "the Italian" and did not care for St. Paul's Cathedral. She did, however, admire the Houses of Parliament, and what had been said against them did not move her, which is a refreshing contrast to those amateurs in the arts who must always consult the authorities who happen to be in fashion before deciding what they may safely admire. In 1860 Harriet lashed out delightfully at those who did not like Milan Cathedral. Its appeal must be *felt*, she declared, and if a man cannot feel it, there is nothing for him to do but bear his misfortune, "but let him not interrupt those who do with any non sense about art."

Harriet's education in painting began very humbly with a picture of two white horses on a sign over a harness store in Hartford. She would have thought that a good beginning, for she believed that people's "love of art ought to begin with its power of representing in pleasing and poetical lights, some portion of their every-day life and experience," and she considered genre pictures "the best adapted for domestic and household ornamentation." She herself developed respectable amateur skill in both painting and sketching. In later years, when *The Christian Union* distributed colored reproductions of famous paintings, she cried "blessings upon chromo-lithography, by which the successful painting of a master can be reproduced indefinitely, and can enter thousands of homes with its educating, quickening, reforming influences." Only a trained eye could "distinguish between the copies and the originals."

As a European traveler she saw all the pictures which travelers see and commented upon many of them, but there can be no point in cataloguing them here. As might have been expected, she tended to concentrate on moral meanings, and of course she had a special interest in paintings on Biblical themes, though she thought pictures of Jesus generally unsatisfactory. For her, artists were among the spiritual types, and painting resembled music in achieving greatness only as it was inspired by the Christian religion.

The Art of ancient Rome was a second-hand copy of the original and airy Greek,—often clever, but never vivid and self-originating. It is to the religious Art of the Middle Ages, to the Umbrian and Florentine schools particularly, that we look for the peculiar and characteristic flowering of the Italian mind. . . . Raphael and Michel Angelo mark both the perfected splendor and the commenced decline of the original Italian Art; and just in proportion as their ideas grew less Christian and more Greek did the peculiar vividness and intense flower of Italian nationality pass away from them.

In Florence in 1860 she was "wholly won over and converted . . . to all the doctrines of those who praise the ancient Pre-Raphaelite artists." In them she found "a gravity, majesty, sincerity, an originality and quaintness, a fulness of poetic feeling, a pathos and moral sublimity, beyond all we had ever dreamed of in art before."

Here again the most appealing thing about Harriet's judgments is their independence. "I . . . look with my own eyes, for if not

the best that might be, they are the best that God has given me."
Egyptian art she considered simply horrible, like something that
had "floundered up out of Nile mud"; so she did not bother to
look at it. If she liked a picture she said so; if she disliked it
she said that too; and she was not in the least disturbed if you
told her that the first picture was unworthy of admiration and
that she would learn to admire the second by-and-by. Art was
created for people, not for critics and other artists, and if the
old masters cannot create something that pleases her, then they
may proceed to Jericho so far as she is concerned. Her reaction
to *The Last Supper* of Leonardo da Vinci differs in tone from
that of Mark Twain but it is equally independent, and she is quite
as frank about the Sistine Madonna, though she admires it greatly
in some aspects. Murillo was "a man of rather a mediocre mind."
Veronese, though refreshingly free of vulgarity, was "the poet of
upholstery and costume," and when he wished to paint Christ and
the apostles, he knew "no better way than to surround them with
the state he loves." Even Michelangelo "expressed only that portion of the religious element which belongs equally to Paganism
and Christianism—that of *vastness and power*." He was "an old
Roman risen from the dead," and his Christ was "a Jupiter with
a handful of thunderbolts," his Moses "a great craggy, Roman
demigod, mighty, mysterious, and cold," and "that bloody-bones
picture," the *Last Judgment*, a positively blasphemous work, with
a Christ less divine than the Apollo Belvidere.[7] In *Pink and White
Tyranny* Mrs. Follingsbee, who admires them because "they are
the thing," sends Charlie Ferrola's long-suffering wife photographs of the *Moses* and the *Night and Morning*, "and I really
wish you would see where she hung them—away in yonder dark
corner!" Lillie says, "I think myself they are enough to scare the
owls," and one cannot but feel that for once Harriet has used her
as a spokesman.

One must admit that Harriet was prudish about Michelangelo's
nakedness. Generally, however, she was quite free of all such
Miss Nancy considerations in her judgment of paintings. As
labels, "sacred" and "secular" did not mean much to her. Com-

menting upon Titian's *Assumption of the Madonna*, she admits
that "generally speaking, the Venetian painting is sensuous, and
not spiritual."

But we are not of that school of thinkers who suppose the spiritual
world differs from ours in being lower toned.... We do not believe
that watery blue, faded pink, and mild suffusions of stone color express
spirituality, and so we find no fault that Titian represents his Madonna
ascending with a pomp of hues like gold and purple clouds of a
glorious sunset.

Her admiration for Rembrandt, whom she compares to Hawthorne—"*The House of the Seven Gables* is a succession of Rembrandt pictures done in words instead of oils"—merely shows her
good judgment, but what is to be said of her love for Rubens—
"to me above all others the painter of *physical life* richness beauty
abundance" and his full-bodied Madonnas, which stand opposed
to "the faded, cold ideals of the Middle Ages, from which he
revolted with such a bound"? At first she detested him "with
all the energy of my soul," but all the time she knew and felt,
"by the very pain he gave me," that he was "a real, living artist,"
and at last she surrendered completely:

But Rubens, the great, joyous, full-souled, all-powerful Rubens!—there
he was, full as ever of triumphant, abounding life; disgusting and pleasing; making me laugh and making me angry; defying me to dislike
him; dragging me at his chariot wheels; in despite of my protests
forcing me to confess that there was no other but he.

Of course the greatest of his pictures was the *Descent from
the Cross* at Antwerp:

My first sensation was of astonishment, blank, absolute, overwhelming. After all that I had seen, I had no idea of a painting like this. I was
lifted off my feet, as much as by Cologne Cathedral, or Niagara Falls,
so that I could neither reason nor think whether I was pleased or not.
It is difficult, even now, to analyze the sources of this wonderful
power. The excellence of this picture does not lie, like Raphael's, in a
certain ideal spirituality, by which the scene is raised above earth to
the heavenly sphere; but rather in a power, strong, human, almost

homely, by which, not an ideal, but the real scene is forced home upon the heart.

She left it "as one should leave the work of a great religious master—thinking more of Jesus and of John than of Rubens."

IV

Music was a part of the Beecher milieu from the beginning. Roxana, as we have seen, played the guitar, and Lyman told one of his sons that if he could play what was inside of him on the fiddle he could beat Paganini. Harriet belonged to the last generation that was exposed to the old Puritan church music of the pre-organ period.

And as there is a place for all things in this great world of ours, so there was in its time and day a place and a style for Puritan music. If there were pathos and power and solemn splendor in the rhythmic movement of the churchly chants, there was a grand wild freedom, an energy of motion, in the old "fuguing" tunes of that day that well expressed the heart of a people courageous in combat and unshaken in endurance. The church chant is like the measured motion of the mighty sea in calm weather, but those old fuguing tunes were like that same ocean aroused by stormy winds, when deep calleth unto deep in tempestuous confusion, out of which at last is evolved union and harmony.... Whatever the trained musician might say of such a tune as old "Majesty," no person of imagination and sensibility could ever hear it well rendered by a large choir without deep emotion.

But alongside this was another livelier, more modern kind of music at home:

Father was very fond of music, and was susceptible to its influence; and one of the great eras of the family, in my childish recollection, is the triumphant bringing home from New Haven a fine-toned upright piano, which a fortunate accident had brought within the range of a poor country minister's means. The ark of the covenant was not brought into the tabernacle with more gladness than this magical instrument into our abode.

My older sisters had both learned to play and sing, and we had boarding in our family an accomplished performer, the charming and beautiful Louisa Watt, whose image floats through my recollection of these days like that of some marvelous little fairy, she was so small, so lovely, so lively, and sang so delightfully.

Father soon learned to accompany the piano with his violin in various psalm tunes and Scotch airs, and brothers Edward and William to perform their part on the flute. So we had often domestic concerts, which, if they did not attain to the height of artistic perfection, filled the house with gladness.

These recollections are among the most cheerful of my life. Our house rang with Scotch ballads, for which Louisa had a special taste, and the knowledge of which she introduced through all the circle of her pupils.

One of my most decided impressions of the family as it was in my childish days was of a great household inspired by a spirit of cheerfulness and hilarity, and of my father, though pressed and driven with business, always lending an attentive ear to any thing in the way of life and social fellowship.

The first great singer Harriet ever heard was Jenny Lind, in New York, in 1852. Considering what they both were, she could not have made a better choice. She was not musical herself, in the narrower sense, but music was very important to her as an expression of both good fellowship and spiritual aspiration. "To me all music is sacred.... All real music, in its passionate earnest, its blendings, its wild, heart-searching tones, is the language of aspiration," far better qualified to express moral and spiritual ideals than painting. And she had the idea that before Christ music had been mainly "in the minor scale." "Music ought not to be looked at mainly as an art. It ought to be a bond of fellowship. A few trying to sing together get united—we agree to overlook each other's discords—the social feeling rises—we feel intimate and it makes a happier circle than any thing else can." So she and her party sang the old Scottish tunes lustily when they were in Scotland, and there is a touching letter to Calvin: "Well, dear old man, I think lots of you, and only want to end all this in our quiet home, where we can sing *John Anderson, My Jo* together." In the same spirit she engineered Sunday evening "sings" in Florida. When church music changed its character and stress came to be placed on congregational singing, her father was important in the new movement, and in the days of Plymouth Church and the very influential *Plymouth Hymnal,* Henry Ward was considerably more so. In her old age she loved all simple music, even street bands, but it was hymns that stayed by her the longest. "I had hymns on the brain. I bless God I have. I love to sing my father's and my mother's old hymns." Her friends noticed that "she always chooses those of a stirring, lively movement. Anything of a slow, melancholy or sentimental order fails to interest her.... A word omitted, or a wrong word used, she notices on the instant and makes the correction."

She mentions Mozart, Beethoven ("on me...Beethoven's Sonatas have a far more deeply religious influence than much that has religious names and words"), and Haydn (*The Creation*). She speaks of *La Favorita, Les Huguenots, Faust,*[8] and *Lohengrin.*[9] *Uncle Tom's Cabin* proves that she was familiar with some Negro spirituals, but in her time it was not the fashion to take them as seriously as they have since been taken. There is one ecstatic expression of her enjoyment of a concert in *Sunny Memories,* but it is a little disappointing that the singer most frequently referred to should be Elizabeth Greenfield, known as "The Black Swan," whose career she tried to encourage. Miss Greenfield seems to have had a phenomenal freak voice, and she engaged in such feats as singing *Old Folks at Home* "first in a soprano voice, and then in a tenor or baritone," whatever that may mean.

V

Finally there was that harlot among the arts, the theater. Both Harriet and her brother Henry Ward said many harsh things about it, though he at least was in a very weak position to do so, for both he and Lyman were very theatrical preachers.[10] In *The American Woman's Home* the theater, though not condemned, is certainly degraded by being classified with dancing and racing as not evil in itself but likely to have unwholesome associations. In *Oldtown Folks* the dangers of the dramatic temperament are presented in Tina, and in 1885 Harriet took a fling at Barnum's "gay, dashing, unprincipled career . . . in which success covers a multitude of sins," and objected to his being accepted by foreigners as a representative American. In "A Winter in Italy" she described a Venetian puppet theater very charmingly, but spoiled her description by condescension, observing that the effort involved was worthy of a better cause. When she was in the mood, she could even make the opposition of the Puritans to public recreation a virtue, presenting them as having attained the stature of Bernard Shaw's Ancients in *Back to Methuselah*, who go to life directly for the needs which, in our stage of development, must be satisfied by art.

Looking over the world on a broad scale, do we not find that public entertainments have very generally been the sops thrown out by engrossing upper classes to keep lower classes from inquiring too particularly into their rights, and to make them satisfied with a stone, when it was not quite convenient to give them bread?

This was not, however, her settled view. Human nature being what it is, she realized that unless wholesome recreation was provided for average people, they would find something worse. "If the Church would set herself to amuse her young folks, instead of discussing doctrines and mere metaphysical hairsplitting, she would prove herself a true mother, and not a hard-visaged stepdame." Elizabeth Stuart Phelps says that some persons in Andover looked askance at Harriet because she was suspected of attending the Boston theaters, and I think she may well have seen more plays than is generally believed. "Presto! like a curtain rising in the theatre, up went the fog"—thus she dared to write in a *Christian Union* paper. "Georgie wanted me to go to the theatre yesterday P.M.," she writes in 1883, "but I declined on the principle of saving my strength—for the same reason I read my Bible and sing my hymns at home this morning instead of going to church." There are neutral references to Rachel, Taglioni, and

Céleste, and there is an 1880 letter to the twins in which she is very anxious for their impressions of Sarah Bernhardt. She entertained Charlotte Cushman, and she did not shrink from citing actresses she admired as arguments for women's rights: "Did anybody ever think that Mrs. Siddons and Mrs. Kemble and Ristori had better have applied themselves sedulously to keeping house, because they were women, and 'woman's noblest station is retreat'?" She rejoiced in the success of Ira Aldridge because it helped refute the myth of Negro inferiority, and she was a great admirer of Joseph Jefferson and lamented that his modesty held him back from Shakespeare. She was clear that attire that would not be acceptable elsewhere was permissible on the stage, and she even managed to mention the famous musical spectacle, *The Black Crook* without a shudder, though many of her contemporaries professed themselves appalled by the nakedness displayed in it. When she visited Toledo she saw the fine new opera house there as a civilizer and a "public blessing," and when some of her fellow guests in the White Mountains put on entertainments for her and others, she spoke of their unselfishness in thus exerting themselves during vacation as manifesting "the dignity of a Christian grace."

There had been amateur theatricals in her own childhood, as there are in Oldtown, and one of her earliest literary enterprises was the abortive play "Cleon." The readings from her own works which she gave in the 'seventies showed her dramatic instinct; one night, preparing for them, she brushed her white hair so that it stood up straight on her head and said to Mrs. Fields: "Now, my dear, gaze upon me. I am exactly like my father when he was going to preach." In Italy, W. W. Story was so impressed by the way she imitated Sojourner Truth's "ringing barytone" that he always wanted her to do it for his friends. In Florida, Harriet and her daughters sponsored dramatic performances as well as dancing parties; once Hattie played in Sardou's *A Scrap of Paper* (the playbill calls him Jardou) for the church building fund, but did not draw a good house.

Mrs. Stowe's connection with the most successful play in American history is spoken of elsewhere in these pages; she did not write it but it could never have been without her. When Asa Hutchinson applied to her for permission to dramatize *Uncle Tom's Cabin*, which was pure courtesy on his part, since under the existing laws she could not have prevented him, she refused on the ground that, theatrical conditions being what they were in this country,

any attempt on the part of Christians to identify themselves with them will be productive of danger to the individual character, and to the general cause. If the barrier which now keeps young people of Christian families from theatrical entertainments is once broken down by the introduction of respectable and moral plays, they will then be open to all the temptations of those who are not such, as there will be, as the world now is, five bad plays to one good.

In other words, the theater is the devil's territory and must not be invaded.

Yet she herself dramatized the novel for the Negro "reader" Mary E. Webb, in whose career she shows more interest than she ever manifested anywhere else in a theatrical connection.[11] She witnessed performances of the Aiken version of *Uncle Tom's Cabin* at least twice, once at the National Theater in Boston, where Francis H. Underwood took her to see the Howards, and once in Hartford, in company with Charles Dudley Warner. She cannot have been too unfavorably impressed, for in *The Chimney-Corner* she cites the success of the play as indicating that impropriety is not a necessary ingredient for theatrical success.[12]

CHAPTER VIII

THE READER

I

Constance Rourke may have been merely echoing a similar earlier judgment in Mrs. Fields's biography when, in *Trumpets of Jubilee* (1927), she set down Harriet Beecher Stowe as "profoundly uninterested in literature." Ruskin, too, had been shocked when, at Durham in 1857, she had chosen to go boating instead of examining the beautiful manuscripts in the cathedral library. The judgment is wrong nevertheless. "Harriet reads everything she can lay hands on." It was written of the child; it was equally true of the woman. Says Edward Everett Hale:

I have seen her come into the house to make a friendly visit, and take up a book within the first half-hour of that visit and interest herself in it, and then sit absorbed in the book, and in nothing else, till it was time for her to go home in the evening. I have known her, simply because she had an interesting book in her hand ... take a street car going out of town, and ride three or four miles without observing that she should have been going in the other direction.

It is true that she believed it more important to be a good woman than a learned one, and she obviously sympathized with Clayton's argument in *Dred*, that "the books that have influenced the world the longest, the widest, and deepest have been written by men who attended to things more than to books." But this argues no indifference to literature; it simply testifies to an understanding of the conditions under which literature is produced. She knew that thought had become a disease in New England and, at times, in her own life, yet she praised the old-time New England mother, who was "not a mere unreflective drudge of domestic toil" but "a reader and a thinker, keenly appreciative in intellectual regions," and both Edmund Wilson and Charles H. Foster have praised her, enthusiastically but not extravagantly, for the vast theological knowledge revealed in her books.[1] A translation of Berquin's *Children's Friend* was the only "story-book" she could afterwards remember from her childhood; Shakespeare and Milton may first have been encountered in *Elegant Extracts in Prose and Verse;* it is no wonder that the Bible was read "hour after hour for mere amusement," nor that, when *Ivanhoe* came into the family when Harriet was twelve, she should have read it through seven times in six months.

Yet she refers with reasonable frequency to the popular nursery tales, several times to "Hänsel and Gretel," which she always misspells. As a woman she wanted books all over the house, not confined to the library, the way some people shut up their children in the nursery, and she seems never to have had much respect for non-readers or even for people who did not buy books. Somewhat surprisingly for so absent-minded and inaccurate a person, she had a phenomenal verbal memory; her son Charley says she could recite the whole *Lay of the Last Minstrel*. In her writings and letters, her great source of quotations is, of course, the Bible, but she often quotes from Shakespeare and Milton, and also turns, with a reasonable degree of frequency, to Tennyson, Longfellow, and other contemporaries. In her own life, she used literature for comfort in time of grief, and she knew, with Clayton, that reading is essentially a matter of the response of the reader's personality to that of the writer. Her comments in *Lady Byron Vindicated* on the connection between a man's personality and his writings, and her analysis of the right and the wrong way to use the writings to understand the personality, are discriminating and sophisticated; so, too, are the passages in *Sunny Memories of Foreign Lands* in which she scrutinizes Shakespeare, Milton, and

Scott for what their work reveals of their own experience and
their differences from each other.[2]

The theological works to which Harriet was exposed in her
father's library might safely be counted upon to kill a modern
child, but she found meat and drink in some of them, not always
of a religious nature. *Harmer on Solomon's Song* fascinated her
because it reminded her of *The Arabian Nights* and *State of the
Clergy During the French Revolution* by its out-and-out horrors.
There was horror, too, in Cotton Mather's *Magnalia*, and the
thrill of consecration besides; as Charles E. and Lyman Beecher
Stowe express it, "no Jewish maiden ever grew up with a more
earnest faith that she belonged to a consecrated race, a people
specially called and chosen of God for some great work on
earth." "The delicious morsel of a *Don Quixote* that had once
been a book" which she one day disinterred from beneath "a
weltering ocean of pamphlets" was a real treasure; so was *The
Arabian Nights* itself, whose wonder she described factually in
her introduction to *A Library of Famous Fiction*,[3] and again
through her fictional self Dolly in *Poganuc People*. The factual
account is the more imaginative of the two:

Then did time and place vanish; howling winds, wastes of snow, and
the solitary dullness of the lone farmhouse, all became things of naught.
A golden cloud of vision encompassed us, and we walked among genii
and fairies, enchanted palaces, jewelled trees, and valleys of diamonds.
We became intimate friends of Sindbad the Sailor; we knew every
jewel in the windows of Aladdin's palace and became adepts in arts of
enchanting and disenchanting.

But even this was not all, nor are all her joys rediscoverable
now. Grandmother Foote read Dr. Johnson as well as theological
writers and talked about Bible characters as if they were real
people, and Aunt Mary Foote was a "beautiful reader" of poetry.
Bunyan, too, was discovered early, and, linking literature with
life, as she had always done from the days when she had seen
the Frog Prince in common undistinguished frogs of her acquaintance, she had made his description of the way to hell more vivid

to herself by brooding over the family smoke house through a chasm in the kitchen chimney. She was so fond of Henry Hart Milman's poem, *The Fall of Jerusalem*, that when she was a celebrity in England, she asked him, through his wife, to copy out a passage for her in his own handwriting.

II

In her school days, Harriet studied Latin, French, and Italian, and made a verse translation from Ovid, but she was hardly a linguist. "My husband chews endlessly a German cud," she writes in 1872. "I must have English." Apparently French was the only foreign language she ever learned well enough to attempt to converse in it. She once, rather coyly, addresses the twins as "*mes chères enfants*," and she signs one letter "*ta mère*." German, despite (or because of) Calvin's love for it, she seems to have disliked, as people who have not troubled to learn it generally do. This shows not only in the "German cud" but, even more, in the snappish reference to her husband's "German class of three young ladies, with whom he is reading *Faust* for the nine hundred and ninety-ninth time." In one of her magazine articles she declares that "German in the mouth of a pretty high-bred woman is just tolerable; but spoken by men in harsh earnest, it seems by the side of Italian like a shower of brickbats and spikes." [4] In Rome in 1857 she thought Italian still had "a grand and resonant sound," reminiscent of "the old Latin." Even French seemed "chippering and insignificant" in comparison.

Perhaps Mrs. Stowe refers to Plato as often as to any classical writer. In *The Minister's Wooing* she speaks of him, playfully and without disparagement, as "an old heathen," and Professor Foster has pointed out that the famous figure of the "rungless ladder" in the same novel is itself a Platonic image. Aesop, Plutarch, and Aeschylus get nods in passing; there is less about Virgil than I should have expected. But her strongest convictions about the classics seem to have been negative. She objected to the formal and mechanical manner in which they were taught in her time, and she resented the education of young Americans being based on classical literature rather than on the Bible and to the obscenities thus introduced into young minds by the very persons vigilant to guard them against obscenity in all later literature (Anacreon, for example, was worse than *Don Juan*). "The adoration of the ancient classics has lain like a dead weight on all modern art and literature; because men, instead of using them simply for excitement and inspiration, have congealed them into fixed, imperative rules." Even classical mythology seems to have appealed little to her, and she disliked what she considered its excessive use in the older English literature. "In some parts of *Paradise Lost*, the evident imitations of Homer are to me the poorest and most painful passages."

Her husband's interests made *Faust* and *The Divine Comedy* inescapable for her, and there are several references to Dante, most notably in *Agnes of Sorrento*, where she also speaks (surprisingly without censure) of Boccaccio; she once asked Fields to get her a *Decameron*. Goethe's vast liberality of spirit she mistrusted at first, and there is a disparaging reference to him in *Sunny Memories;* on the whole, however, he fares better than might have been expected. She did sense his largeness and benignancy: "That remarkable and many-sided man was capable of appreciating a religious sentiment, in which he did not sympathize, and believing the facts of another's experience, even although not 'set down in his philosophy.'" She certainly intended a compliment when she compared George Eliot's "peculiar insight into the workings of the moral faculties and the religious development through all its phases" with that of Goethe. She speaks briefly of Heine and of Tieck, and Lillie Ellis thinks, on her deathbed, of La Motte Fouqué's *Undine*, which had also been recalled, under happier circumstances, by Nina Gordon. When her son Charley took to reading Kant, Harriet expressed her pleasure, praising the philosopher for his "common sense and reason."

There are more references to French literature, but here the moralist gets in the way again, with some suggestions of a taste for prurience. In *Pink and White Tyranny* Lillie Ellis's taste for French novels is an element in her depravity. There are conventional references to *Paul and Virginia*, Victor Hugo, and Balzac (quoting, of all things, the famous "enchanted cigarettes" passage). She admired Fénelon, and in her *Bible Heroines* she quoted Montalembert. She also admired Edmond About, partly at least because she considered his novels wholesome. Less conventional are her references to Madame de Staël, whose *Corinne* fired her in her youth as no mature reader can be fired by anything, and to Sainte-Beuve, whom she admired as a later, more discriminating New Englander, Gamaliel Bradford, was to admire him, for "his capacity of seeing, doing justice to all kinds of natures and sentiments." When *Oldtown Folks* was published she wanted a copy sent to him.

But what is to be made of the fascination she found in Eugène Sue and in George Sand (whom she is fond of calling Sands)? Of the former she wrote her husband in 1844 that she had been reading him attentively with a view to writing a critique. His atmosphere is "like the air of a forcing house at 90—or so—tho full of luscious blooms and fruit make you stagger and pant for the air—not the first discernment of any boundaries between right and wrong in them—talented—so much the more!" She wonders whether if she were to write "a condemnatory article" about his novels, "will all the saints go and read them to see if it is true? If they feel as I did after it they won't be hurt—it is a perfect outrage on the language to have them done into English." But why, then, devote so much time to them, especially since literary criticism was never her forte, and the article seems never to have appeared?

George Sand shocked and fascinated her even more. In one of her articles on writing she quoted her approvingly, and when she reached the Lido, she remembered that

this beautiful shore is the spot where Madame Sands represents her Consuelo and Anzioletto as gathering shells during the times of their childish betrothals—one of the prettiest and the purest pictures that great artist ever painted, and which makes one regret that she should ever have written otherwise.

But the long undated letter she wrote Mary Livermore from Stockbridge does as thorough a hatchet job on Sand as the editor of a modern scandal sheet could hope to achieve. In France Harriet had expected to meet her but was told that she was not considered a proper person to receive in society. She gives a great deal of scandal about her life: "her course and her principles have been those of Ninon d' Enclos" [sic]. She "broke Chopin's heart and caused his death." "Her connection with Alfred de Musset was a notorious scandal." The "*physicalness*" of her descriptions of sensual love is disgusting. Harriet even believes that the shock her license gave the French conditioned them to accept "the despotism of Napoleon." If she is now to be connected with the cause of women's rights, as Mrs. Stanton seems to threaten, the effect will be similarly disastrous.

III

To all intents and purposes, then, Harriet Beecher Stowe was a reader of English and American literature. Yet of early English literature she knew little. "I certainly do not worship the old English poets. With the exception of Milton and Shakespeare, there is more poetry in the works of the writers of the last fifty years than in all the rest together." There are a few references to Spenser, Bacon, Jonson, and Donne, and that is about all. Donne's

> That you might almost say her body thought

seems to have impressed her; she quotes it in two novels. She objected to Chaucer's Griselda as a false ideal of womanhood, yet her most interesting reference to early English literature concerns Chaucer:

I read Chaucer a great deal yesterday, and am charmed at the reverential Christian spirit in which he viewed all things. He thought of marriage as "a most dread sacrament," just as I do; and surely, if our catechism says truly, a sacrament is an outward and visible sign of an inward and spiritual grace.

If this seems a non-literary, pietistic approach to a great poet, it at least evidences a more penetrating grasp of the profound Christianity that underlay all his worldliness and *savoir-faire* than many of the older Chaucerians grasped.

As for her two exceptions, she frequently quotes Shakespeare—in her novels and articles, on the title page of *Sunny Memories*, even in the *Key to Uncle Tom's Cabin*. One of her most interesting quotations occurs in the sketch "A Scene in Jerusalem," [5] where she quotes Hamlet's words concerning the Ghost ("Remember Thee!/Yea, from the table of my memory/I'll wipe away all trivial fond records") and makes them an expression of the Christian's concentration upon Christ. A magazine article of 1869 invokes *Romeo and Juliet* in connection with her hopes for a real reconciliation between North and South:

Young people will see, like, love, in spite of meaning not to do so, and love will be born of hate, and the Montagues and Capulets cannot keep the Northern and Southern States apart more than a generation.

Yet the only important dramatic use of a Shakespearean theme is in *The Pearl of Orr's Island*, where her own early delighted discovery of *The Tempest* is transferred to Mara, and one chapter is actually called "The Enchanted Island."

But Shakespeare does not get a clean slate; he was not enough of a Puritan for that. "He who hath a good old English Bible is much mistaken when he goes to Shakespeare to study human nature." It is not surprising that she should have particularly liked *Macbeth*, where there is more black and white and less gray than in most of the other tragedies:

It has always seemed to me that this tragedy had more of the melancholy majesty and power of the Greek than any thing modern. The striking difference is, that while fate was the radical element of those, free will is not less distinctly the basis of this. Strangely enough, while it commences with a supernatural oracle, there is not a trace of fatalism in it; but through all, a clear, distinct recognition of moral responsibility, of the power to resist evil, and the guilt of yielding to it. The theology of Shakespeare is as remarkable as his poetry. A strong and clear sense of man's moral responsibility and free agency, and of certain future retribution runs through all his plays.

When she visited Stratford, she attempted ambitiously to ponder biographical and critical problems, and though she completely misunderstands Mistress Hall's epitaph and somewhat forces the note on Shakespeare's religious implications, on the whole her observations show considerable sensitiveness and acuteness, the state of Shakespearean scholarship being what it was in her time. There is another interesting little Shakespeare lesson in *Dred*, where we are obviously intended to admire Nina for saying frankly that she does not like Shakespeare and cannot understand him, in contradistinction to the hypocrisy of more conventionally minded persons who profess admiration without feeling it because that is what they think they are expected to do, thus giving the wise Clayton a chance to instruct her—and the reader—concerning both Elizabethan dramatic conventions and the changing nature of language.

Milton, too, is often quoted, nowhere else quite so often as in *Oldtown Folks*, and when she visited Vesuvius she speculated on the possibility of his having derived thence the inspiration for his description of hell. But the surprising thing about her references to Milton is the amount of disparagement applied to a writer with whom one might have expected her to be *en rapport*. She found him cold, lacking in the tenderness and sympathy of Dante, and she thought that he failed "to represent worthily, unassisted by the direct inspiration of the Holy Ghost, the words of one wholly divine." In comparing him, as "a magnificent imitator of old forms, which by his genius were wrought almost into the energy of new productions," with the "Gothic" Shakespeare ("I think Shakespeare is to Milton precisely what Gothic architecture is to Grecian"), she absurdly underestimates both his romanticism and his dazzling technical originality.

But there was another seventeenth-century writer who meant a great deal to her, and this was "that Shakespeare of the Christian allegory," Bunyan. I am sure she refers to him more often than to any other non-Biblical writer. Sometimes she quotes him directly; more often she takes one of his great figures and applies it to the character or situation that she is describing, a mode of treatment to which, as allegorist, he was peculiarly susceptible. Once a whole meditation was directly derived from him.[6]

Among eighteenth-century writers she refers to, or quotes from, Pope, Cowper, "Ossian," and Gray, and when she was in England, she wept over the wrong country churchyard, a blunder by which she was afterwards much amused. Burns's poetry and Scott's came into her life together, and both were assimilated into her very being. In *We and Our Neighbors*, Dryden, Dr. Johnson, and Young's *Night Thoughts* are cited to exemplify the old-fashioned tastes of Mrs. Betsy and Miss Dorcas, but Harriet had imitated Johnson when a schoolgirl,[7] and there is a magazine piece on "The Happy Valley" which blends *Rasselas* and *The Pilgrim's Progress*.[8] She has many references to Defoe, whom she considered one of the gretat models of English prose. She recognized Swift's genius but considered him too obscene to be read without expurgation. I have one reference to Sterne but I recall none to Fielding or Smollett. Richardson presumably meant more to her. I have already spoken of her mother's devotion to *Sir Charles Grandison*, and in *Bible Heroines* Harriet herself achieves a far-fetched comparison between that hero and Ruth's Boaz. In *The Minister's Wooing* she calls the novel a "seven-volumed, trailing, tedious, delightful old bore," but she once got so absorbed in it that she forgot to come down to dinner as an invited guest. *The Mysteries of Udolpho* is mentioned in *The Pearl of Orr's Island*, and *Caleb Williams* plays an important part in *Lady Byron Vindicated*. She admired Maria Edgeworth—especially *Frank*—from the days of her youth, yet in her paper on Mrs. A. D. T. Whitney she tends to disparage her, Mrs. Whitney, as a kind of American Edgeworth, being given the edge in spirituality.

Among the Romantics were two of the great passions of Harriet's life. Byron was her splendid sinner. He mingled with her other guilty admiration, Aaron Burr, to produce the Burr of *The Minister's Wooing* and the Ellery Davenport of *Oldtown Folks*, and even, in a milder form, Cleon and the skeptical disillusioned St. Clare of *Uncle Tom's Cabin*. Her love for him, inherited from her father, went back to her early years—"I remember well the time," she wrote of *Childe Harold's Pilgrimage*, "when this poetry, so resounding in its music, so mournful, so apparently generous, filled my heart with a vague anguish of sorrow for the sufferer, and of indignation at the cold insensibility that had maddened him"—and it was bitter irony indeed that life should finally bring her to the place where she could not, as she conceived it, fulfil the sacred obligations of friendship toward the woman she honored above all others, his wife, without blackening his name. He died before she had reached her thirteenth birthday, and she took her strawberry basket and went out to Chestnut Hill. "But I was too dispirited to do anything; so I lay down among the daisies, and looked up into the blue sky, and thought of that great eternity into which Byron had entered, and wondered how it might be with his soul." The next Sunday she heard her father preach a memorial sermon from the text: "The name of the just is as brightness, but the memory of the wicked shall rot."

She had encountered, at a cruelly early age, the bitter truth that the moral realities of life are not set aside for the convenience of those we love, perhaps even the sadder and sterner truth that it is possible to love a human being devotedly and still be perfectly clear that he is a moral and spiritual bankrupt. She never glossed over Byron's sins; neither did she ever cease to care for him. A Beecher ought to have been able to understand him if anybody could, for Byron too was brought up on the God of Wrath that, in their early days, darkened the sky for them, and, unlike them, he never found his way out of the shadow; who better than they could afford to pity him? Being a Puritan does not mean not knowing sin. Perhaps, indeed, the Puritan is the only one who does know it, sexual sin at any rate; others simply accept the physical basis of life and enjoy it without guilt. I am sure Mrs. Stowe would have understood Gamaliel Bradford's penetrating analysis of her hero:

Byron was not in the least like Casanova or Aaron Burr, men who kept up a sexual revel for the endless varied delight of it, without a moment of compunction or remorse. To Byron, the remorse was the stamp of sin, without which the whole exhibition would have been worthless. Nor again was he like Pepys, who sinned against his will and suffered the pricks of conscience afterwards, real pricks. To Byron the pricks were theoretical, like the sin, and both made gorgeous material to flaunt before a gasping world.[9]

Scott she took much less emotionally, but his effect on her work was more important. Though Dickens fancied he saw himself in *Uncle Tom's Cabin*,[10] Scott was worth more to her as a literary influence than all other writers put together. We should suspect that she had reread his novels before writing *Uncle Tom's Cabin* even if we did not know the fact, for the book recalls him not only in its specific techniques of story-telling but even more in its grasp and vision of the life of a people and the sure, easy mastery with which it marshals and controls large masses of disparate materials.[11] And this is quite as true of *Dred*, which is *Old Mortality* transferred to a Southern setting.

This, too, was an influence of long standing, dating back to the time in Harriet's childhood when her sister Catharine inherited Alexander Fisher's library. "You may read Scott's novels," said Lyman, having made his examination. "I have always disapproved of novels as trash, but in these is real genius and real culture." They read them to such purpose that when they made apple sauce thereafter, they caused the evening to pass by taking turns to see who could "tell the most out of Scott's novels."

Harriet wrote an article about "Sir Walter Scott and His Dogs," thus getting two of her great passions together, and she was capable of using a character's fondness for Scott as a touchstone of his worth and good sense. Thus the admirable Rose Ferguson of *Pink and White Tyranny* "was old-fashioned enough to like Scott's novels; and though she was just the kind of girl Thackeray would have loved, she never could bring her fresh young heart to enjoy his pictures of world-worn and decaying natures."

But Harriet would not have been Harriet if she had been able to accept even Scott without moral reservations. In *Sunny Memories* she takes up the objections that have been made to his work and carefully plays them down, making a possible exception of his attitude toward war, an odd reservation for her, for if Scott's vision was defective at this point, her own was certainly no less so. But her discussion of him in her first article on "Literary Epidemics" takes him sternly to task for his treatment of the Puritans,[12] and even twenty years later she could write coldly of "Walter Scott, who always took the most frigid and coolest views upon religious subjects."

Outside of Byron and Scott among the Romantic poets, the most frequent references are probably to Coleridge and Tom Moore (I have found none to Keats), but the most interesting are those to Wordsworth. In *Pink and White Tyranny*, John Seymour, infatuated with Lillie Ellis, quotes "She Was a Phantom of Delight" to himself. In an 1869 article, suggestively entitled "Sunday Afternoon," in which she argues that everybody needs something to do which he does merely because he wants to, Harriet quotes from and refers to Wordsworth admiringly, even approving the controversial, and certainly non-Puritan, "wise passiveness" of "Lines Written in Early Spring," against which Irving Babbitt once brought up all his heavy artillery.[13] In "Summer Studies," one of her few nature poems, Harriet herself echoes this piece.

Mrs. Stowe presumably admired Tennyson, since she quotes him a number of times, but she has left no considered judgment of his work. She met the Brownings in Europe, and became friendly with Mrs. Browning at least; in 1925 Lyman Beecher Stowe wrote a correspondent that she "had two favorite poems just as she had two favorite legs in walking. They were Mrs. Browning's 'Human Life's Mystery' and 'We Sleep' (first line 'He

giveth His beloved sleep') Psalm CXXVII." What she thought
of Robert Browning nobody knows. Rossetti and Swinburne seem
to have shocked her.[14]

She wrote Macaulay admiringly, presumably when she sent
him *Uncle Tom's Cabin*, stressing her early interest in his essay
on Milton; he is said to have been much annoyed with her later
for having quoted his conversation inaccurately. She admired
Carlyle also—she once told Mrs. Claflin that his life of Cromwell
had done her more good than most sermons—but she was closer
to Ruskin, who once spent a week with her and her daughters in
the Alps and, as she says, "made a special pet of my Georgia."
He seems to have come close to falling in love with Georgia's
mother, but it all remained on a high plane. "He is an original
and one of the most delightful of men and a true Christian whom
I hope to meet hereafter." Among the minor Victorians mentioned are Hood, Dr. John Brown, Sydney Smith (whom she
greatly admired), and Rhoda Broughton (whom she did not).
She once scornfully dismissed Edmund Yates and Miss Braddon
as "sensation mongers of the day." She displays a surprising liberality when she makes Froude and Lecky a kind of test case
for the frivolity of Lillie Ellis, who cannot be drawn into a reading circle which studies them.

Among novelists, Mrs. Stowe has a good deal to say of Bulwer-
Lytton, objecting to his flashier qualities but apparently seeing
more capacity in him than it is fashionable to discern nowadays.
In her "Olympiana," published in *Godey's* in 1839, she condemns
what she considered his glorification of criminals and lawbreakers.

Apollo lay stretched, *a la Pelham*, on a couch of gold and purple,
picking his teeth, and admiring his own handsome image in a golden
door opposite, which answered all the intent and purpose of a mortal
looking glass.

In 1870 she praised *Lothair* not as a novel but for its earnestness
of tone as showing the change that had come about in Disraeli
since *Vivian Grey*. She could find no such talent in Marryat as
Bulwer and Byron possessed, but she thought his tone much

healthier. Conventional as his standards were, he was less injurious to the reader because he made "no pretension either to philosophic morality or to sentimental virtue."

In an 1868 letter to her daughter Hattie, she called *Phineas Finn* "Trollope's best, as yet," but the very next year she denounced him as "a regular Tom Tulliver," in a letter to George Eliot, for his treatment of women—surely a curious judgment of a novelist who created some of the most delightful heroines in our literature. *Jane Eyre* is surely echoed in *Oldtown Folks*,[15] but nothing could be worse than the reference to it in *Little Foxes:* "The authoress of *Jane Eyre* describes the process of courtship in much the same terms as one would describe the breaking of a horse." With Charles Kingsley she shared moral and religious interests of which their personal contacts made them both more conscious.[16] Charles Reade she herself influenced importantly, for it was from her *Key to Uncle Tom's Cabin* that he derived the idea for his documented fiction.[17] But the novelist to whom she felt closest in spirit was George Eliot, which is less surprising than it might seem in view of George Eliot's overwhelming moral earnestness and Harriet's own amazing lack of prudery, especially in her contacts with people whom she happened to like. "Why do I love you you once asked. Because you are altogether lovely for one reason—and because as Adam Bede said God gave me this love." She read *Daniel Deronda* "like scripture," and sometimes, even when alone, she talked to George Eliot "so earnestly that I should think you must know it even across an ocean." Even when taking communion, she felt "so drawn" to her "darling Friend" "that it seemed as if my heart bore you and your trials to the infinite Love and I felt sure that He would help you." Only with *Middlemarch* does she seem to have had reservations. "I have enjoyed reading it because it is you tho by no means the highest and best in you. As *art* it is perfect, but perfect art as an end—not instrument—has little to interest me." At one point she seems to have given George Eliot the embarrassing idea that she thought Casaubon a portrait of Lewes!

Did you think for one moment that I fancied a resemblance between Mr. Lewes and Casaubon? Oh thou of little faith. Don't I know all about him? and the perpetual admiration system he very properly keeps up to you? Oh my dear, I know all about you, but all wives and husbands have *general* points of resemblance to all others.[18]

Religious writers, Victorian and others, stand, of course, in a class apart. She considered herself to have been influenced by Baxter's *Saints Rest*, but she does not often refer to it. She praises Keble's *Christian Year*, and she was much interested in Mrs. Jameson. She was strongly of the opinion that Isaac Watts, considered as a poet merely, deserved a much higher rank than had been accorded him.

But for all her kinship of spirit with George Eliot, the Victorian writer of whom Harriet had most to say was Charles Dickens. When *Uncle Tom's Cabin* was published, she sent Dickens a copy addressed "To the Author of *David Copperfield*," and the *Key* pays tribute to his service in alerting Englishmen to the horrible conditions around them. In *Pink and White Tyranny*, Judge Ferguson, a devotee of the older English literature, confesses to a "toleration" for Scott, "and had been detected by his children both laughing and crying over the stories of Charles Dickens; for the amiable weaknesses of human nature still remain in the best regulated mind," and in *We and Our Neighbors* the even more conservative Miss Dorcas

had sat up all night surreptitiously reading *Nicholas Nickleby*, and had hidden the book from Mrs. Betsey lest her young mind should be carried away, until she discovered, by an accidental remark, that Mrs. Betsey had committed the same delightful impropriety while on a visit to a distant relative.

When Harriet was in England, Dickens was a guest and a speaker at a dinner in her honor; she seems to have been favorably impressed by him, but since she was almost equally taken with Mrs. Dickens, this does not get us far. She once cancelled an engagement at his house because of fatigue; later, when she called on him, he was too ill to see her. He himself admired *Uncle Tom's*

Cabin generously, though with reservations; later he was repelled by what he considered her cant; still later he was violent about her Byron article without saying why.[19]

Catharine Beecher's preface to *The Mayflower* praises the seriousness and morality of the sketches contained in that book as showing what fiction can be without the frivolity of Dickens. Harriet never descends to such silliness as this, though in her introduction to the works of Charlotte Tonna she does prefer that writer's descriptions of low life to those of Dickens because, if less graphic, they are also less seductive. But a writer does not often get a better chance to make a fool of herself than Harriet seized upon when she annihilated Dickens in the second of her "Literary Epidemics" articles in the *New-York Evangelist*. Though he had at this time only reached *Martin Chuzzlewit*, she was sure that he was already on the wane, especially in America. "He had a vein of original matter and imagery, but not a very deep or broad one, and we think his performances begin to show, and will increasingly show that vein to be about exhausted." He lacked "the breadth and solidity of mental capacity" of Scott and Edgeworth—or even of Bulwer and Irving. It was a mistake ever to have thought of him as a moral writer, "a sort of literary Martin Luther." He wrote for fame and money, not "moral design or purpose." Nature had given him "a generous, warm heart, a true appreciation of what is tender and magnanimous, a downright and full-hearted contempt and detestation for all meanness and oppression," and his tendency to throw "the warmth of poetic coloring around the every day walks and ways of men" had been a useful corrective to Byron and Bulwer. He drew "the whole class of the oppressed, the neglected, and forgotten, the sinning and suffering, within the pale of sympathy and interest." But his pictures of vice in *Oliver Twist* had encouraged "trash literature" to "run very much in a foul and muddy current, full of the slang and filth of low and depraved society." She found his depiction of "characters of almost angelic sweetness and purity [like Oliver himself] as springing up without religious culture" unconvincing, but thought that, since young readers are influenced by sympathy, not logic, this would probably do no real harm. Other characters, however, were different:

A sensible and enlightened parent would dread to have his son associate, day after day, with a low-bred, drinking stage-driver, without any religious or moral education; and he would dread such association the more, if the man was good-natured, witty, and agreeable; and yet this precisely is the effect of the fictitious association of the two Wellers, father and son. To hear the language of religion burlesqued, and connected with low and ludicrous associations—temperance societies, and religious meetings and ministers caricatured, and burlesqued in a style of the lowest slang, must surely be an injury to the young mind in any connection; and the more injurious if it be done with real wit and genius.

For that matter, Dickens's novels in general are open to objection as "anti-temperance tracts." She also objects to his unworthy religionists and particularly to the elder Weller's witticisms on the subject of the "new birth," and he makes it worse because, unlike Scott, he gives no "counter representations." Little Nell and Rose Maylie talk "sentimentally of angels and heaven" and "delightfully of dying," but there is no recognition of "such a person as Jesus Christ" or "such a book as the Bible." "Thoroughly good-hearted and amiable" as Dickens is, "he evidently has no religious perceptions and sympathies, and therefore, could not be expected to realize their existence from anything in himself." All his remarks on religion evince "frivolity of mind, a want of enlargement of view, and a shallowness of moral capacity." His was indeed "but a second rate order of mind," inferior to Byron's, Bulwer's, or even Tom Moore's.

I do not argue that this is completely without penetration, nor that Harriet has nowhere put her finger upon any shortcoming of Dickens. It must be remembered, too, that the Dickensian novels which might have been expected to appeal most to her were still, at this date, unwritten. As a considered record of her response to the greatest writer of her time, the *Evangelist* article is still, however, a sufficiently sad one, and if Dickens deserved what she wrote about him for his excoriation of hypocritical clerics in *The Pickwick Papers* and elsewhere, then she too deserved all the strictures to which she was subjected for what she said about pro-slavery sectarians in *Uncle Tom's Cabin* and *Dred*, though it must be admitted, of course, that she does present the other side also. I have encountered no evaluation by Mrs. Stowe of Dickens's later novels, but I think she was not fully aware of his quality until after his death. In 1872 Fields sent her his *Yesterdays with Authors*. "I read it with deep interest," she wrote him, "particularly that about Charles Dickens. He had his faults of nature but it is not often that more good and less evil are mingled. I am quite won over to him." [20]

<h1 style="text-align:center">IV</h1>

Except for Cotton Mather, American literature was for Mrs. Stowe largely contemporary literature. Among the great New England writers of her time, Oliver Wendell Holmes was her best friend. Barring his Quaker pacifism, Whittier was closest to her ideologically. Lowell printed her work (notably *The Minister's Wooing*, which he greatly admired) in the *Atlantic*. But Longfellow was the one from whom she quoted most frequently.

Holmes's Unitarianism might have been expected to act as a barrier between them, but they discussed even religious matters with perfect frankness and good humor. She never forgot his loyalty to her at the time of her Byron article. In 1870 she wrote Fields urging him to bring out a uniform edition of Holmes's works. "Next to Hawthorne he is our most exquisite writer and in many passages he goes far beyond him." Even in 1890, when her light was far spent, she wrote Holmes touchingly, thanking him for his picture, "which I look at dozens of times a day and smile at, and say 'good day, dear Doctor.'" She adds: "How I should rejoice to see you in my parlor and how much we could say to each other. *Do come—do do* DO come dear friend and we will renew life together." [21]

Whittier, of course, would have been endeared to her by his antislavery work alone. In 1853 she sent some of his poems to the Duchess of Sutherland: "I am anxious that he should become known in England for he is *truly* a poet. He is *himself* a poem— one of nature's lyrics." She adds that "Massachusetts to Virginia" is "the noblest lyric of modern days." She often urged Whittier to visit her in Florida. When his seventieth birthday was cele- brated in 1877, she paid him perhaps the most eloquent tribute he ever received:

It has been his chief glory, not that he could speak inspired words, but that he spoke them for the despised, the helpless and the dumb; for those too ignorant to honor, too poor to reward him. Grace was given him to know his Lord in the lowest disguise, even in that of the poor hunted slave, and to follow him in heart into prison and unto death.

When he died in 1892 she was beyond such eloquence, but she saved all the newspaper clippings she could find on him, and she wrote a touching letter to a friend who had sent her sympathy:

Of course, I had already learned, from the papers, of the going home of his pure spirit. To such as he the transition from this world to the next is but slight. It would be selfish to sorrow. Ours is the loss, and his the eternal gain. I wish I might send a fitting tribute, but my days are almost numbered and my pen halts in my hand.

The most significant reference to Lowell is that to *The Biglow Papers* in *My Wife and I* as "the spirit of the Sermon on the Mount translated into the language of Yankee life, and defended with wit and drollery." In 1889 she sent him a birthday letter in which she described herself as "one of the thousands who have laughed and wept over your magic verses." She paid Longfellow the compliment of taking an epigraph from him for "The Mourn- ing Veil," her contribution to the first number of *The Atlantic Monthly*, and she quotes "The Arrow and the Song" complete in *My Wife and I*. When she was in Maine she found the roots of some of his poems there, and even thought they sounded better on their native heath. But probably her most interesting, and cer- tainly her most unconventional, reference to Longfellow was made when the dirt in Notre Dame Cathedral reminded her New England soul of Lucifer's soliloquy in *The Golden Legend:*

What a darksome and dismal place!
I wonder that any man has the face
To call such a hole the house of the Lord
And the gate of heaven—yet such is the word.

What, now, of the others? One of the Claflin letters in which she quotes "The Mountain and the Squirrel" suggests that she thought Emerson an old bore, but it is not quite certain that she meant this. She once had "an Emersonian cat from Concord named *Bramah*, being of the race of the 'Red Slayer,' " and when she went to visit the Claflins she took the cat with her. In another letter to Mrs. Claflin, she quotes a Transcendentalist as saying that he believed in God but not the God of Abraham, Isaac and Jacob. "He is just the God I do believe in—the God I find real and living now as then in the first dawn of time." On Poe I have found only one humorous reference to "The Raven" in *We and Our Neighbors*. Cooper is mentioned in "The Happy Valley," which includes a visit to Cooperstown. She speaks in passing of both Prescott and Parkman. There is an epigraph from Bryant in *Uncle Tom's Cabin*. Judging by the number of her references to him, she seems to have known Irving fairly well.

There is more on Hawthorne. She mentions a number of his works—"The Celestial Railroad" furnishes an epigraph for the Greeley article—and Professor Foster has argued reasonably that *The Blithedale Romance* importantly influenced *Oldtown Folks*.[22] The romantic atmosphere of old England more than once seemed to her more congenial to his genius than America's cold light of day. "If our Hawthorne could conjure up such a thing as the Seven Gables in one of our prosaic country towns, what would he have done if he had lived here?" In her *Hearth and Home* articles on writing she praised him for his ability to describe homely scenes in *The American Note-Books* and such sketches as "The Old Apple Dealer," and for his freedom from clichés. His temperament may not have been much like hers, but she lost patience with him only when he defended Franklin Pierce.

She also had considerable interest in the minor writers of her day, and in her later years she encouraged numerous juniors and inferiors, especially, but by no means exclusively, when their work had a pious or evangelical cast. When she moved to Cincinnati, her uncle Samuel Foote brought her into touch with such writers of the Semi-Colon Club as James Hall, Caroline Lee Hentz, and Salmon P. Chase, and Professor Adams is certainly right when he argues that Hall's *Western Monthly Magazine* served Harriet well by providing a pattern "less remote than Scott and Edgeworth, or even Sedgwick and Sigourney." She speaks of Caroline Kirkland; in "Betty's Bright Idea" she quotes a poem of Mrs. Sigourney's without naming her; she did not even shrink from quoting Sam Slick. She liked James Parton's biographical writings.[23] Late in life she relished the work of her Hartford neighbors, Mark Twain and Charles Dudley Warner, and was particularly fond of *The Prince and the Pauper*. Cable and Bret Harte interested her also,[24] and in 1893 she wrote the young Fred Lewis Pattee a really charming letter, thanking him for a volume of his poems.[25] The Huntington Library has a letter to Fields proposing that he should encourage Miss Josephine Ruggles to rework a story under her direction, with the idea of its running through three or four *Atlantics*. But I do not know where her combined kindness and discrimination are more nicely shown than in the letter of introduction to Lady Byron which she wrote for that phenomenally popular novelist, Mrs. E. D. E. N. Southworth, when that personage went to Europe in 1859:

Mrs. Southworth is a writer of a very voluminous class of novels—which have very glaring defects, but have genius. She is almost the only instance I know of a really original creative southern author but she is one of the old decayed Virginia stocks—a thoroughly southern woman tho a strong anti slavery one and her novels contain pictures of that strange mediaeval exceptional sort of life which exists at the south, which were it not for exaggeration and overdrawings would have made her immortal.

Mrs. Southworth was fond of boasting that she never met anyone who had not read at least one of her novels. I wonder was she including Lady Byron.

CHAPTER IX

THE WRITER

I

Writing in *Hearth and Home* in 1869, Mrs. Stowe told a girl correspondent that when she was "ten, twelve, or thirteen years of age," her "two leading passions" were reading and writing, but that she wrote "without praise and without encouragement—without any body to express either admiration or approbation, or to put it in a newspaper." This was rather ungrateful to her remarkable composition teacher at Litchfield Academy, John Pierce Brace, who became Jonathan Rossiter in *Oldtown Folks* and who was the great-grandfather of the twentieth-century novelist, Gerald Warner Brace. "I was very much interested in poetry," she says, "and it was my dream to be a poet." In a way, the dream never died, and many years later she forced her only collection of poems upon a reluctant publisher, who finally brought them out as a small book and included them in her collected works but would not use any of them in the *Atlantic*.

A writer of fiction derives his materials from experience, observation, hearsay, reading, and imagination; Mrs. Stowe used all these sources. The influence of literature may be illustrated by reference to *The Pearl of Orr's Island*, where both Shakespeare and Theocritus make themselves strongly felt, yet the use of Shakespeare also indicates experience, for Mara's discovery of *The Tempest* and her love for it were young Harriet's own. It was quite impossible to predict what might stimulate so wayward an imagination as hers; there is nothing to support Harry Birdoff's wicked suggestion that she might have taken the name Topsy from *Toplady on Predestination,* but I must admit I think her quite capable of it.

Uncle Tom's Cabin and *Dred* have perhaps had their sources explored most fully, notably in *Tom's* case by Charles H. Foster, who gives an excellent summary of the possible literary influence "of Mrs. Trollope, of Richardson and the sentimental novel, of Defoe and a method of realism, of Scott and the expanded tale of travel, of Hall and Drake and the challenge for a Western-Southern literature." [1] There was also, of course, a great deal of non-literary antislavery writing, most notably Theodore Weld's *African Slavery As It Is* (1839).

Insofar as they furnished Mrs. Stowe with literary models, guided the bent of her genius, and taught her her trade, the importance of the novels mentioned by Professor Foster and others can hardly be overestimated; as actual sources of material I think experience was more important. She was capable of what James calls "the suddenly determined absolute of perception": "One bright evening, as I was entering the old gateway, I saw a beautiful young girl sitting in its shadow selling oranges. She was my Agnes [of Sorrento]." But she was also capable of seizing an idea out of the air and then going to work to authenticate it: "I seem to have so much to fill my time, and yet there is my Maine story waiting. However, I am composing it every day, only I greatly need living studies for filling in of my sketches." She lived with her childhood memories all her life before turning them into *Poganuc People* and with Calvin's many years before she wrote *Oldtown Folks,* but she got Simon Legree from her brother Charles's account of a brutal overseer who proudly exhibited a fist like an oak burl and boasted that he had got it from "knockin' down niggers." This is not to say that Legree has the kind of authenticity which the *Oldtown* material possesses, but his vitality as myth is very great, and if Jay Hubbell is right when he conjectures that the overseer's statement "sounds suspiciously like a tall tale told for the benefit of the credulous outsider," this does not lessen our impression of Harriet's ability to make much of little. Like other artists, she had her own way of paying attention to things. When she visited a Kentucky plantation in 1833, she "did not seem to notice anything in particular that happened, but sat much of the time as though abstracted in thought. When the negroes did funny things and cut up capers, she did not seem to pay the slightest attention to them." But she had got all she needed for the description of the Shelby estate.

Scholarly accuracy was beyond Harriet Beecher Stowe; she told different stories concerning the origin of *Uncle Tom's Cabin* and ascribed Eliza and the ice-crossing episode to a number of different sources, both literary and experiential.[2] There have been rival Uncle Toms too, and at least three originals have been suggested for Miss Ophelia. But Cincinnati was a station on the underground railroad, and though not all the details can now be authenticated, we can see Harriet's own experiences with slave-holders and abolitionists in many incidents and episodes. I do not mean that she never tried to get her novels "right"; she was capable of looking up materials and consulting the informed for specialized knowledge, and there is a rather charming story about her daughters coming into her room one night, when terrified by a thunderstorm, to find their mother lying calmly in bed with all the curtains up: "I have been writing a description of a thunder-storm for my book, and I am watching to see if I need to correct it in any particular."

She used public figures and public events—the slave uprisings involving Nat Turner and Denmark Vesey in *Dred* and perhaps Sojourner Truth for Milly. She changed *Dred* substantially, and made it considerably less conciliatory than it would otherwise have been, because of the gains the slavery forces made while she was writing it; perhaps the most blatant journalistic reference in all her fiction is her biting denunciation in this novel of Preston Brooks's attack on Charles Sumner in the United States Senate:

This time the blow felled Clayton to the earth, and Tom Gordon, precipitating himself from the saddle, proved his eligibility for Congress by beating his defenceless acquaintance on the head, after the fashion of the chivalry of South Carolina.[3]

Her use of Aaron Burr has already been noted. The Doctor of *The Minister's Wooing* is Dr. Samuel Hopkins, crossed and mingled, of course quite legitimately, with others.[4] Though she specifically denied it in her Preface, *My Wife and I* is a *roman à clef* in its portrayal of Victoria Woodhull as the emancipated Audacia Dangyereyes and of the much more respectable suffrage leader, Elizabeth Cady Stanton, whom Mrs. Woodhull had so strangely taken in, as Mrs. Cerulean. The disclaimer may have had some legal value in saving Harriet from a libel suit, but she could not possibly have expected it to be believed.[5]

Harriet also used herself and her family in her writing, both with great freedom. As has already been noted in part elsewhere, she is Dolly in *Poganuc People*, and her husband is Horace Holyoke of *Oldtown Folks*. Dolly's father, Parson Cushing, is Lyman Beecher, and Tina of *Oldtown Folks* is Georgiana Stowe. "The passage in *Uncle Tom* where Augustine St. Clare describes his mother's influence is a simple reproduction of my own mother's influence as it has always been felt in her family," and the high church Episcopalians in *Oldtown Folks* were based on Roxana's people. The reported drowning of James Marvyn in *The Minister's Wooing* and its aftermath were based on the death of both Alexander Fisher and of Harriet's own son Henry. The sorrows of the Negro women who lose children in *Uncle Tom's Cabin* probably gained power and pathos from Harriet's own loss of her son, the first Charley, and she herself wrote George Eliot of the "slave mammy" who comforted her afterwards.

Mary Scudder of *The Minister's Wooing* suffers (or supposes she has suffered) a loss like Catharine Beecher's, but temperamentally she is much more like Catharine's (and Harriet's) mother than she is like Catharine. Dr. Foster has pointed out that in Mary's letter to Dr. Hopkins, Harriet used whole passages from a letter of Roxana's to Lyman Beecher. "At the center of *The Minister's Wooing*," he says, "Mrs. Stowe thus placed in a fictionalized portrait of her mother the clearest vindication of Puritanism furnished by her father's autobiography." Harriet may have taken the suggestion for Mary's visit to Mrs. Marvyn from Catharine's visit to the Fishers after her fiancé's death, but the purpose of the two visits was quite different. And if Mrs. Marvyn is indebted to Mrs. Fisher, there is some Catharine too in her statement, "I am quite sure there must be dreadful mistakes somewhere." Such things show that Harriet used her sources creatively; she was no copyist. In the Preface to the *Key* she declared that "in fictitious writing, it is possible to find refuge from the hard and the terrible, by inventing scenes and characters of a more pleasing nature." She was of the opinion that she had done this even in *Uncle Tom's Cabin*, and when she comes to *Agnes of Sorrento* she disclaims authenticity altogether, declaring that her story "is a mere dreamland" which neither assumes nor will have responsibility for historical accuracy. But there was nothing too intimate, too painful, too personal for her to make copy of—not even Henry's death or Fred's alcoholism. Perhaps it helped her, in *My Wife and I* and *We and Our Neighbors*, to give Fred's struggle a happy ending.

II

Harriet Beecher Stowe would probably not have developed a very elaborate theory of fiction under any circumstances, but she was not helped by the vestiges which clung to her of the old Puritan belief that there was a faint odor of brimstone about it all. As a schoolgirl she had been required to write compositions "On the Disadvantages of Novel-Reading," and there is an undated letter to her son Charley in which she laments the tendency of young people to devote Sunday to novels because it "emasculates and runs out the mental and moral energy." She adds that "the amount of people who never read anything but fiction is sad to contemplate." Sometimes she uses fiction as an element in the demoralization of her spoiled young girls. She once wrote a clerical correspondent, expressing the hope that Christians would

not permit "conscientious scruples" to prevent them from reading *Uncle Tom's Cabin* because it was a work of fiction; it was,
she assured him, "*fiction truer than fact.*" And in Hartford days
she wrote a letter in behalf of a sick friend to James T. Fields,
begging "some pamphlet novels and other of the magazine literature that you have an overstock of. If you will make me up a
bundle of such light trash as will amuse a sick mind I can do some
good with it and will be much obliged to you." It was not the
kind of letter by which one could expect a publisher to be greatly
charmed.

If anything, this attitude was more fully expressed in age than
in youth. *Dred* very sensibly presents the claims of good fiction
over bad history; *The Minister's Wooing* boldly promises the
hypothetically restive reader that the novel is going to turn out
a love story and nothing else; in *The Pearl of Orr's Island* we are
assured that "works of fiction, as we all know, if only well gotten
up, have always their advantage in the hearts of listeners over
plain, homely truth." But *My Wife and I* was prefaced with a
waspish attack on fiction and the interest therein: "It appears to
me that the world is returning to its second childhood, and
running mad for Stories. Stories! stories! stories! everywhere;
stories in every paper, in every crevice, crack, and corner of the
house." Five years later she was still of the same mind: she would
rather write another *Footsteps of the Master* than devote herself
to *Poganuc Papers*.

Yet she will not commit herself to an extreme position. One
of her most interesting utterances is her preface to *A Library of
Famous Fiction*. "The propensity of the human mind to fiction is
one of those irresponsible forces against which it has always
proved vain to contend." On the one hand, she is apologetic.
"Since the world must read fiction, let us have the best in an
attractive household form, that they may not be overlaid and
shuffled out of sight by more modern but less effective tales."
But she cannot leave it there. "Even in the strictest households,
certain permitted works of fiction" have not been tolerated as
a necessary evil but cherished "as one of the choicest delights of

life." Nor does she scruple to bring man's higher spiritual nature itself into the involvement. "The boundaries of the present life have everywhere, in all lands and countries, proved too narrow and too poor for the wants of the soul," and "the possession by human beings of the glorious faculty of living an unreal life, and seeing things invisible, is a sufficient answer to those who doubt the uses of fiction."

When this would not do, one could always fall back on the usefulness of fiction to an end beyond itself. "The use of the novel in the great questions of moral life is coming to be one of the features of the age. Formerly the only object of fictitious writing was to amuse. Now nothing is more common than to hear the inquiry of a work of fiction, 'What is it intended to show or prove?'" After reading Anna Dickinson's *What Answer?* she wrote her, "Don't mind what any body says about it as a work of art. Works of art be hanged! You had a braver thought than that." But of course when others attacked, or she thought they were getting ready to, she could always defend:

Many, in this hard and utilitarian age, are wont to underrate the faculty of the imagination, and all that ministers and belongs thereto, as of no practical value. But, for all that, it is nonetheless a fact, that such a faculty does exist, burning and God-given, in many a youthful soul, and, for the want of some proper aliment, seeks the strange fire from heathen altars, and culls poisonous fruits and flowers from hot-beds of the god of the world.

One advantage of specially consecrated literature was that one could always judge it by special standards. "By a parable, we mean a work of fiction written solely for the moral intent, and in which the artistic is merely incidental." In an age as mad for stories as her own, she was willing to concede that "truth must be offered to the people in the way they will take it best. When a person does this, the work is to be judged of not mainly as a literary or artistic work, but as a moral instrument." The application of such standards may have helped salve Harriet's Puritan conscience, but it was certainly bad for her as an artist.[6]

III

Actually, however, none of this mattered very much; temperamentally Harriet was enough of an artist to succeed in spite of it. Her failure to give a consistent account of even the origin of *Uncle Tom's Cabin* has been much ridiculed, and her final conviction that "God wrote it!" [7] has been taken as proving that she suffered from a Messianic complex. I find this an uncomprehending judgment. Artistic creativity is as much a mystery to the uninitiated as mystical awareness; it cannot be described except in terms of parable. And Harriet's background being what it was, it was inevitable that her parable should take a conventionally religious form. Even so unmystical a writer as George Eliot said that "in all she considered her best writing, there was a 'not herself' which took possession of her, and that she felt her own personality to be merely the instrument through which this spirit, as it were, was acting." There may have been a touch of Messianism in Harriet, but it would be quite as reasonable to argue that she was a genuine artist of the type who depends upon her intuitions.

Some of her meditations on literary technique seem naïve enough. Look at the notes on how to begin a story at the beginning of *The Minister's Wooing*,[8] on suspense in *The Pearl of Orr's Island*,[9] and, most of all, on structure, in *Oldtown Folks*.[10] It is also true that she was capable of professing complete indifference to *Uncle Tom* in its aesthetic aspect: she "no more thought of style or literary excellence than the mother who rushes into the street and cries for help to save her children from a burning house, thinks of the teachings of the rhetorician or the elocutionist." But this is the voice of the Christian reformer which Harriet perhaps thought she ought to be; it is far from giving a complete indication of what she actually was. Read her articles on writing in *Hearth and Home* and see if you can believe that they came from a writer who had not studied her craft. She champions a Saxon style, urging simplicity, concreteness, and avoidance of affectation, hackneyed expressions, and effects suitable in foreign languages but not in English, with the Bible, Bunyan, Thackeray, Hawthorne, Irving, and Holmes as models.

It is an overstatement to say, as we often do, that she began the New England local color movement; as Professor Adams reminds us, Catharine Sedgwick, Lydia H. Sigourney, and others were in the field before her. But she built nobly on the foundations which they had laid, and she had a far greater influence upon her successors in this field than, say, Hawthorne, who was too tragic, too specialized, too individually great to be the founder of a school. Harriet committed herself in the sketch of "Uncle Lot" at the very beginning of her career:

And so I am to write a story—but of what, and where? Shall it be radiant with the sky of Italy? or eloquent with the beau ideal of Greece? Shall it breathe languor from the orient, or chivalry from the occident? or gayety from France? or vigor from England? No, no; these are all too old—too romance-like—too obviously picturesque for me. No; let me turn to my own land—my own New England; the land of bright fires and strong hearts; the land of deeds, and not of words; the land of fruits and not of flowers; the land often spoken against, yet always respected; "the latchet of whose shoes the nations of the earth are not worthy to unloose."

She had no need to explain why she did not write of "the sky of Italy." She was to try that in *Agnes of Sorrento,* and it added nothing to her fame. It might have been more to the point to contemplate the skies of Cincinnati, where she never laid the scene of a story, though she certainly knew it better, through her long residence there, than she ever knew the South. But her Cincinnati residence stimulated her for all that and enlarged her vision; without it she might have remained a provincial writer, never achieving the imaginative grasp of the life of a nation which *Uncle Tom's Cabin* embraces. Yet the desire to picture and interpret New England remained with her all her days, and she causes Horace Holyoke to express it in the preface to *Oldtown Folks,* though I gravely doubt that either he or Harriet ever made the mind "as still and passive as a looking-glass, or a mountain lake," or succeeded in presenting without judging. She herself told George Eliot that she had "put heart soul and life blood into this book which cost me more to write than any thing I ever wrote." She knew that she was conscious of treating marriage more realistically in *Oldtown Folks* than it was commonly handled in fiction, and she was conscious of breaking new ground in *Uncle Tom's Cabin* also, allying herself with the world-wide contemporary democratic movement in the novel, seeking out and embellishing "the common and gentler humanities of life." Closing a scene between those two scoundrels Marks and Loker in Chapter VIII, she remarks

If any of our refined and Christian readers object to the society into which this scene introduces them, let us beg them to begin and conquer their prejudices in time. The catching business, we beg to remind them, is rising to the dignity of a lawful and patriotic profession. If all the broad land between the Mississippi and the Pacific becomes one great market for bodies and souls, and human property retains the locomotive tendencies of this nineteenth century, the trader and catcher may yet be among our aristocracy.

Despite the propaganda and the sarcasm, she is basically in harmony here with Chaucer's plea for the realistic use of low-life materials in *The Canterbury Tales* and with the multitude of her successors who have introduced us to undesirable fictional company since.[11]

What I am saying of course is that, whether she completely knew it or not, Mrs. Stowe wrote *Uncle Tom's Cabin* like an artist.

My vocation is simply that of painter, and my object will be to hold up in the most lifelike and graphic manner possible Slavery, its reverses, changes, and the negro character, which I have had ample opportunities for studying. There is no arguing with *pictures,* and everybody is impressed by them, whether they mean to be or not.

The story took its own way, and she followed where it led, regardless of money payment or her own strength. She had contracted with *The National Era* for a short serial, to run about three months. *Uncle Tom's Cabin* ran ten months, and she received only the $300 agreed upon. This did not trouble her much; neither did she heed the cries of the prospective book publisher that a double-decker antislavery novel would be a commercial impossibility. So it might very well turn out to be, but how did that concern her? "Your Annie reproached me for letting Eva die," she told her friend Mrs. Howard. "Why! I could not help it! ... it affected me so deeply that I could not write a word for two weeks after her death." Just so did Dickens feel about Little Nell.

Perhaps the complete sense of possession she experienced with *Uncle Tom's Cabin* never came again (there is only one first novel in any writer's life). Nevertheless her son-biographer says she dictated much of *The Minister's Wooing* "under a great pressure of mental excitement," and this was not a unique experience. Even her occasional writing sometimes possessed her. "I had planned an article gay sprightly wholly domestic," she wrote Fields in Civil War days, "but as I began and sketched the pleasant home and quiet fireside an irresistible impulse *wrote for me* what followed an offering of sympathy to the suffering and agonized, whose homes have forever been darkened." When she writes in one of her *Palmetto Leaves*, "It is vain to propose and announce subjects from week to week. One must write what one is thinking of. When the mind is full of one thing, why go about to write on another?" it is easy to dismiss the statement as feminine lawlessness and caprice, but what then are we to say about Mark Twain's method in his *Autobiography* and often even in his fiction? Harriet always insisted that writing must make its own laws. "A story *comes,* grows like a flower, sometimes will and sometimes won't, like a pretty woman." If this is naïve, then Keats is naïve too when he insists that poetry must come as naturally as leaves to a tree, and that otherwise it had better not come at all. She says she wanted to write about the Negroes again after emancipation, but the story would not come. Nor did she ever want the trumpets blown before her, to mark out the way she ought to go. If that had been done with *Uncle Tom's Cabin* she probably could not have written it at all. "Nobody expected anything, nobody said anything, and so I wrote freely. Now what embarrasses me is to be announced as an attraction—to have eyes fixed on me and people all waiting."

Sometimes she emphasizes the agony of creation. She is "a poor sinner laboring under a book." Her idea of luxury was to be free of writing. "I feel like a poor woman I once read about,—

> Who always was tired,
> 'Cause she lived in a house
> Where help wasn't hired,

and of whom it is related that in her dying moments,

> She folded her hands
> With her latest endeavor,
> Saying nothing, dear nothing,
> Sweet nothing forever."

She tells us too that she wrote *Uncle Tom's Cabin* "with my heart's blood. Many times . . . I thought my health would fail utterly; but I prayed earnestly that God would help me till I got through, and still I am pressed beyond measure and above strength." She did not always judge her work wisely. She knew the value of *Oldtown Folks*—"it is my résumé of the whole spirit and body of New England"—and, perhaps for that very reason, she labored over it as she had never labored over any other book. But at one time she seems to have thought *Dred* better than *Uncle Tom*, and she definitely preferred the gimcrack *Agnes of Sorrento* ("my little darling") to the contemporaneous *Pearl of Orr's Island*. But she always rejoices in her successes, large and small, and when she thinks she has "done well," she says so. Sometimes, like Dickens, she lovingly quotes her own characters.

IV

Harriet seems to have managed the externalities of the writer's career with reasonable success also. Theoretically she could be as fussy about writing conditions as anybody. She once declined an invitation from Mrs. Fields on the ground that it would "disturb the composure and quietude" needed for the inception of a new work. "To move my writing desk from its quiet corner and disturb my moorings by new scenes would be like sweeping down a half built spider's web." She could not write in very hot weather nor yet in cold—"cold weather really seems to torpify my brain"—and in later years she even thought that Hawthorne and Emerson could have done better work in Florida! "I have really been unable to write this story. I can give no other account of the matter than this, that sometimes I can and sometimes I can't write a given thing." She also had the idea that deadlines worried her, and that it troubled her to write under pressure or for financial need, though she never wrote any other way. Moreover, she was a scatterbrain, forever conceiving good and bad ideas which distracted her from the work in hand—it is probably just as well that we do not have James T. Fields's private reaction to her suggestion that she take time out from the already badly-stalled *Oldtown Folks* to write an article on planchette!—and so susceptible to influence that she feared to read a new novel lest she should imitate it in the work in hand.

Actually, however, Harriet could write anywhere, under any conditions, and at any time; as a badly-harassed and, at the beginning, poverty-stricken, wife and mother, without so much as a room of her own, how could she ever have produced anything otherwise?

When I have a headache and feel sick, as I do to-day, there is actually not a place in the house where I can lie down and take a nap without being disturbed. . . . If I lock my door and lie down someone is sure to be rattling the latch before fifteen minutes have passed.

And again:

Since I began this note, I have been called off at least a dozen times; once for the fish-man, to buy a codfish; once to see a man who had brought me some barrels of apples; once to see a book agent; then to Mrs. Upham's to see about a drawing I promised to make for her;

then to nurse the baby; then into the kitchen to make a chowder for dinner; and now I am at it again, for nothing but deadly determination enables me ever to write; it is rowing against wind and tide.

I have no desire to minimize what Harriet accomplished under these difficult conditions, but I do not believe that the zeal with which she overworked herself as a writer was a mere tribute of devotion to her family. She was a born writer—as she once said, her mind "bubbled" with stories—and when she took her pen in hand, even in pain and weakness, she came into her kingdom. "My writing is the least of my cares," she wrote her daughter Hattie in 1861, "and takes probably the least time." Two years later she repeats this: "Now it is very easy for me to write—writing is my element as much as sailing is to a duck." This, too, must be discounted somewhat. She is making a case for the agony that household accounts and other domestic chores cost her ("Arithmetic was always as hard to me as it is to Eliza. When I was a girl I thought I could not even make change in a store"), and she wishes to be relieved of them. But essentially I believe she was telling the truth.

Yet she stood in perpetual need to be reassured of the worth of what she had created, and from her family she always had it. "Do come and hear, and tell me how you like it." One wonders how she could have survived without this. "And is it not true," she asks George Eliot, "that what we authors want is not *praise* so much as sympathy? A book is *a hand* stretched forth in the dark passage of life to see if there is another hand to meet it." As we have seen, she sent *Uncle Tom's Cabin* to a number of distinguished Englishmen; much later, she wrote Horace Greeley, as editor of the New York *Tribune,* a long letter about *Lady Byron Vindicated.* Newspaper critics, on the other hand, she tried to take in her stride.

One hundred thousand copies of *Dred* sold in four weeks [she writes her husband from England]! After that who cares what critics say? ... It is very bitterly attacked, both from a literary and a religious point of view. The *Record* is down upon it with a cartload of solemnity;

the *Athenaeum* with waspish spite; the *Edinburgh* goes out of its way to say that the author knows nothing of the society she describes; but yet it goes everywhere, and Mr. Low says that he puts the hundred and twenty-fifth thousand to press confidently.

Yet as late as *Oldtown Folks* she could be indignant over a bad review in *The Nation*, "the general drift of which," as she wrote Mrs. Fields, "is that there is nothing in it—not a character and never was in anything I wrote and that they are tired and sick of it and vote it a bore. There's criticism for you!" She adds that "the book is not sensational and can make no headway with those whose taste is formed by Lady Audley and Mrs. Henry Wood," but goes on to cite the *Examiner* and another English paper as having been more appreciative than she had expected. Later in the year she was delighted with another English review. "To-day comes the London *Times* with three columns of discriminating appreciative praise of *Oldtown Folks*. I never saw any review of it that gave me so much pleasure. It is quite a triumph."

From one point of view, Mrs. Stowe was an easy writer for her publishers to deal with: she frankly left all the mechanical matters to them. "My manuscripts are always left to the printers for punctuation—as you will observe; I have no time for copying." She goes further yet, for there is a letter to H. O. Houghton in which she says that when she repeats the same word too often, she hopes it may be changed! Of course the demand for such services created its own problems. Once at least she wanted a quotation verified, and once she wanted Howells to turn a couplet for her. Actually she deserves less credit for her agreeableness than one might suppose, for she did not think such things very important: "perhaps it is not necessary to be so fearfully correct." "I wish . . . she would give more local coloring to her picture," wrote Whittier, "so that we may know what part of the world we are in, in what age, as respects costume, etc., and what climate." She was careless too about the names and relationships of her characters and sometimes forgot what she had told the reader about them, as Scott did.

But one must not exaggerate Harriet's carelessness. One letter to Fields reports being slowed down by revising something that had not pleased her, and she was always very particular that her dialectal spellings should not be tampered with. She defended her author's rights when they seemed important to her, and she sometimes overrode the publisher's. There cannot have been many writers to whom Fields made more generous advances, and there cannot have been many who were so irregular even in delivering work that had already been paid for. "Proofs were not ready when they were promised," writes Mrs. Fields with studied patience, "the press was stopped, and both author and publisher required all the tender regard they really had for each other and all the patience they possessed to keep in tune."

The things she did understand Mrs. Stowe brooded over with scrupulous care. She took an intelligent interest in format and in illustrations.

I want a funny gold cover designed for *Pussy Willow* with Pussy Willow ferns and hepaticas in gold on a blue ground. Make it pretty and taking—and I think you will make a sale of it.

On *Lady Byron Vindicated* she was even more specific:

I want the book size of *Chimney Corner*—printed handsomely. As there will be much quoting of documents which I want to have in a marked different type I propose that they be put in leaded in smaller type. But first choose a good clear plain type for the *documents* so that *nobody may skip them as fine print* and then have a larger type for my own words.

She expected "an avalanche" on this book, and there was no question in her mind that her publisher must stand by her: "You must be up and doing and help me. This is war to the knife and the enemy are perfectly unscrupulous." Because she had referred to Godwin's *Caleb Williams* in the course of her argument, she did not hesitate to advise:

Bye the bye you had better publish in clear type with paper covers an edition of *Caleb Williams* at once for there will certainly be a call for it after reading my book—don't forget this.

These are not the words of a woman accustomed to being refused; *Caleb Williams* was advertised facing *Lady Byron's* title page.

Like most authors, Mrs. Stowe sometimes interceded with her publishers for a friend, but her tone was a bit more peremptory than is customary nowadays. In 1867 she wrote Howells about a story by her niece Mary Hooker Burton: "It seems to me well worthy of a place in the *Atlantic* and I shall feel personally obliged by its acceptance." She took over Fields's editorial functions on occasion, sending him one kind of article when he had asked for another, or even proposing the establishment of a whole new series, even on domestic science, and sending the first installment along with the suggestion. She crammed *Agnes of Sorrento* down the *Atlantic* maw when what Fields wanted was a new New England story. The latter—*The Pearl of Orr's Island*—went to *The Independent*. But when she found that between the two stories she had bitten off more than she could chew, she wrote the *Independent* editor, Theodore Tilton: "With this number ends Part First of *The Pearl of Orr's Island*. Part Second will be ready to appear in the autumn, and will extend through the year." Only she did not give him the real reason for the delay. "In order to give the story the finish and completeness I wish, it will be necessary for me to revisit those scenes once more and see them in their summer glory. Time has somewhat dimmed my recollection." She was not pleased when, announcing PART II, Tilton called it "MRS. STOWE'S GREAT STORY," and insisted on his running a "card":

That a story so rustic, so woodland, so pale and colorless, so destitute of all that is expected ordinarily in a work of fiction should be advertised ... as "Mrs. So-and-so's *great* romance," or with words to that effect, produces an impression both appalling and ludicrous.

In itself this sounded charmingly modest, but the implied rebuke to the editor was anything but that.

V

The economic aspect of Mrs. Stowe's literary life calls for special attention. As we have seen, she grew up in poverty. Though her father, Lyman Beecher, was one of the famous men of his time, he was an object of charity in his old age; at the height of his fame he earned less money than many college boys make today in their spare time. And her husband would have been no better off without his wife.[12]

When the publication of *Uncle Tom's Cabin* was in prospect, the Stowes hoped Harriet might get a new silk dress out of it. Because they had no money to risk on printing bills, they turned down an offer of half-profits and accepted a 10 per cent royalty.[13] When sudden, overwhelming prosperity came, her thankfulness was not untouched by uneasiness: "God, to whom I prayed night and day while I was writing the book, has heard me, and given us of worldly goods *more* than I asked. I feel, therefore, a desire to 'walk softly,' and inquire for what has He so trusted us?" But her financial problems were not over; the more money she earned, the more she needed; she would certainly have had fewer creature comforts if she had not found prosperity, but she might also have been considerably less driven, and she was quite right when she wrote of herself, "There's no earthly use in having anything—Lordy Massy, no!"

Calvin thought her extravagant, and in a way she was. She spent a good deal on rushing about the world, she sent her daughters to fashionable schools in Europe, and she poured money into the first Hartford house, which, partly because of bad planning, and partly because it was soon swallowed up in an industrial neighborhood, had to be abandoned for a fraction of its cost. Extravagance was not, however, the root of the matter. She was fantastically generous (she was always clear that good wages were better than charity), and she had many dependents.[14] She and Henry Ward both lost money on *The Christian Union*. If the Hartford house was a disaster, the orange grove at Mandarin was another; the only good thing she got out of it was that a parcel of land she had purchased for $200 appreciated to $7,000; she used the money to buy a parsonage for Charley in Hartford. "I have invested thirty-four thousand dollars in various ways," she once wrote, "none of which can give me any immediate income." [15]

Her interest in the economic aspects of writing she displayed from the beginning:

I have seen Johnson of the *Evangelist*. He is very liberally disposed, and I may safely reckon on being paid for all I do there. Who is that Hale, Jr., that sent me the *Boston Miscellany,* and will he keep his word with me? His offers are very liberal,—twenty dollars for three pages, not very close print. Is he to be depended on? If so, it is the best offer I have received yet. I shall get something from the Harpers some time this winter or spring. Robertson, the publisher here, says the book [*The Mayflower*] will sell, and though the terms they offer me are very low, that I shall make something on it. For a second volume I shall be able to make better terms. On the whole, my dear, if I choose to be a literary lady, I have, I think, as good a chance of making profit by it as any one I know of. But with all this, I have my doubts whether I shall be able to do so.

I am not suggesting that Harriet was incapable of generosity toward her publishers. She was very understanding when the publisher of *Hearth and Home* fell into financial difficulties. To one English publisher who paid her for *Uncle Tom's Cabin* she wrote:

When American publishers have helped themselves to so many English works I have felt that it was no more than just that English publishers should have the same advantage of American ones.... The success of the book is their reward. They do it as a speculation and they gain by it. I am satisfied.

As a service to Fields, Osgood she went over their accounts with Gail Hamilton in an attempt to convince that doubting author that her publishers had dealt justly with her. But she squeezed every word of her own writing for every penny it could be made to yield. Her letters are full of requests for what is due, for estimates of what is going to be due, and even for advances on what was not due at all. Like Hawthorne, she used her publisher as a banker, drawing against her account in case of need, even when there was nothing there to draw on. "I write it just now," she says of a manuscript, "because I want a little of the ready." Between 1866 and 1869 Fields paid her $10,000, largely in the form of advances, and then, when *Oldtown Folks* was finished at last, she refused to permit him to serialize it in the *Atlantic*, partly because she thought she could make more out of it unserialized. Often she set her own price for *Atlantic* articles, later demanding increases because economic conditions had changed or merely because she was in need. She might agree to write for the *Atlantic* exclusively, but if driven by financial need afterwards, she never hesitated to repudiate the treaty unilaterally. Nor did she ever hesitate to suggest new editions or special exploitation—*Oldtown Folks* and *Agnes of Sorrento* with photographic illustrations picturing the scenes of the stories and once a new, illustrated edition of *Uncle Tom's Cabin*, aimed at the Southern Negro trade, to be sold by subscription. When *My Wife and I* was selling like hotcakes, she wanted the sales figures published. "I like people to know it for very many reasons." And did any author ever make a better job of teaching a publisher his business than she did when, on December 22, 1871, she wrote Osgood:

I called at your store yesterday and from appearances there I should infer that people would conclude that I was not among your authors. On the Christmas counter were the works of every other of your authors but none of mine. The new book which I supposed was got up for holiday sales was not on the counter although examples of even past issues of other authors were.

At Roberts brothers I saw large shop bills announcing a new Holiday book by Miss Alcott—and in consequence, he will probably sell many copies of a collection of little stories which she has prepared for Xmas.

Nobody could guess by any appearance at your store that there was a new book in the market by Mrs. Stowe.

Yet the stories there have been proven to be popular, have been separately quoted and noticed—have recently one of them been chosen for a public reading in Lawrence. It is a book that people would buy by hundreds if they only had it *showed* to them and their attention called to it. In short it is a book that will pay for pushing.

Both my other books have been the successes of the season. Each sold from 10 to 14 thousand in a week and this might do at least half as well.

Nothing in a literary way was too close to Mrs. Stowe to have its money value scrutinized. Her vindication of Lady Byron was a sacred duty, but she did not forget to ask that the publisher's check be forwarded promptly. Six days after the assassination of Lincoln she wrote:

I sent my June no yesterday—it would have come five days sooner but I was struck dumb by the news. I have something more to say of our lost President. Would it not be well to take my piece on him and that on Andy Johnson and publish them together in a little book with mourning decorations? I think we might sell thousands and I want to say something to thousands.

This is startling enough, but another letter, about her own late husband is even more startling. After he died in 1886, she wrote Henry Houghton that she had been asked to do an obituary article. She would rather have it in the *Atlantic* than anywhere else; did Houghton care for it? "It may run through two nos— of 12 pages each and I must request the same rate of compensation I used to receive from $1 to 200 per article." And I fear it would be difficult to comment on that.[16]

CHAPTER X

THE REFORMER

I

Harriet Beecher Stowe, says James C. Austin, "was not only a rabble rouser . . . but a fanatic who could be expected to pursue relentlessly any cause to which she attached herself." [1] It would be difficult to find a more uncomprehending judgment of any American writer. There was certainly a touch of fanaticism in Lyman's attitude toward the Roman Catholic Church. Isabella too showed signs of fanaticism at times, but, as I have said, Isabella probably was not quite sane. Generally speaking, fanaticism was not in the Beecher temper. Judged against the background of their times and in comparison with their contemporaries, they were all moderates. Harriet in particular seldom took up an extreme position on any issue: she was always for "the best possible." This temperamental bias has already appeared in many connections in these pages; it must be displayed now in connection with the causes she served.

Such immoderation as she did display was, for the most part, an expression of her devotion to the things she loved. One of these was, as we have seen, what she conceived as the Christian home. Another was New England. In an 1876 letter to J. F. Clarke she praises "the old Yankee type." "God bless it with all its faults. It was a glorious type and I don't want the memory of it to perish." Nothing could be more provincial than the glorification of New England in the *First Geography*. The Pilgrims left England because they could not obey the King's laws "without breaking the laws of God." They did not stay in Holland because "there they found that their children were tempted to do a great many wicked things." And she becomes as smug as the friends of Job when she continues that "no people in the world have been more prosperous in every kind of business than those in New England; for God always makes most prosperous those who are most obedient to his laws in the Bible." [2]

In *Men of Our Times* she shows great interest in "family stock," and she is never happier than when she can trace anything she admires back to New England. In *Pink and White Tyranny* John Seymour would not live in New York City "if it would give me the mines of Golconda," and his sister Grace "was one of those women formed under the kindly severe discipline of Puritan New England, to act not from blind impulse or instinct, but from high principle." In this same novel she admits that some members of the Boston aristocracy are not "otherwise distinguished than by a remarkable talent for being disagreeable." But, on the whole, "those 'true-blue' families . . . have claims to respectability; which makes them . . . quite a venerable and pleasurable feature of society in our young, topsy-turvy, American community." In *The Minister's Wooing* we are even told that "it is impossible to write a story of New England life and manners for a thoughtless, shallow-minded person." But I think the climax is in what seems to be a Preface to a proposed French edition of *The Mayflower*, attached to a letter to the publisher Charpentier, preserved in the New York Public Library. Here New England is called

the heart of the whole country. From it, enterprise energy and education have gone out through all the other states. It has been said that each section of the United States has its peculiar produce. The southern states have their cotton sugar and rice, the western states cattle and grain, but the New England states produce *men and women!*

Harriet's interest in Negroes being what it was, it may be interesting to glance at her attitude toward certain other minority groups. What she says about Jews is all favorable. Their moral superiority she attributes to the wise, humane provisions of the Law of Moses. But I do not find that she had any real interest in Judaism except as it prepared the way for Christianity. In 1854 she wrote to Isaac Meyer Wise, who had sent her his *History of the Israelitish Nation,* of "that singular and sacred nation to whom I, in common with all the world, am indebted for the preservation and transmission of the oracles of God." She added that she never meets a Jew or enters a synagogue without thinking of these things.

In her New England, the Irish, too, were something of a race apart. It fell to her to comment upon them mainly as servants, especially in the *House and Home Papers.* It would be too much to say that there was no condescension in her attitude, but she gives the impression of a genuine friendliness:

People may mourn in lugubrious phrase about the Irish blood in our country. For our own part, we think the rich, tender, motherly nature of the Irish girl an element a thousand times more hopeful in our population than the faded, washed-out indifference of fashionable women, who have danced and flirted away all their womanly attributes.... Give us rich, tender, warm-hearted Bridgets and Kathleens, whose instincts teach them the real poetry of motherhood; who can love unto death, and bear trials and pains cheerfully for the joy that is set before them. We are not afraid for the republican citizens that such mothers will bear to us.

In Indians she seems to have had little interest. In *Oldtown Folks* they shelter Tina and Harry; in one of *Sam Lawson's Old-time Fireside Stories* ("Colonel Eph's Shoe-Buckles"), which involves Indian warfare, they are very savage, though not incapable of being Christianized. In her sketch of General Sheridan she remarks of one tribe, "These turbulent savages have no more self-control than so many tigers." But the most interesting passage is her description in *The Christian Union* of 1877 of the Christianizing and civilizing of a band of captured Indians at St. Augustine,

Florida. "We have tried fighting and killing the Indians.... We have tried feeding them as paupers in their savage state.... Suppose, now, we try education."

More interesting are Harriet's references to what we would now call the class conflict. Professor Adams and others have commented on St. Clare's utterances in *Uncle Tom's Cabin:* "One thing is certain,—that there is a mustering among the masses, the world over; and there is a *dies irae* coming on, sooner or later. The same thing is working in Europe, in England, and in this country." But Adams adds, "Incredible as it may seem, the sense of social economic responsibility implied in St. Clare's speeches was utterly foreign to Mrs. Stowe's thought."

St. Clare's utterances do not, however, stand alone. It is true that her friendship with the Duke and Duchess of Sutherland and other aristocrats seems to have turned Harriet against English republicanism, and that when she inadvertently patronized an English sweatshop, her defense showed her a mistress of all the feminine illogic that has ever existed among Eve's descendants.[3] As late as *Pink and White Tyranny* she could praise standpatism in Mr. Van Astrachan, who did not believe "that pitching everything into pi once in fifty years" was quite necessary. "Blessed be the people whose strength is to sit still!" But she was not unaware of Van Astrachan's limitations, and she was as clear as Mark Twain that the day in which labor was to rule was at hand. "Numbers is the king of our era." (This, as Constance Rourke remarked, anticipated Matthew Arnold by a decade.) "The power is passing out of the hands of the cultivated few into those of the strong, laborious many."

I do not believe that any reader of *We and Our Neighbors* has ever been strengthened in his admiration for capitalistic manipulations by the author's account of how Miss Dorcas and Mrs. Betsey are impoverished by the company in which their savings are invested, in spite of the fact that business is good. In *Men of Our Times* class feeling is invoked again and again. "In looking through the list, it will be seen that almost every one of these men sprang from a condition of hard-working poverty." In her sketch of Sheridan she remarks that "it might almost be said that in our country poverty in youth is the first requisite for success in life." Of Senator Henry Wilson she says that "the plain working-man was taken by the hand of Providence towards the high place where he, with other working men, should shape the destiny of the labor question for this age and for all ages." But the Lincoln paper is the one in which she goes farthest. "*For* us and our cause, all the common working classes of Europe—all that toil and sweat, and are oppressed. *Against* us, all privileged classes, nobles, princes, bankers and great manufacturers, all who live at ease." God "chose the instrument for this work, and He chose him with a visible reference to the rights and interests of the great majority of mankind, for which he stood." And she adds, "Abraham Lincoln was in the strictest sense *a man of the working classes.*"

Of course none of this means that Harriet was a Marxist, or that there has not been much in Marxianism since her time that she would have regarded with horror. But there were what we would call Marxian elements in her thinking nevertheless, and she was certainly not blind to the capitalistic abuses against which the Christian Socialists and others protested. In *Footsteps of the Master* she declares bluntly that "the Sermon on the Mount was, and still is, the most disturbing and revolutionary document in the world."

II

The test case for Harriet Beecher Stowe as a reformer is of course the slavery issue. Because *Uncle Tom's Cabin* was the one unquestioned work of genius which the antislavery movement produced, it is tempting to regard her and her family as having been in the forefront of the abolition movement from the beginning. Indeed she herself was so tempted—and she yielded to temptation.[4] But this is so far from having been the case that when she began work on her great novel she wrote her editor, Dr. Gamaliel Bailey, that up to this time she had felt "no particular call to meddle with this subject, and I dreaded to expose even my own mind to the full force of its exciting power." She was still flirting with such ideas as gradual emancipation through purchase and colonization in Liberia, but she did not really expect to see the slaves freed during her lifetime. In 1886 she was to tell James Lane Allen that it was the Fugitive Slave Law that set her off,[5] and this agrees with what she told others. Her first anti-slavery piece was "The Two Altars," written in 1851 and included in the 1855 edition of *The Mayflower;*[6] there had been no anti-slavery piece in the 1843 edition. Of her four contributions to *The National Era* before *Uncle Tom's Cabin* only one had even mentioned the slavery issue.

Moreover she intended *Uncle Tom's Cabin* itself as a pacificator. "I shall show the best side of the thing," she said, "and something *faintly approaching the worst.*" And later, to Lord Shaftesbury:

It was my hope that a book so kindly intended, so favorable in many respects, might be permitted free circulation among the... [Southerners] and that the gentle voice of Eva and the manly generosity of St. Clare might be allowed to say those things of the system which would be invidious in any other form.

She had expected attacks from the North rather than from the South, and this is just what, at the outset, she got, which should not surprise those who remember her statesmanlike insistence that slavery was a national, not a sectional, problem, with the North thoroughly involved in it through its economic interest in the cotton trade, or her bitter, sometimes subversive, attacks on the federal laws which protected slavery and her criticism of the clergymen, both North and South, who defended it. There are more kind masters in the book than cruel ones, and she deliberately made her worst villain, Simon Legree, a Vermonter.

If all this was clear in *Uncle Tom's Cabin*, it was made equally clear in other writings. Take "Uncle Sam's Emancipation," which appeared in 1853 in the book of that title:

The great error of controversy is, that it is ever ready to assail *persons* rather than *principles*. The slave system as a *system*, pehaps concentrates more wrong than any other now existing, and yet those who live under and in it may be as we see, enlightened, generous, and amenable to reason. If the system alone is attacked, such minds will be the first to perceive its evils, and to turn against it; but if the system be attacked through individuals, self-love, wounded pride, and a thousand natural feelings, will be at once enlisted for its preservation.

One could hardly be more conciliatory than this, and Harriet expanded in an 1853 letter to Daniel R. Goodloe: [7]

It has been my earnest desire to address myself to southern minds, for I have always believed that there was slumbering at the South, energy enough to reform its evils, could it only be aroused.

It has seemed to me that many who have attacked the system, have not understood the southern character, nor appreciated what is really good in it. I think *I* have, at least I have tried, during this whole investigation, to balance my mind by keeping before it the most agreeable patterns of southern life and character....

It seems to me that truly noble minds ought to consider *that* the best friendship which refuses to defend their faults, but rather treats them as excrescences which ought to be severed, and what is true of individuals is true of countries.

I respect and admire the true chivalric, noble ideal of the southern man, and therefore more indignantly reprobate all that which is no part of him, being the result of an unnatural institution, and which is unworthy of him, and therein, I think, show myself more fully a friend than those who undertake to defend faults and all.

It is true that she was more bitter in the *Key* and in *Dred*, but even here her moderation had not been utterly destroyed. Right up to Fort Sumter she oscillated between warnings that if the South persisted in sowing the dragon's teeth the whole country would reap the whirlwind and the conviction that war was unthinkable. In the *Key* she says that "human nature is no worse at the South than at the North," that the guilt of slavery rests upon both sections, that Maine itself is committed to a contemptuous attitude toward the Negro and "an unchristian feeling of caste," and that "while the irresponsible power of slavery is such that no human being ought ever to possess it, probably that power was never exercised more leniently than in many cases in the Southern States." There is even a remarkable passage on a young Southerner who had killed a Negro and escaped punishment. She granted that in himself this young man might be "as generous-hearted and as just . . . as any young man living; but the horrible system under which he has been educated has rendered him incapable of distinguishing what either generosity or justice is, as applied to the negro." Developing this idea she steers straight toward a moral determinism very similar to that which was to be developed by Mark Twain: "As this educational influence descends from generation to generation, the moral sense becomes more and more blunted, and the power of discriminating right from wrong, in what relates to the subject race, more and more enfeebled."

After the war she supported Johnson's (and Henry Ward's) conciliatory Reconstruction policy and opposed the radical Republicans, and it says a good deal for both her and her southern neighbors that they should have welcomed her in Florida as cordially as they did. In 1876 she was attracted by the Confederate war memorial in Savannah, which reminded her of Scott's monument in Edinburgh. The inscription from Ezekiel 37 particularly impressed her.

All forces of life and nature and society tend to healing. Flowers grow over battlefields, kindness and good will spring up where alienation has been, and the veiled figure with the fingers on the lip is the fittest emblem for a monument that perpetuates the memory of strife among brothers.

But none of this means that Harriet was in any sense insincere toward the Negro or that her interest was not deeply enlisted. In March 1852 she wrote Horace Mann:

Today I have taken my pen from the last chapter of *Uncle Tom's Cabin* and I think you will understand me when I say that I feel as if I had written some of it almost with my heart's blood. I look upon it almost as a despairing appeal to a civilized humanity—in the close of it I think you may trace the result of some of your suggestions.

And she added that "so deeply has the cause I speak for enwoven itself with my life, that sympathy for that, seems to me almost a personal favor." I am willing to take this at face value, and I would add that though after *Dred* Harriet never devoted a whole novel to slavery, she never lost her interest in it nor, later, in the freed Negro.[8] Her unpublished letters show many kindnesses to individuals, both before and after emancipation, and during her residence in Florida she several times repudiated as "a vile slander" reports that her southern residence had caused her to regret that she ever wrote *Uncle Tom's Cabin*.[9] She favored desegregated schools, and though she never glossed over the Negro's faults or viewed him through rose-colored glasses, she always sought to give him the benefit of any possible doubt.[10]

But an antislavery worker in the sense in which Lucretia Mott, Lydia Maria Child, the Grimké sisters, John Greenleaf Whittier and others were antislavery workers she was not; neither did she bear with them the burden of the heat of the day. She was a professional writer but not a professional agitator; moreover she was a creative writer, and she could only deal with subjects that fired her imagination.[11] "Instead of requiring a sacrifice from her," writes Professor Adams, "abolition brought wealth, fame, and self-assurance. Slavery was the tool by which she found herself." This is not disparagement, but it is a fact, and there is no sense denying it to make a martyr of her. F. B. Sanborn recognized it;[12] so did Frederick Douglass. So, in a different way, did Mary Boykin Chesnut, whose famous *Diary from Dixie* shows an imagination haunted by Mrs. Stowe. Mrs. Chesnut hated slavery, and she never denied that the kind of thing Harriet described in *Uncle Tom's Cabin* could happen, but she did feel that Harriet, writing about slavery, had a much easier role than hers, which was to live with it on a plantation.[13]

If Harriet found it convenient, in her latter days, to forget her late conversion to abolitionism, she also preferred to forget some things about her earlier attitude toward Lincoln.[14] Her sketch of him in *Men of Our Times* was admiring without giving any suggestion that she had been extremely critical of him until late in the war. The closest she comes is to say that "there was a time when he pleased nobody." "He was, like the great Master whom he humbly followed, despised and rejected of men, a man of sorrows and acquainted with grief; we hid, as it were, our faces from him, he was despised, and we esteemed him not." [15]

When he was elected in 1860 she hailed the Republican victory in *The Independent*, though it was "far from being up to the full measure of what ought to be" on the slavery issue. But her attack on the First Inaugural Address was outrageous, culminating in a quotation from Sojourner Truth: "Is God dead?"

Lincoln's crime was partly that he had, "with perfect naïveté," identified himself with the South and partly that he had blamed the North for the existing situation, but, still more, "the coolness with which from first to last, he ignores the existence of any moral or religious sense as forming any important element in national movements." This inspires another quotation: "The fool hath said in his heart there is no God."

It was left for the XIXth century to show a specimen of a state-paper, proposing to a Christian nation to become more formally than ever they have been before robbers, kidnappers, and pirates—without betraying through a line that a God had ever been heard of in America—unless it be in certain customary rhetorical phrases at the close.

By September 5, 1861, she was calling for immediate emancipation by Presidential proclamation. She was furious when Lincoln overruled Frémont's liberating the slaves in captured territories and removed him from his command, and when the President said that his "paramount object" was "to save the Union and . . . not either to save or destroy Slavery," she produced a bitter parody by rewriting his statement as she thought Christ would have made it:

My paramount object in this struggle is to set at liberty them that are *bruised* and *not* either to save or destroy the Union. What I do in favor of the Union, I do because it helps to free the oppressed; what I forbear, I forbear because it does not help free the oppressed. I shall do less for the Union whenever it would hurt the cause of the slave, and more when I believe it would help the cause of the slave.

If Harriet knew what she was talking about here, and was not simply intoxicated with her own rhetoric, then she was willing to go to war to free the slaves but was otherwise indifferent to whether the nation lived or died. So far as she was concerned, the Civil War was a war for emancipation: she gives no sign of understanding any other issues. When the time came to address her "Reply" to the "Affectionate and Christian Address" of the Englishwomen on the slavery issue, she did not write it until she had had a personal interview with Lincoln to make sure that he would "make good" on emancipation. Her letter, which was in the January 1863 *Atlantic*, was a stinging rebuke to Britain for her friendliness toward the Confederacy. "I have often wondered," wrote Lyman Beecher Stowe, "whether President Lincoln knew she was going to issue it and how sorely pressed Minister Adams felt about it."

III

Of all the causes she might have been expected to serve, the one to which Harriet would seem to have been least sensitive was peace. Her background in this area was a very respectable one, for while she had one Revolutionary commander, General Andrew Ward, in her immediate ancestry, her grandfather, David Beecher, decided, under Revolutionary War pressures, that he could not bring himself to kill a human being, and both Lyman and Roxana opposed the War of 1812. In *Sunny Memories* Harriet herself calls the English-speaking peoples "the Romans of the nineteenth century."

We have been the race which has conquered, subdued, and broken in pieces other weaker races, with little regard either to justice or mercy. With regard to benefits by us imparted to conquered nations, I think a better story, on the whole, can be made out for the Romans than for us. Witness the treatment of the Chinese, of the tribes of India, and of our own American Indians.

But this is hardly typical. In *Poganuc People*, Dolly, who is Harriet, has a fine patriotic spasm all by herself upon hearing the Declaration of Independence read at a Fourth of July celebration:

She was a girl—there was no help for that; but for this one day she envied the boys—the happy boys who might some day grow up and fight for their country, and do something glorious like General Washington.

Like Henry Ward, Harriet was quite militantly-minded in the face of the riots provoked by slavery men in her Cincinnati days ("If I were a man, I would . . . take good care of at least one window"). Later Plymouth Church was so active in equipping the Kansas emigrants that the Sharpe's rifles sent out to them were popularly known as "Beecher's Bibles." [16]

If Harriet was committed to anything, it was to the thesis that on all moral and religious issues, the Bible, and especially the teaching of Jesus, was the supreme authority. Yet the pacifism of Jesus and of New Testament religion received little direct recognition from her. In *Bible Heroines* she praises Moses for trying to restrain war, and in the *Key* she argues at some length that the purpose of Deuteronomy 20:5-10 was to put an end to military expeditions. But over against this must be placed a really horrible passage from the sketch of Delilah: "There are a few representations of loathsome vice and impurity left in the sacred records, to show how utterly and hopelessly corrupt the nations had become whom the Jews were commanded to exterminate."

In the *Key*, again, she takes a fling at "those casuists among us who lately seem to think and teach that it is right for us to violate the plain commands of God whenever some great national good can be secured by it," but it does not seem to have occurred to her that this had any application to the commandment "Thou shalt not kill." In one of the *Oldtown Fireside Stories* ("Oldtown Fireside Talks of the Revolution") she does admit, in effect, that

Christian ethics cannot be applied in wartime. In *Footsteps of the Master* she acknowledges that Jesus antagonized his enemies by rejecting violence, but she makes little or nothing of it. In her account of the Temptation, she sees him as rejecting political compromise but says nothing of his rejection of the war method. One need only turn to *Paradise Regained* to understand how differently this might have been handled. Through most of *Men of Our Times*, too, she simply ignores the incompatibility of Christianity and war, then, rather surprisingly, raises the question as prologue to her portrait of Oliver O. Howard: "Can there be a Christian Soldier?" Obviously, Howard was a man of noble character, but in view of the number of other Civil War generals who professed Christianity and were serious about their religion, it seems odd to discuss the problem only here. In all her writings about Quakers, there is nowhere any stress on Quaker pacifism. Sumner's peace addresses at the time of the Mexican War she approved, apparently because they were directed against a slave power. Garrison's non-resistance she reported without comment in her sketch of him, and added, apparently with approval, that he made no effort to keep his son out of the Union army.

When the war began, Harriet warned in *The Independent* of the long hard road ahead. "Even Mrs. Partington has discovered that there are really bad-meaning fellows in this world who can't be talked to, and must be put down by force." The cause she found "a cause to die for—and, thanks be to God, our young men embrace it as a bride, and are ready to die." "If war be an evil [she is no longer sure even of that!] it is less evil than many others, and one attended by many and high forms of good." By June 13 she was rejoicing that in Andover the theological students were drilling and the Phillips Academy boys too. The theologues seemed to her to have an "improved appearance of health and manly vigor. We venture to say if this state of things prevails, there will be no dyspeptic views of theology so far as this generation of ministers is concerned." By September 4, 1862, she was crying, "Better, a thousand times better, open, manly, energetic war, than cowardly and treacherous peace." At some time during the conflict she presented a flag to a company of Andover recruits, and Agnes Park, who witnessed the ceremony, writes with noble restraint: "Many of those young lives were sacrificed to their country. Some endured imprisonment at Andersonville, and yet lived to forgive, if not forget." To forgive—let us hope —more than the South.

She praised John Brown—"the man who has done more than any man yet for the honor of the American name"; credited insane reports of Southern barbarism (violating graves, making drinking-cups of skulls, wearing cameos "cut from bones and treasure scalps," and such obscenities) even before the war; damned Hawthorne for his fidelity in friendship when he dedicated *Our Old Home* to former President Franklin Pierce; [17] and after the war beat the drums for a political career for both Grant and Sherman (whose march of depredation from Atlanta to the coast of Georgia she called "romantic"!). In her sketch of Farragut she quoted with approval a horrible piece of "Homeric military ardor baptized by Christian sentiment," written by one Henry Brownell:

> His kingdom here can only come
> In chrism of blood and flame.

And she herself contributed a piece called "The Holy War" to a patriotic anthology; [18] the text comes from Revelation 19 but what war she is thinking of is quite clear.

Even the children had to be inured to killing, and in *Queer Little People* she commented on the swallowing up of little Mr. Frog by Mr. Water-snake and Mr. Bullfrog:

It seems a sad state of things; but then I suppose all animals have to die in some way or other, and perhaps, if they are in the habit of seeing it done, it may appear no more to a frog to expect to be swallowed some day, than it may to some of us to die of a fever, or be shot in battle, as many a brave fellow has been of late.

If no more, I should certainly think that would be enough. But the most revolting combination of blood lust with religiosity and bland assumption of a knowledge of God's ways seems to me to have been achieved in these generalizations about the Civil War in the Grant sketch:

It was God's will that we should have a four years' war, and therefore when we looked for a leader he sent us Gen. McClellan.

It was God's will that this nation—the North as well as the South—should deeply and terribly suffer for the sin of consenting to and encouraging the great oppressions of the South; that the ill-gotten wealth which had arisen from striking hands with oppression and robbery, should be paid back in the taxes of war; that the blood of the poor slave, that had cried so many years from the ground in vain, should be answered by the blood of the sons from the best hearth stones through all the free States; that the slave mothers, whose tears nobody regarded, should have with them a great company of weepers, North and South—Rachels weeping for their children and refusing to be comforted; that the free States, who refused to listen when they were told of lingering starvation, cold, privation, and barbarous cruelty, as perpetrated on the slave, should have lingering starvation, cold, hunger and cruelty doing its work among their own sons, at the hands of those slave masters, with whose sins our nation had connived.

General McClellan was like those kings and leaders we read of in the Old Testament, whom God sent to a people with a purpose to wrath and punishment.

Having heard Harriet at her worst on this issue, we should also, to be fair, hear her at her best. In Italy in 1859 she was shocked by an Italian woman's rejoicing over the Austrian blood that had been shed.

It is pitiful to think of on both sides! One longs for the day when nations will strive only in noble deeds, and all the splendor that now invests war will be spent in solemn celebrations of peace and fraternity.

And in 1877 she wrote to an English friend:

As to the Eastern question we agree with Gladstone. Let Russia take charge of the Christian provinces if she will and fight her own battles but for heavens sake let not England go to war again. War is like fire, and Europe now is like tinder and every nation ought to keep out of it lest a general conflagration put back the course of civilization for centuries. My experience of war leads me to dread it. War is wasteful, cruel, devilish and Christian nations ought to find some better way. Arbitration should take the place of armament.

IV

A somewhat amusing, yet troublesome, footnote to Harriet's reforming interests is furnished by her attitude toward the use of alcoholic beverages and related indulgences. Though there are a number of admirable old New England women in her stories who take snuff without being rebuked by their creator, I think it may be said that her references to tobacco are consistently hostile. She knew that there was a great tea and coffee controversy," but she refused to become involved in it, and apparently accepted both drinks, though there is one letter to James T. Fields in which she orders some dandelion coffee. "Coffee that not only does not make one ill but *does* make one better is an approach to the millennium." But the alcohol business is more complicated.

Lyman Beecher came out of a world innocent of temperance movements, where the air at ministers' meetings was as foul with whiskey fumes and tobacco smoke as it is in night clubs today, and where it was not at all unusual to see some of the brethren considerably elevated. Against all this he revolted, becoming one of the early important influences toward committing American Protestantism to an anti-liquor point of view, a work which his son, Henry Ward, carried on after him.[19]

Officially Harriet takes up a total abstinence position. In *Uncle Tom's Cabin* and *Dred* liquor is consistently associated with degradation; St. Clare turns against his occasional dissipations when he sees the grief they cause Uncle Tom. Bolton in *My Wife and I* exemplifies the good man who must drink immoderately or not at all; out of consideration for such, Harriet argues, social drinking should be abandoned. In *Pink and White Tyranny* John Seymour holds out against Lillie in refusing to serve wine in his home though he gives way on all else, and in *Poganuc*

People the revival of religion converts, among others, the tavern-keeper, who thereupon shuts up his tavern.

The non-fiction writings and the letters bear the same testimony. Governor Buckingham of Connecticut is praised as an abstainer in *Men of Our Times.* One of her "Letters from Maine" hails the dry law "as marking an *era* in the history of elections, because there, for once, men of principle forsook all party lines and measures, to vote for PRINCIPLE alone." When James Parton's book on drinking and smoking came out, Harriet wrote his wife, Fanny Fern, that she hoped it would sell by thousands. Echoing her husband, she believed that "the wine that Christ used was undoubtedly the simple sour wine of the peasantry of Palestine and not intoxicating"; hence she preferred the unfermented juice of the grape in the communion service.[20] In England she and her party seem to have made a point of refusing wine, declaring that "the view of your great cities, flaming nightly with signs of 'Rum, brandy, and Gin' is to the eyes of an American as appalling as the slave-market of our Southern States to an Englishman." And according to Thomas Wentworth Higginson, she once insisted in advance, with rather comical results, that no wine be served at an *Atlantic* dinner which she was expected to attend.

But in this matter Harriet's professions did not quite match her practice. She was not a teetotaler, or at least not a consistent one, and at this point alone I think it is not possible wholly to acquit her of hypocrisy.

In 1856, when she was working on *Dred*, she was faint one day in the office of her publisher. They refreshed her with two glasses of champagne, and after she had gone home they sent her some Catawba wine. On July 13 she wrote from Andover, "I should like half a dozen more bottles of Catawba to support the hot weather and the *long pull.*" In a letter conjecturally dated June 5, 1862, she tells Hattie that she is sending home two boxes of claret prescribed by the doctor and that Calvin must be prepared to pay the charges. And on December 1, 1883, she writes like a real connoisseur: "As to that old wine it is very choice old Burgundy, which Brother Henry got on purpose for your Father and me and I hope it will come safe and sure what ever way you send it for it is worth its weight in gold so to speak." [21]

More interesting than any of these items are two undated letters to Hattie in the Women's Archives:

My publishers offer $200 a number if I will write recollections of my life. In this way with very little labor I can gain $800 a month.

In order to do this there must be a change which I now will indicate.

1—The wine &c I have usually taken at 11 o'clock to be placed *in the dining room closet where I can get it* at 6 o'clock in the morning. I can then *do my morning's walk before breakfast* and have the forenoon clear for work. If you will begin this tomorrow—please tell me.

And the other:

The changes I wish to make are two.

1st Directly after breakfast give me that portion you have hitherto given at 11 o'clock.

I shall take it and take a walk of an hour and a half to equalise the stimulant that it may not rush to the brain—and be home ready to go to writing at 11 o'clock and write two hours.

2 Directly after dinner give the same—and I shall take my afternoon walk and have two more hours to devote to writing. *The stimulus* will be used up in active out of door exercise which will strengthen my general health.

Certainly this is a novel health regimen, by anybody's standards.

In her *Crowding Memories*,[22] Mrs. Thomas Bailey Aldrich told the highly entertaining story of the visitation Harriet made her, self-invited, when Mrs. Aldrich was a young married woman. Somewhat appalled at the idea of entertaining so distinguished a guest all by herself, she regaled her with claret cup, of which Harriet partook generously,

and very shortly afterwards complained of the unsettled character of the room. . . . And the sea turn—everything is in a blue mist—did we often have such sudden fogs? She would lie down if the sofa had not such a momentum: to her eye it was misbehaving as badly as a berth at sea.

Lie down she did, and her skirts, "like Hamlet's words, 'flew up,' revealing very slender ankles and feet encased in prunella boots.... The stockings were white, and the flowery ribbon of the garter knots was unabashed by the sunlight." As the hour for her husband's arrival drew near, Mrs. Aldrich tried to cover her guest with a "gossamer scarf," but at the first touch she sat up, "and with dim, reproachful eyes asked: 'Why did you do it? I am weak, weary and warm as I am—let me sleep.'" On the question of propriety she was even firmer: "I won't be any properer than I have a mind to be."

Before Aldrich arrived, however, "Mrs. Stowe had had a strong cup of coffee, her skirts had resumed their normal shape, and she was herself again." During the dinner she held forth on how "the heat of the day and the motion of the train" had produced "a strange dizziness which she had never experienced before."

Amusing as this is, there is a wryer and more ironical twist in another story, told by Harriet herself in a letter to Calvin. On January 4, 1865, she had "a stiff neck and a raging angry tooth ache." She turned first to ether and camphor, which relieved her temporarily. Then:

In the forenoon it came on again till I was wild with despair and bethought me that I might get sleep with brandy—I took a stiff dose and slept from eleven till four without waking tho the salute of over hundred cannon were fired and all the Bells of Boston rang for joy at the final wiping away of our national shame and reproach.

And she adds: "Strange that when the consummation of my life's desires was announced I should be lying vanquished by toothache."

By toothache? Well, never mind. It sounds much better that way, and Mrs. Stowe, as Lowell observed, had the mind of a romancer.

Chapter XI

THE DAUGHTER

I

This study of Harriet Beecher Stowe began with a chapter called "The Daughter"; it ends designedly with another identically titled. For Harriet had a Father in heaven as well as a father on earth, and her relationship to Him was the central fact of her life.

Yet, oddly enough, its characteristic note was rebellion, for before her heart could find rest, even in God, she had to fight her way out from her inherited Calvinism.

The Calvinistic view may well be stated in the words of her sister Catharine, who, as we have seen, rebelled against it before her:

Up to the age of sixteen my conceptions on the subject of religion were about these: that God made me and all things; that he knew all I thought and did; that because Adam and Eve disobeyed him once only, he drove them out of Eden, and then so arranged it that all their descendants would be born with wicked hearts; and that, though this did not seem either just or good, it was so; that I had such a wicked heart that I could not feel or act right in anything till I had a new one; that God only could give me a new heart; that if I died without it, I should go to a lake of fire and brimstone, and be burned alive in it forever; that Jesus Christ was very good and very sorry for us, and came to earth and suffered and died to save us from this dreadful doom; that revivals were times when God the Holy Spirit gave people new hearts; that, when revivals came, it was best to read the Bible, and pray, and go to meetings, and that at other times it was of little use. By "revival preaching" I was taught to look at God as a great moral governor, whose chief interest was to sustain his law. Then there seemed to be two kinds of right and wrong, the common and the Evangelical. According to this distinction, I could not feel or do anything that was right or acceptable to God, till my birth-gift of a depraved heart was renewed by special divine interposition.... The selection of the recipients of this favor was regulated by a divine decree of election without reference to any acts of a being who did nothing but evil and only evil till this favor was bestowed.

A more colloquial expression of the Calvinistic system was achieved by Sam Lawson:

Parson Simpson's a smart man; but, I tell ye, it's kind of discouragin'. Why, he said our state and condition by nature was just like this. We was clear down in a well fifty feet deep, and the sides all round nothin' but glare ice; but we was under immediate obligations to get out, 'cause we was free, voluntary agents. But nobody ever had got out, and nobody would, unless the Lord reached down and took 'em. And whether he would or not nobody could tell; it was all sovereignty. He said there wa'n't one in a hundred,—not one in a thousand,—not one in ten thousand,—that would be saved. Lordy massy, says I to myself, ef that's so they're any of 'em welcome to my chance. And so I kind o' ris up and come out, 'cause I'd got a pretty long walk home, and I wanted to go round by South Pond, and inquire about Aunt Sally Morse's toothache.[1]

Sam Lawson, obviously, was not disposed to break his heart over his doomed condition, and Harriet realized that he did not stand alone. She knew that

man was mercifully made with the power of ignoring what he believes. It is all that makes existence in a life like this tolerable. And our ministers, conscious of doing the very best they can to keep the world straight, must be allowed their laugh and joke, sin and Satan to the contrary notwithstanding.

And besides the Sam Lawsons, there were the more sensitive souls who, while giving an intellectual assent to the doctrines, treated damnation as Addison treated witchcraft, believing in it in the abstract yet refusing to credit any particular instance of it. Such was Parson Avery of *Oldtown Folks,* who "was a firm believer in hell, but he believed also that nobody need go there, and he was determined, so far as he was concerned, that nobody should go there if he could help it."

Harriet had been brought up by just such a minister. "Oh, my dear son," cried Lyman Beecher, when Edward was struggling with religious difficulties in 1821, "*agonize* to enter in. You *must* go to heaven; you *must not* go to hell!" Harriet later objected, to George Eliot, that her father applied the methods of "a priori metaphysical discussion" to theology in a way for which she could find no justification in "the *facts* of daily observation and universal human consciousness." And she added, "When I married, I found a man of universal reading and great love of facts whose first work was to upset all of *technical* orthodoxy my own reflections had left—and replace it by a wise insight into *facts* which his reading in many languages gave him the command." But this does not quite do Lyman justice. He was emphatic in pointing out that he did not believe in infant damnation and that Calvin had not believed in it either. His was a "clinical" theology, which "relieved people without number out of the sloughs of high Calvinism." Compared to Jonathan Edwards, none of the Beechers would have taken high rank as logicians, but they developed philosophies that men could live by, and if they had gone into medicine none of them would have reported, as a modern physician is said to have done, that the operation was successful but the patient died. According to Harriet her father believed "that it was both unwise and unphilosophical for young Christians ... to subject their religious emotions to the test of close metaphysical analysis, at least to the extent often practiced." Once when, having arranged to exchange pulpits with another pastor, he was told that the exchange had been foreordained, he replied, "Is that so? Then I won't do it!" and went home.

But the Beecher temperament is not the only temperament, and Harriet knew too that "on some natures theology operates as a subtle poison, and the New England theology in particular."

Her own conversion, at fourteen, after hearing her father preach a particularly simple and appealing sermon on the love of Christ, was as peaceful and sensible as anybody could have asked for. She went home, fell into his arms, and said, "Father, I have given myself to Jesus, and He has taken me." And Lyman, his glad tears falling, accepted the offering in the spirit in which it had been made. "Is it so? Then has a new flower blossomed in the kingdom this day." But Catharine, not yet as sensible as she afterwards became, wondered if the lamb could come so easily into the fold, and the pastor of the First Church of Hartford asked Harriet silly questions which sowed doubts in her mind and induced unnecessary years of spiritual struggle and agony.

Ultimately she distinguished sharply between Jonathan Edwards and "good, motherly Cotton Mather." [2] Edwards she rejected completely:

President Edwards had constructed a marvelous piece of logic to show that, while true virtue in man consisted in supreme devotion to the general good of all, true virtue in God consisted in supreme regard for himself.... The whole of it falls to dust before the one simple declaration of Jesus Christ, that, in the eyes of Heaven, one lost sheep is more prized than all the ninety and nine that went not astray, and before the parable in which the father runs, forgetful of parental prerogative and dignity, to cast himself on the neck of the far-off prodigal.

And when her son Charley read Edwards she wrote him:

The effect produced on you by reading Edwards is very similar to that produced on me when I took a similar mental bath. It is a mind whose grasp and intensity you cannot help feeling. He was a *poet* in the intensity of his conception and some of his sermons are more terrible than Dante's Hell.

But his God is not a Father. Not the God that *Jesus* meant when he said to Philip, He that hath seen *Me* hath seen the Father—from henceforth ye know him and have seen him.

It is still not generally realized how far she went, for her pietistic nineteenth-century language has obscured it. There was a Prometheus element in Harriet Beecher Stowe; for all her sense of reverence she went out to justify the ways of men to God. As early as 1829, still desperately beset with her own doubts and fears, she wrote: "The wonder to me is, how all ministers and all Christians can feel themselves so inexcusably sinful, when it seems to me we all come into the world in such a way that it would be miraculous if we did not sin." Ultimately she embraced Oliver Wendell Holmes's generous plea for all moral invalids in his *Elsie Venner*: "Elsie is one of my especial friends,—poor, dear child!—and all your theology in that book I subscribe to with both hands." But the most daring passage of all is in a letter to Martha Wetherill (December 15, 1860), which has so far been printed only obscurely [3] and is consequently still largely unknown, for here we see her not only denying Calvinistic foreordination and election and extending salvation to non-Christians, but even rejecting the necessity for what Calvinists understood as conversion. When Harriet had written this letter she was through, once and for all, with the Monster God whom her later Hartford neighbor Mark Twain was to excoriate in *The Mysterious Stranger*, and whom she herself had described in *Dred* as one "that creates myriads only to glorify himself in their eternal torments."

The things I said to you in parting, when we walked together in the great Hall at Chalkley, I said hoping perhaps they might have at least some influence in relieving your good heart of a burden which our own Father never meant us to carry—the awful burden of thinking that every person who does not believe certain things and is not regenerated in a certain way *in this life* is lost forever. I say this is nowhere explicitly stated in the Scriptures, and if it were true, it ought to be, and it is contradicted by every one of those numerous passages which state that God has for all creatures He has made the feelings of a Father. Because if it were true that this kind of belief and regeneration is absolutely the only way to Heaven, and this life the only time, it can be proved by very simple arithmetical calculation—it is nearer correct than the contrary to say—that all the human race up to our time, and about all in our time, are lost or going to be. Any map of the world will show you that the proportion which have even heard of

Christ is in the minority—and the minority of that [is] the Protestant world—and in that, the majority are the utterly ignorant and uninstructed who, from their circumstances, are like Heathen, and of those who *do know* and have opportunity, a great proportion still even of good people do not believe orthodox doctrine, and of those (who do believe orthodox doctrine), how small the number who show any signs of such a regeneration as we believe in. So that, instead of Christ having brought a glorious gospel of salvation, He has only brought the news of damnation, and we learn the appalling fact that the whole human race, with some small exceptions, is made for everlasting misery, for the number who have been true saints is certainly, in comparison to the human race, only in the proportion of one in a million.

But the Calvinistic ghost still walked. It walked even for Mark Twain. An inverted Calvinism has been discerned in Mark's mechanical determinism,[4] and I am sure Johanna Johnston is right when she perceives a trace of it, lingering gentle and amiable, but transformed almost out of recognition, even in Harriet's comfortable seventieth-birthday conviction that "everything that ought to happen is going to happen." In Europe she thrilled to ruins because she felt that, in the religious sense, she, like all human beings, was a ruin herself. Even as late as *Oldtown Folks* the orthodox are "my people," and she feels for them when the *Atlantic* or Harvard College antagonizes them. She might criticize the clergy as freely as she liked, but when anybody else did it she sprang at once to their defense.

But where did you get Alton Locke's mother [she wrote Kingsley]? Tho sprung of a Calvinistic stock I have never seen such an exhibition of Calvinism—nor such Calvinistic ministers. I don't know but I shall take up arms yet for that grave decorous respectable old Calvinism in which I was born, tho sooth to say it has fallen into my mind as the apostle says "sowing not what shall be but bearing grain"—it has been the seed out of which has sprung a new belief more ethereal as I think yet with somewhat of the woody fibre of that positive old system to support it.

In an introduction to a British edition of *The Minister's Wooing* she said it more formally:

The author has executed the work with a reverential tenderness for those great religious minds who laid in New England the foundations of many generations, and for those institutions and habits of life from which, as from a fruitful germ, sprang all the present prosperity of America.[5]

Moreover, nature herself seemed to Harriet to have her Calvinistic aspects. She says this again and again, but the best statement is in *Sunny Memories of Foreign Lands:*

Calvinism, in its essential features, never will cease from the earth, because the great fundamental facts of nature are Calvinistic, and men with strong minds and wills will always discover it. The predestination of a sovereign will is written over all things.... All this I say, while I fully sympathize with the causes which incline many fine and beautiful minds against the system.

Nor is it only physical nature of which these things are true. As Ellery Davenport puts it in *Oldtown Folks:*

If you had been in England, as I have ... you'd see that pretty much the whole of the lower classes there are predestinated to be conceived and born in sin, and shapen in iniquity; and come into the world in such circumstances that to expect even decent morality of them is expecting what is contrary to all reason.

Such considerations place difficulties in the way of accepting the God of Love in whom Harriet finally came to believe, and it may be that she did not solve all of them. "After seeing nature, can we reason against any of the harshest conclusions of Calvinism, from the character of its Author?"

II

Though her famous essay at the age of twelve, "Can the Immortality of the Soul Be Proved by the Light of Nature?" shows what most of us would regard as a remarkable theological capacity in Harriet Beecher Stowe, she herself seems to have considered theology somewhat antipathetic to women.

Theologic systems ... [she has Horace Holyoke tell us in *Oldtown Folks*] have as yet been the work of men alone. They have had their origin ... with men who were utterly ignorant of moral and intellectual companionship with women, looking on her only in her animal nature as a temptation and a snare.

She never had any truck with denominationalism, and her attitude toward even what have been regarded as essential Christian doctrines may best be described as pragmatic. Though she opposed with all her might the danger of her son Charley's becoming a Unitarian, I have nowhere found any discussion by her of the doctrine of the Trinity.

Your uncle is precisely the model I would hold up to you [she wrote Charley], of how a manly and honest man should guide himself in the ministry in an age when God is shedding new light on religion thro the development of his own natural laws in Science. What he could not conscientiously preach he let alone. He did not ridicule—he did not denounce—he simply confined himself to teaching that of whose truth he was *certain*. He never said anything about Adam's fall one way or the other, but preached simply that all had sinned and needed to repent. He preached Christ as the Savior from Sin—as the Friend, Comforter and Guide. He preached a certain punishment of sin here and hereafter. The need of God's Holy Spirit—God's willingness to give it. Prayer—and its answer. The Bible—and its inspiration and how to use it.

She probably clung to some ideas which many today would be inclined to regard as Christian superstitions. She seems to have believed in the devil. Though one passage in *Footsteps of the Master* shows that she was aware of the difficulties involved, she apparently believed in the Second Advent also; in 1858 she even suggests that it may be imminent. But she certainly did not stress these things or permit them to inspire fanaticism, as so many have done. And she only believed in the Puritan Sabbath to the extent that it could justify itself in terms of its fruits.[6]

Prayer she believed in—and practiced—devoutly, and when her prayers were not answered she often tried to persuade herself that they had been, as when the wounded President Garfield succumbed in spite of all her efforts to save him:

I think the All Wise often looks beyond the *words* of our prayers and gives us the *real thing*. What we sought was the peace and prosperity of this great nation and God by allowing this suffering and death has united north and south in one grief, one tribute of sympathy. Our *real reunion* will be cemented by the blood of this martyr.

On the Bible, again, she is pragmatic. Its power, she says, is beyond that of mere literature, and we may be sure she would have agreed with the Christian worker who met the skeptic's query "How do you know that the Bible is inspired?" with the reply "Because it inspires me." Certainly it inspired Harriet. She knew all its great words and promises by heart, and they sank to the depths of her soul, whence they rose to comfort and nourish her in all the trials and crises of her life.

There are passages where she seems impatient of scholarship and gives the impression of considering the Bible most valuable to those who take it most simply. But she was married to a distinguished Biblical scholar, and her attitude toward these matters was not obscurantist. Though she takes her Bible pretty literally, she still ponders many scholarly problems. Thus she believed that St. Luke got the materials for his birth narrative from Mary, and she reports and evaluates the views of competent scholars on the two different genealogies of Jesus. She is very sensible in defining the difference in quality between the canonical and the apocryphal Gospels, and she corrects the popular idea that Jesus, at twelve, instructed or lectured to the doctors in the Temple. She grasps the basic principle of historical scholarship when she writes that "the Creator revealed himself to man, not at once, but by a *system* progressively developing from age to age." [7] Pharaoh's sending Sarah away with gifts and presenting her with Hagar as a handmaid is "a legend savoring more of national pride than of probability."

Intellectually she would probably not have accepted the Quaker principle that when the sacred record contradicts the witness within, the sacred record must be denied, but in practice this is what she does. Her explanation of why the New Testament writers did not, or could not, attack slavery directly, and her argument that they were consistent with their general attitude in opposing "the *spirit* of an abuse first, and leave the *form* of it to drop away, of itself, afterwards" is very ingenious, even though one may not be quite convinced that the men of the first century saw slavery quite with the eyes of Mrs. Stowe, but she meets the issue when she declares that "as sure as there is a God in heaven is the certainty that, if the Bible really did defend slavery, fifty years hence would see every honorable and high-minded man an infidel." She was capable of calling upon woman's intuition to settle a question, as when she ascribed Psalm 90 to Moses because it "has an internal witness in the character of the sentiment." She could be arbitrary, as when she denied that Jephthah's daughter was sacrificed ("human sacrifice was above all things abhorrent to the Jewish law and to the whole national feeling"); she was "simply taken from the ordinary life of woman, and made an offering to the Lord." And she was just plain silly when she saw the presence of Jesus Christ in every supernatural incident recorded in the Old Testament.

Her liberalism shows in the way she encourages Charley to apply her views concerning theology in general to the central Christian doctrines of sin and redemption:

Whether the account of the Fall in Adam is to be literally or symbolically interpreted is a question for scholars and archaeologists and makes no practical difference in preaching to a parish where every man woman and child are sinners according to the law of God and the teaching of Christ, and need to be called to repentance. I have my own opinion on that point but I feel no call to talk about it—it is enough that every body has sinned and come short of the Glory of God.

As to the atonement too, there is no call for any controversy. None of the modern orthodoxy of our day hold or teach that God needed Christ's sufferings and blood to *reconcile him to us*—on the contrary they hold and teach with St. John that "Here is love—not that we loved God but He loved us, and sent His son to be a propitiation for us."

When you say ... you do not believe in any Hell I do not understand you for first you must see in this life that there is suffering mysterious and unalterable, awful, the fruit of sin. There is before our eyes the hell of the drunkard, the murderer, the dishonest, and there are Christ's awful sayings that it is better to cut off a right hand or pluck out a right eye than that soul or body be destroyed in hell. There is a hell, a fearful one—it is so certain a fruit of sinning that the only escape from it is escaping from Sin and the only Savior who can save His people from their sins is Jesus.

God did not need Christ's suffering and blood "*to reconcile him to us.*" Here Harriet stands with that other great Hartfordian who did so much to save us all from theological barbarism, Horace Bushnell. Yet she seems a little afraid of Bushnell,[8] and she certainly does not always reach his level. She falls far below it when she writes Charley that "there is no provision in human life or government offering pardon or repentance. Such a declaration would be a virtual repeal of all law," or when she develops an absurd parable about the heir to the Czar going to "live with the condemned Nihilists in Siberia and if necessary to die for them to manifest his father's love." Her insight was much deeper when she wrote, "The atonement is not merely a contrivance by which we escape the punishment of sin—it is a salvation *from* sin itself. As the full spirit of Christ on the cross pervades our heart sin dies." And she asks her daughters: "Till you have loved somebody better than yourselves, how can you understand the love of God, whose whole life is outward, whose existence consists in giving?" [9]

III

As for the church as an institution, Harriet finally moved out of the Presbyterian-Congregational communion, into which she had been born, into the Episcopal Church—Mr. St. John's "blessed medium." We shall see in a moment why she could not surrender to Rome; neither could she have taken the more common direction of New England Calvinist rebels into Unitarianism, for this would have inhibited the close, emotionalized sense of union with a supernatural Christ which her nature craved. In *Poganuc People* the appeal of the Episcopal service to the children of the Calvinist minister, and especially to Dolly, is winningly described:

It was in truth a very sweet and beautiful service, and one calculated to make a thoughtful person regret that the Church of England had ever expelled the Puritan leaders from an inheritance of such lovely possibilities.

But though she loved the liturgy, she thought the Episcopal sermons tended to be dull, and when she was in England she missed the close logical demonstration on which her New England ears had been trained. Of course Episcopalianism was no late discovery for her. She learned the Anglican catechism before the Calvinist one, and when she visited Nutplains as a child she always heard the Episcopal service, whose appeal to her must have been subtly strengthened through its connection with the thought of her adored dead mother. Though she apparently did not become an Episcopalian until after moving to Hartford in 1864, she was clearly already inclined in that direction by January 1862, when she wrote Hattie:

I not only consent to your joining the Episcopal Church as you have often expressed the desire to do but I desire it so much that I will remove any obstructs in your way. I have applied for a seat in the church in town and I shall sometimes go with you—always to sacrament because I find that service is more beneficial to me than ours.

I have found nothing to support Forrest Wilson's statement that Harriet almost turned Catholic in Rome and have no idea on what he based it. It is true, as Foster has shown,[10] that *Agnes of Sorrento* reworks *The Minister's Wooing* in Catholic terms, but though Harriet did her best to be fair to Catholicism in this novel, she brought her heroine at last to reject the cloister for the Christian home and to present her petitions directly to Christ, like "the veriest Puritan maiden that ever worshipped in a New England meeting-house." I should say that Italy must have been the last place that could attract Harriet to Catholicism, for she

felt that the spirit of the old Rome lived on in the new, and that
changing the name from Jove to Christ had accomplished little.
The Vatican pile gave her nothing of the spiritual thrill she had
derived from the cathedrals of the north. Venetian churches
she thought showy, and the theatrical sounding of the silver trumpets from the dome of St. Peter's at the elevation of the Host
contrasted most unfavorably with the simplicity of "the little
quiet upper room when Jesus broke the bread and gave the wine
to twelve simple fishermen." In 1859 she hoped for a genuine
Protestant movement in Italy "if it should please Providence to
continue to the Pope that auspicious blindness and stupidity, that
conscientious dullness of religious obstinacy, which has marked
his course hitherto," and if he should "only be foolish enough to
try launching an excommunication at Victor Emmanuel." The
next year she saw the Pope, with "great light-brown eyes" like
"a soft, sleek leopard's, as he came smiling and benignant, blessing
from right to left, with the pikes of his Swiss soldiers around
him." And she comments: "Fancy St. Paul or St. Peter with a
guard of pikemen!" The poems "The Garden of the Vatican"
and "St. Peter's Church" are distinctly hostile.

It will not do to overstress Harriet's scornful references to
relics and impostures, like "the bones of the eleven thousand
virgins, who, as the chronicle says, were slain because they would
not break their vows of chastity" ("Did the worship of Egypt
ever sink lower in horrible and loathsome idolatry?") or the
miracle-working bambino, said to have been carved of wood
from the Mount of Olives and painted by St. Luke, which struck
her as "the ugliest little wooden doll that eyes ever rested upon."
Many good Catholics would agree with her about such things.
Perhaps they might even overlook her scornful reference to "the
celebrated pervert Archdeacon Manning." But such outrageous
statements as the one in the *Key* where, having quoted Southern
churchmen on slavery, she brands the utterances "as truly Anti-
christ as the religion of the Church of Rome," would be harder
to take, and when, in *Bible Heroines*, she calls Judges "the record
of the period which may be called the Dark Ages of the Jewish

Church, even as the mediaeval days were called the Dark Ages of Christianity," one can only wish she might have lived long enough to read *Mont-Saint-Michel and Chartres.*

Fortunately, Harriet was not always so intolerant. She always granted that the Catholic Church "preserves all the essential beliefs necessary for our salvation," and though she objected to the Catholic attitude toward the Blessed Virgin on the ground that she usurps the place of Christ, so that "there comes to be at last *no God but Mary,*" she did not like Protestant depreciation of Mary either. She was pleased when the Catholic Bishop Purcell praised her geography for its unprejudiced handling of Catholic matters, and she was pleased when she found Catholic hymns in the *Plymouth Hymn Book.* She praised the church for making marriage a sacrament. She objected to New England mistresses who tried to make Protestant converts out of their Irish servant girls, advocating that instead they seek the broad basis of Christian love upon which both could stand together. "What matter, *in extremis,* whether we be called Romanist, or Protestant, or Greek, or Calvinist?" In *My Wife and I* she has an eloquent passage on the advantages of being a nun. She could even understand the converts who turned "from the unbelief coldness atheism of this age, seeking a shelter in a church strong and definite and to poetic natures very attractive." Though they had not chosen the best way, they had still chosen something better than unbelief.

The note of condescension here certainly does not need my pointing out, and I am sure many Catholics will find it more offensive than out-and-out hostility. It is, I think, typical of its author's mind. She had the peculiar notion that while Catholicism stimulated the religious nature, it did not satisfy it. Even when rebuking Americans who behave irreverently while sightseeing in Catholic churches, she declares that the devotion shown there "is an idolatrous one, and that we know a more excellent way." To one seeking assurance of salvation, as Luther did, "the whole Catholic system" was "one great and gloomy barrier standing between it and its Redeemer." She knew that the church can answer questions over which conscientious New Englanders have tortured themselves into death or insanity, and for that reason she understood the value of the confessional, but she was sure spiritual genius would be required to operate it properly, and she shrank from the idea of an intermediary stepping between God and the soul. Ellery Davenport of *The Minister's Wooing* would like to be a Catholic "if I could get my reason to sleep; but the mischief of a Calvinistic education is, it wakes up your reason, and it never will go to sleep again, and you can't take a pleasant humbug if you would," and Harriet herself declares that Catholic schools must be inferior because "it is the great aim of education to teach every person to think for himself," and because Catholic schools do not teach the Bible. Like all spiritually-minded people Harriet admired Catholic saints, who "ascended to heights of love, prayer, self-abnegation and spirituality," but when she finds a Catholic like Fénelon whom she especially admires, she is likely to find that "the excellences of his character resulted, in no instance, from the *peculiarities* of the Catholic system; but that they were the result simply of that close imitation of the character of Jesus which is inculcated alike by Catholic and Protestant."

IV

Immortality Harriet of course took for granted. "Our friends shall be restored to us in bodily form and shape, perfect in an immortal youth and bloom, never to die." That was in 1857. By 1872 she was less naïve. She now sees the doctrine of the resurrection of the body as a concession to human love. It means the preservation of individual human identity. Beyond that she does not care to push it.

Her most individual note was her decided rejection of the idea that probation ends at death. She had been distressed over the fact that the cruel doctrine of hell was so much more heavily stressed in the New Testament than in the Old, which was popularly regarded as much more severe.

The whole life of Christ, the whole of his sufferings and death was designed to show us that our Heavenly Father does not refuse to suffer for and with his children that he may redeem them. Nor do I believe the shocking cruel doctrine that his infinite patience and tenderness ends at death. Not a word of this in the Bible and I believe our Father's love pursues every soul thro all worlds, till every possible means of restoration has been tried—and that none are lost but they who resist all.

The parable of the rich man and Lazarus was not, she thought, to be taken literally, but even if it were, it would not necessitate our ruling out further probation after death: it teaches that anguish is "the immediate result of an unreligious sensual selfish life . . . but it does not forbid the idea that there as here anguish may be salutary and lead to a better life." She is not a Universalist, but she is obviously doing her best to have as few lost as possible.

I do not . . . see any evidence in the Bible that anybody at death goes directly to the states known as Hell or Heaven. It is remarkable that the doom of having gone to Hell so freely pronounced by theologians over this or that sinner is *never* pronounced of any one person in the Bible. Even Judas is simply said to have gone to his own place. It is only human imagination that changes that indefinite expression into Hell.

Keen interest in the future life lies next door to occultism, and one would not have to read far in Mrs. Stowe without becoming aware of her curiosity about psychic phenomena. Perhaps the most abundant evidence occurs in the *Oldtown Fireside Stories,* several of which are ghost stories, but there are ghosts in the novels also [11] and suggestions of the same in the poems. As Jim Larned says, "folks may say what they're a mind to: there are things that there's no sort o' way o' countin' for—things you've jist got to say, 'well, here's suthin' to work that I don't know nothin' about.'" Nor is this utterly "unnatural," for "there are times and tones and moods of nature that make all the vulgar, daily real seem shadowy, vague, and supernatural, as if the outlines of this hard material present were fading into the invisible and unknown." This was Harriet's personal experience at times. "I *do* have hopes of inexpressible beauty and sweetness, and of late they come oftener and oftener,—they come between dawn and daylight when I seem to be asleep and am not, but am conscious as near to God—*almost* as I could ask." This is the note she strikes in her poems:

> It lies around us like a cloud,
>   A world we do not see;
> Yet the sweet closing of an eye
>   May bring us there to be.

And again:

> The veil between this world and that to come
> Grows tremulous and quivers with their breath;
> Dimly we hear their voices, see their hands,
> Inviting us to the release of death.

And, most directly and characteristically of all, in the only poem of Harriet's that can really be said to have lived:

> Still, still with Thee, when purple morning breaketh,
>   When the bird waketh and the shadows flee;
> Fairer than morning, lovelier than the daylight,
>   Dawns the sweet consciousness, *I am with Thee!*

That was what she really wanted from life, and when the spiritualist movement really got under way during her lifetime, she could hardly have been expected to turn away, especially since, having lived with Calvin, it was not possible for her to accept the easy, superficial explanation that all the phenomena were the product of trickery. "Tell that to the Marines!" she wrote Fields with quite delightful vulgarity. "It is quite too late in the day to tell it to sensible folks who have seen as much as I have, and as you or Annie has, for all you keep still about it—like the rest of us. That cock won't fight."

Yet she knew that incidental trickery might well appear, and she guarded herself carefully against it. Publicly she never wished to be committed. Sometimes the puerility of what purported to be messages from the dead disgusted her. "If the future life is so weary, stale, flat, and unprofitable as we might infer from these readings, one would have reason to deplore an immortality from which no suicide could give an outlet." In other moods she realized that such doubts did not reach to the heart of the question: "I do not know of any reason why there should not be as many foolish virgins in the future state as in this." She was brave enough to write to the rationalistic George Eliot about an experiment in planchette which purported to be guided by the spirit of Charlotte Brontë. She also told her that when grief-stricken persons came to her, she always told them that "this field is a dangerous one for you with your weakened nerves and suffering heart to explore. It is a *real* force but an *unknown*, unregulated one, and one which in the present state of knowledge would be unsafe for you to trust yourself to." For herself, she writes again, "*I* do not need their signs or wonders. I do not ask to see or speak to *my* lost ones. *My God* is my ever present medium of communication with the unseen, and communion with Him is the firmest of realities to me." And she adds that spiritualism "is full of that which leads to danger. Alas is there *any*thing in our present mortal state that is not?" Yet "of the reality of the facts there can be no manner of doubt," and the dogmatic, superior scorn of the scientists achieves nothing except to warn off the very people who could investigate the phenomena in a discriminating, responsible fashion.

The caution (and the New England common sense) are obvious here. So is the unwillingness to be seduced into accepting anything not quite reconcilable with Christianity. But the appeal is even more obvious. "I cannot get over the feeling that the souls of the dead do somehow connect themselves with the places of their former habitation, and that the hush and thrill of spirit which we feel in them may be owing to the overshadowing presence of the invisible." Sometimes she would tell herself and others that spiritualism was an unsafe basis upon which to build a religion but still a perfectly legitimate subject for scientific investigation. And sometimes, writing to a scientific man like Oliver Wendell

Holmes, she would express the belief "that the marvels of spiritualism are natural, and not supernatural, phenomena,—an uncommon working of natural laws." The one thing she could not do was to deny the phenomena or surrender her interest in them.[12]

V

Science never frightened Harriet Beecher Stowe. Her brother was one of the first prominent American clergymen openly and boldly to accept the evolutionary hypothesis and to insist that it was not irreconcilable with a spiritual interpretation of life; in her way his sister was equally courageous.[13] Of course she was never in any danger of becoming a materialist, for as she found physical nature hard and cruel, so she believed also that "the *mere* physical, scientific view of man leads directly to inhumanity." She even once called Agassiz a "dear old pig headed philosopher" because he was not open-minded about planchette. But she never denied the close interrelationship between the body and the soul, and she was never in danger of supposing that one could be strengthened by abusing the other.

One reads the histories of St. Theresa, John of the Cross, and Francis de Sales with a mixture of admiration and pain. One cannot help regretting that these glorious beings wasted so much of their strength in wrestling down and destroying those laws of their physical nature which might have been their strongest support in their quest of holiness.

She even admits that there are spiritual crises in which devotional exercises are a hindrance and not a help. "What the soul wants is to be distracted for a while,—to be taken out of its old grooves of thought, and run upon entirely new ones." I do not recall that Harriet anywhere mentions Whitman, but if she could have got around what I suppose would have seemed to her the exaggerated sexuality of *Leaves of Grass,* the two might have found themselves not so far apart. As it was, she was probably more in conscious harmony with Thomas Wentworth Higginson, whose famous *Atlantic* essay, "Saints and Their Bodies," reprinted in his *Outdoor Papers* (1863), was but the opening gun in a gallant, lifelong campaign to break down the curious idea that "physical vigor and spiritual sanctity are incompatible" and which contributed so importantly to the physical culture movement in America. "Guarantee to Americans health," cried Higginson, "and Mrs. Stowe cannot frighten them with all the prophecies of *Dred*; but when her sister Catharine informs us that in all the vast female acquaintance of the Beecher family, there are not a dozen healthy women, one is a little tempted to despair of the republic."

Interest in science did not enter the Beecher family with Henry Ward. "Who scrubs a floor to the glory of God/Makes that and the action fine." But the old New England bluestocking cultivated her mind as well as her heart and read Greek while she rocked the cradle. How quaint and strangely touching is Roxana's letter to her sister-in-law Esther Beecher:

Mary has, I suppose, told you of the discovery that the fixed alkalies are metallic oxides. I first saw the notice in the *Christian Observer*. I have since seen it in an *Edinburgh Review*. The former mentioned that the metals have been obtained by means of the galvanic battery; the latter mentions another, and, they say, better mode.

And she adds, "I think this is all the knowledge I have obtained in the whole circle of arts and sciences of late; if you have been more fortunate, pray let me reap the benefit." Esther, too, "had read on all subjects—chemistry, philosophy, physiology, but especially on natural history, where her anecdotes were inexhaustible"; she once told a sick child "*nineteen rat stories* all in a string!" which would be quite enough to make some children sicker. And Lyman himself sometimes shocked despairing religious inquirers "by a series of questions as to *air, exercise, diet*, such as are generally the introductory examinations of a physician."

The American Woman's Home, which Harriet wrote with her sister Catharine, is religiously motivated throughout, but it is both scientific and technical in its method, based upon and summarizing current scientific knowledge, whether always correctly or

not I cannot say. Harriet recognized the dominance of temperament too, even in religious matters, and saw human nature as
molded by circumstances. The unpleasant Crab Smith and his
unlovely sister are the products of social forces, and good humor
may be the product of a person's bodily make-up rather than a
Christian virtue. Unpleasant home conditions drive men outside
to vice, and a badly ventilated church makes the finest sermon
ineffectual. "A sermon on oxygen, if one had a preacher who
understood the subject, might do more to repress sin than the
most orthodox discourse to show when and how and why sin
came." She can accept a material explanation for a spiritual
change, and it does not shock her to find the source of what
seems like a gift of prophecy in women in their nervous intensity.
"It is often held to be a medical fact that morbid appetites are
the blind cry of nature for something needed in the bodily system
which is lacking." Her praise of good health in her *Chimney-
Corner* paper "Bodily Religion: A Sermon on Good Health" is
not Christian Science, but it comes close enough in some particulars to remind us that Mrs. Eddy too revolted wholesomely
against that glorification of bodily weakness which both Higginson and Harriet excoriated:

The hygienic teachings of the New Testament have never been sufficiently understood. The basis of them lies in the solemn declaration,
that our bodies are to be temples of the Holy Spirit, and that all abuse
of them is of the nature of sacrilege. . . . The doctrine of the resurrection of the body, and its physical immortality, sets the last crown of
honor upon it. That bodily system which God declared worthy to be
gathered back from the dust of the grave, and re-created, as the soul's
immortal companion, must necessarily be dear and precious in the eyes
of its Creator. The one passage in the New Testament in which it is
spoken of disparagingly is where Paul contrasts it with the brighter
glory of what is to come: "He shall change our vile bodies, that they
may be fashioned like his glorious body." From the passage has come
abundance of reviling of the physical system. Memoirs of good men
are full of abuse of it, as the clog, the load, the burden, the chain. It is
spoken of as pollution, as corruption,—in short, one would think that
the Creator had imitated the cruelty of some Oriental despots who

had been known to chain a festering corpse to a living body. Accordingly, the memoirs of these pious men are also mournful records of slow suicide, wrought by the persistent neglect of the most necessary and important laws of the bodily system; and the body, outraged and downtrodden, has turned traitor to the soul, and played the adversary with fearful power. Who can tell the countless temptations to evil which flew in from a neglected, disordered, deranged nervous system,— temptations to anger, to irritability, to selfishness, to every kind of sin of appetite and passion? No wonder that the poor soul longs for the hour of release from such a companion.

But that human body which God declares expressly was made to be the temple of the Holy Spirit, which he considers worthy to be perpetuated by a resurrection and an immortal existence, cannot be intended to be a clog and a hindrance to spiritual advancement. A perfect body, working in perfect tune and time, would open glimpses of happiness to the soul approaching the joys we hope for in heaven. It is only through the images of things which our bodily senses have taught us, that we can form any conception of that future bliss; and the more perfect these senses, the more perfect our conceptions must be.

This seems to me a remarkable passage and, despite the fragments of ancient modes of thinking which cling to it here and there, a remarkable one, but Harriet shows even more boldly and attractively in an unpublished letter to her daughter Hattie: [14]

As long as we are in mortal bodies the view of things spiritual must always be subject to cloud and eclipse and when we put up our telescope to see the heavenly bodies some crawling thing or other will come between us and them and appear a magnified monster shutting out their beauty.

Hattie had apparently said that she hated God, but Harriet met even this without hysteria:

No poor suffering child, you do *not* hate your Father in Heaven any more than you do me and the horrible image that rises before your mind and which you think you hate is the fly that has crept between the glasses of the telescope and is magnified as a monster.

It was from just such mental weariness, the result of inward sorrow that you sometimes thought *me* your loving mother cold and estranged and wanted to go away from me.... Turn from the false image which you call God and justly hate to the real God which manifests itself to you in your mother's heart. No cold no selfish no unfeeling being could ever have made me capable of what I feel for you my darling— a mother's love is God revealed.

She adds:

I shall no more press you my dear, I will not weary you—neither am I alarmed nor astonished as if some strange thing happened to you. The kind good Friend who gave *me* to you will bring you out all clear.

And finally:

Do not blame yourself for any thing—do not force yourself, endeavor to do what is easiest to you—above all have faith in

Your affectionate
Mother

Perhaps there is a touch of smugness here, along with Harriet's familiar glorification of motherhood. But there is also enough insight and charity to excuse far more serious sins than she ever dreamed of committing.

VI

The heart of Harriet's religion, like Henry Ward's, was a personal devotion to Christ, and to Christ conceived as loving a man "in his sins for the sake of helping him out of them." "I am not in sympathy alone with *the Church*," said Beecher, "but with *the whole human family*." And Harriet herself said, "I feel that I love God,—that is, that I love Christ," and again, of her brother and herself, "He and I are Christ-worshippers, adoring Him as the Image of the Invisible God." Beecher even prayed to Christ, finding in him a close reality he could not find in the idea of God, and telling those who came to him from Unitarian instruction that they too prayed to Christ without knowing it because God was real to them only as he was revealed in Christ. As we have seen, Harriet criticized Roman Catholics for permitting Mary to swallow up the Trinity. It might perhaps be fairly retorted that she herself permitted the Second Person to absorb the other two.

Since Jesus Christ as men knew him was a man, some may find a species of idolatry in this, but begging all question of the Divinity of Christ, I do not believe Harriet would have been greatly disturbed by this, for she believed that God's character can only be inferred from the best which exists in human character (like Browning in "Saul," she argues that God could not possibly create a being greater than Himself), and Christ being the best and greatest of men, he therefore becomes the supreme revelation of God. In working out her interpretation of Christ, she made much use of Geikie, Farrar, and other scholars, but her basic reliance was upon her own religious experience.

For who is this Jesus? Not a man who died eighteen hundred years ago; but a living God, who claims at this moment to be Prince of the kings of the earth—to be the great reigning and working force, who must reign till he hath put all things under his feet.

Or, as she once put it to Calvin:

He is so infinitely, so eternally, so inexpressibly good, so trustworthy, so beautiful, so glorious—it is such a joy to worship Him, to give up one's self and take him instead, I am comforted for being such a poor unworthy wretch by thinking of what He is. Of myself I will not glory, but of Him. Oh, who can say what glory there is in Him. How little He is known, how few know how endless is his goodness, his tenderness, his infinite endless generosity to those who trust Him. How little do they know how truly indulgent He is, what perfect rest is his service, what perfect freedom his yoke.

In 1876 she wrote George Eliot that it was now fifty years since Christ

became a living presence to me and ever since He has been the Inspirer Consoler and Strength of my life, and to read of those who struggle for goodness without knowing *him* is painful to me as to read of those who die of hunger when there is bread enough and to spare. Christ is my Life—all I ever have been able to do or suffer, all my hope for the poor and oppressed has been my feeling sense of his living presence and that He is ruling all things.

And in 1885 she added: "For you too dear I believe in the infinite love tho perhaps thro your tears you do not see Him."

There is only one type of composition to which such utterances can possibly be compared, and that is the love letter. The Beecher rebellion against Calvinism was the rebellion of the heart. Lyman himself yearned over Byron and Napoleon and shed tears over Milton's Satan. Henry Ward never preached anything but God's love, and Harriet's novels exemplify it again and again. There are blessed spirits in them like Harry and Tina Perceval in *Oldtown Folks* who recognize it almost instinctively and consequently bypass the Calvinistic nightmare altogether.

His conclusions were all intuitions.... In him was seen the beginning of that great reaction which took place largely in the young mind of New England against the tyranny of mere logical methods as applied to the ascertainment of moral truths.

Esther in the same novel is less fortunate, and the old Edwardian logic nearly kills her, but even she is finally saved by love. In *The Minister's Wooing* an ignorant slave woman Candace explains it all to Mrs. Marvyn. Candace would not have been capable of Catharine Beecher's logical refutation of Edwards, but she had no need for it either. Though she does not pretend to understand it all, she knows that "dar's a drefful mistake somewhar," as indeed there was. "Why, Jesus didn't die for nothin',—all dat love ain't gwine to be wasted. De 'lect is more 'n you or I knows, honey!" But always and everywhere it was love, the love of a God who can help suffering humanity because He is a suffering God. And it was not only the whole world that He had in His hands, but as Henry Adams was to perceive in the case of the Virgin of Chartres, He "knows each one of us by name," and none of us is a means toward an end but each is an end in himself and infinitely precious in His sight. In 1884 she wanted Calvin to take a message to a bereaved woman that Christ "loves her *personally* —feels for her individually, that he loves her even as she loved the child and that he will hereafter show her the reason why he has done this."

Love—love—love. "The inconceivable loveliness of Christ!" She found it when she was a child. She kept reaffirming it until she died. "I love everybody," she said in her pitiful old age. The last words she spoke on earth, to her Irish nurse, were "I love you." Then she went away from the helpless, broken lovers of earth into the Love that can never be frustrated or denied and that can never die.

NOTES

INTRODUCTION

1 "Uncle Tom's Measure," *NR*, LXXVI (1933), 212-13. Young recorded that he grew up in the South without knowing the book or

knowing anybody who had read it. Now, having read it himself, he could find few, North or South, who had read it, which, in view of its continuing sales and circulation, would indicate that his acquaintance was strangely limited. Though a drama critic by profession, he had never seen it on the stage either. When he did read the book he found the death of Eva funnier than anything in *Three Weeks*, and he was disappointed in Eliza's escape because he had expected bloodhounds. But he rather liked the brutal and "Gothic" ending, and he did not deny that in concentrating on the menace of slavery to the integrity of the family and stressing the iniquity of a system which permitted human beings to pass under the control of brutal masters, Mrs. Stowe had struck sources of irresistible emotional appeal.

2   William Sloane Associates.

3   *Love and Death in the American Novel* (Criterion Books, 1960).

4   *New Statesman*, LXIV (1962), 490.

5   *Spectator*, CCVIII (1962), 761.

BIOGRAPHY

1   The letters from Hattie Stowe, who accompanied her mother, to her twin sister Eliza, in WA, give many interesting details of the tour.

2   According to Mott also, *UTC* sold 50,000 copies during its first eight weeks and 120,000 by November. "By January 1853 the figure was 200,000 copies for the United States, according to *Putnam's Monthly*, with thirty editions in England and Scotland, two translations in French, and one in German." See his *A History of American Magazines, 1850-1865* (HUP, 1938). Sampson Low estimated the sales in England and her possessions as 1,500,000 during the first year and a half. In 1887 Florine Thayer McCray stated that the novel was selling 1,500 copies a month. In 1951 David Dempsey reported that the New York Public Library had replaced forty worn-out copies during 1950. On March 18, 1962, *The New York Times Book Review* reported that 21,342 copies had been sold during 1961 in the United States, in eight different editions. Edmund Wilson was surely in error when he asserted, in *Patriotic Gore*, p. 3, that *UTC* had been out of print at the time it appeared in "The Modern Library" in 1948. It is the belief of the authorized publishers, Houghton Mifflin Company,

as expressed in a letter of Priscilla C. Smith to me, December 11, 1963, that the firm has never allowed the book to go out of print since taking it over in 1862. Miss Smith further stated that on November 1, 1955, HM's total sales figures on *UTC* stood at 1,017,040. It must be remembered that the novel has been issued by many other American publishers; one Chicago firm alone issued 740,000 copies.

3   In 1896 Rogers had a *UTC* teaspoon. Uncle Tom and the cabin were in the bowl, with Topsy, Eva, and Harriet herself on the handle, and her autograph on the back. Along with Sherlock Holmes, the great Dickens characters, and a few others, the people of this book have also had a long life in cartoons and advertisements. In 1919 the great Hearst cartoonist F. Opper, creator of "Happy Hooligan," celebrated the housing shortage with a picture of Uncle Tom renting his cabin to a wealthy couple at $200 a month while he moved out to the dog house, and the displaced canine queried disconsolately, "Where do I go from here?" In the 1930's the novel still had enough vogue in Germany to cause the Nazis to ban it "because it runs counter to our racial ideals," and in 1940 the Atlanta author of *Gone With the Wind* took a crack at it, inspiring Lyman Beecher Stowe to suggest that she had never read it. Some Southerners have admired the book greatly. Joel Chandler Harris, creator of Uncle Remus, maintained that Mrs. Stowe defended "the system she intended to attack." "She declaimed . . . against the possibilities of slavery, but something or other she found in it attracted her sympathy, so that the spirit and purpose of her book is almost entirely different from what it was intended to be." "All the worthy and beautiful characters in her book —Uncle Tom, little Eva, the beloved Master, and the rest—are the products of the system that the text of the book is all the time condemning." See Julia Collier Harris, ed., *Joel Chandler Harris, Editor and Essayist* (University of North Carolina Press, 1931). There is a wry variation of this in Agnes Repplier's amusing essay, "Books That Have Hindered Me," in her *Points of View* (HM, 1891). On the other hand, Leslie Fiedler has recorded how, as a boy, he got from *UTC*, the first book he ever bought with his own money, and read and wept over in secret, the beginning of his implacable opposition to racial discrimination. See *No! in Thunder: Essays on Myth and Literature* (Beacon Press, 1960).

4   According to Richard Moody, *UTC* was under canvas as early as 1854, and there were between 400 and 500 troupes operating in the

'nineties. Troupes might be as small as three or as large as fifty persons, with a wide variety of animals. In the 'eighties there were "Ideal Double Mammoth" shows; sometimes characters were tripled or quadrupled; there was even a nine-act version, anticipating *Strange Interlude*. The recent history of *UTC* in the theater has abounded in contradictions surpassing the fantastic and bordering on the insane. In 1942 Billy Bryant visited New York City with a showboat troupe and failed. In 1945 Negro leaders of Bridgeport, Conn., supported by queerly-assorted bedfellows drawn from the Communist Party and "the local pastor's association," suppressed a musical version, with the American Civil Liberties Union protesting. Another production starring Barbara Bel Geddes was reported suppressed at Arden, Del., in 1952. Yet Uncle Tom has had fresh triumphs in our time, some of them of a distinctly odd variety. In 1932 a version produced by the Moscow Second Art Theater stressed the woes of the Negro, made Topsy Eliza's daughter, saved Eva's life, and omitted all the religion. In 1933 The Players achieved a very successful revival of the Aiken version, revised by A. E. Thomas. In 1935 e. e. cummings's ballet scenario *Tom* appeared. In 1962 a new opera by Luigi Ferrari Trecate, *La Capanna dello Zio Tom*, based partly on Negro spirituals, was staged in Rome. Current theatergoers will not need to be reminded of the Uncle Tom ballet in the Rodgers and Hammerstein musical, *The King and I* (1951), based on Margaret Landon's book, *Anna and the King of Siam*. Anne Harriette Leonowens was herself an Uncle Tom enthusiast; she introduced the book to one of the king's wives, who translated it into her own language, and whose whole life was influenced by it. The Huntington Library has a letter from Mrs. Stowe to Mrs. Fields in which Harriet tries to get information concerning Mrs. Leonowens and her use of *UTC* in Siam. (See also the letter from Mrs. Leonowens in "RE," Vol. I, p. lxxxviii.) The first film production was Edwin S. Porter's one-reeler for Edison in 1903. In 1918 Paramount did a feature production, with Marguerite Clark playing both Topsy and Eva, and in 1927 there was an elaborate production from Universal, but there has been no sound version. By far the most continuous use of *UTC* in the modern theater, however, has been that of the Duncan Sisters, who, in 1923, turned the story into a musical comedy, *Topsy and Eva*, with book by Catherine Chisholm Cushing and music by themselves. Its greatest success was in Chicago, where it ran for more than a year and made its stars the toast of the town, but they continued to play the same characters in vaudeville and night club engagements across the world until Rosetta was killed in an auto crash late in 1959. The success of these remarkable performers was due primarily to their ability to "kid" their ancient materials and at the same time treat the characters involved with charm, compassion, and understanding. Kenyon Nicholson's play, *Eva the Fifth* (1928) deals with a *Tom* troupe. In 1943 Helen Hayes had a great success in *Harriet*, a biographical play about Mrs. Stowe by Colin Clements and Florence Ryerson, and in 1947 a play by Ian Hay, *Hattie Stowe*, was acted at the Embassy Theater, London.

5 Syracuse University has a letter to "Dear Sir," not in Harriet's hand, dated Oct. 25, 1852, which shows well how she went about gathering materials for the Key.

6 See Ruth Suckow, "An Almost Lost American Classic," *College English*, XIV (1953), 315-25.

7 Those who believe these novels strike a radically new note in Harriet's work have not taken her serials into account. Much of *Pink and White Tyranny* was anticipated in "The Only Daughter," *Godey's Lady's Book*, XVIII (1839), 115-22. In "Olympiana," *Godey's*, XVIII (1839), 241-3, she presented the Greek gods in a fashionable, frivolous parlor discussion.

Chapter I: THE DAUGHTER

1 His sister.

2 At some point every writer confronts the Freudian ordeal. Harriet met it with Janet A. Emig, "The Flower in the Cleft: The Writings of Harriet Beecher Stowe," *Bulletin of the Historical and Philosophical Society of Ohio*, XXI (1963), 223-38, which concerns itself mainly with the implications the author can read into Harriet's treatment of fathers, mothers, and children in her fiction, all about as convincingly done as such things generally are.

Chapter II: THE SISTER

1 For Thomas K. Beecher, see, besides Lyman Beecher Stowe, *Saints, Sinners and Beechers*, the intimate portrait in Max Eastman, *Heroes I Have Known* (Simon and Schuster, 1942).

2   Kenneth R. Andrews, *Nook Farm: Mark Twain's Hartford Circle* (HUP, 1950), p. 56. This book contains the best account of Isabella Hooker available.

3   Milestones on her way were *Letters on the Difficulties of Religion* (1836) and *Common Sense Applied to Religion; or, The Bible and the People* (1857). For a good popular account of the matter (and of Alexander Fisher), see Martha Bacon, "Miss Beecher in Hell," *AH*, Vol. XIV, No. 1, December 1962, pp. 28-31, 102-5.

4   When J. C. Derby asked Henry Ward Beecher whether he had read all the books written by members of his family, he replied, "I have made it a rule of my life to read none of the writings of my relatives, and with two or three exceptions have adhered to that rule." According to Mrs. Beecher's account to Edward Bok, her husband never read serials, but did read *UTC* in book form as soon as it appeared, all one day and through the evening, then threw it down saying, "There, I've done it! But if Hattie Stowe ever writes anything more like that, I'll—well! she has nearly killed me."

5   There is, however, a curious letter of Harriet's to Henry, written from Mandarin, March 4, 1873 (WA), about some matter which had provoked him: "Now, the old lesson of forgiving enemies Henry you have got pretty perfect. That page is thumbed and dog's eared; the Devil has about given you up on that track." If he would be perfect, she would have him also learn to forgive awkward friends. "Scripture nowhere says 'Love your friends' and somebody must be sworn at or we shall burst." She continues: "We are old Henry— our mother is waiting for her children to take us home. Let nothing separate the love that should unite us to her and to them. We have *got to bear with each other*—a little while and we shall be glad of every kind word said and every harsh one repressed."

6   *Henry Ward Beecher, An American Portrait* (George H. Doran Company, 1927).

7   Alfred A. Knopf, 1954.

8   The fullest account of Victoria Woodhull's career is in a distinctly popular book by Emanie Sachs, *The Terrible Siren* (H, 1928).

9   Harriet wrote, presumably to Mrs. Fields, Dec. 24, 1872: "By the bye in reply to what you said, Tilton *does* deny the story in the most indignant manner.... But all parties advise that no public notice be taken of a slander from such a source. You see what a precedent it would be if women of that class could throw into the community

such stories about respectable people and call on them to disprove them. What man or woman would be safe from the most loathsome persecution." On September 9, 1874 Harriet wrote Leonard Bacon that she perceived danger in a mere man trying to be wholly Christlike toward his enemies. The Library of Congress has a very interesting letter from Mandarin, dated merely "Jan. 28," in which Harriet speaks of a time when Henry had bravely and lovingly upheld his wife in years when "thro physical causes she was in very trying state, and also how his patience and love had guided her into serene waters." Eunice "always had a woman's instinctive hatred of Bowen and Tilton." If she was ever jealous, it was not of Mrs. Tilton but of Tilton himself, who tried to monopolize Henry's time and attention.

10   See Lyman Abbott, *Henry Ward Beecher* (HM, 1903) and "Henry Ward Beecher, Prophet of the Love of God," in *Silhouettes of My Contemporaries* (D, 1921).

11   The owner of *The Independent*, who is said to have believed, on the basis of an alleged deathbed confession of his late wife, that Beecher had committed adultery with her.

Chapter III: THE WIFE

1   *Mark Twain's Autobiography* (H, 1924), II, 243.

2   Edmund Wilson has quoted from some of them in *Patriotic Gore*.

3   Calvin admitted an appetite for liquor and pretty girls but does not seem to have got into trouble on either count. His real temptations were food and sloth. In 1869 Harriet sent greetings through Elizabeth Agassiz to a lady "whose dark eyes made a deep impression on the too susceptible heart of my poor Rabbi." A few days later she says that a "susceptibility to female charms appears to increase with years with him." This does not sound like a worried woman. But in September 1870 she writes Calvin himself:

Dr. Taylor in a letter says that he thinks there is nothing in your constitution that would prevent your being a long lived cheerful and happy man.

He says it is only you have too great an appetite which gets an amount of food into your system which there is not enough brain force to dispose of. He says the secret of Henry's great power of work is his being so small a consumer that every particle is used up entirely and there is no *burden* on the system.... You have practiced the most wonderful self control in respect to all other appetites, few men have done as much, and perhaps God has appointed you to vanquish this last one as the last step to victory.

Dr. Taylor's physiology seems to have been as odd as Harriet's. This was not the only connection in which she had held up Henry as a model to her husband.

4 *Chapters from a Life* (HM, 1896). Forrest Wilson's idea, inexplicably derived from this book, that Elizabeth Stuart Phelps did not like Mrs. Stowe, is one of the curiosities of criticism.

5 "RE," VIII.

CHAPTER IV: THE MOTHER

1 "RE," XV.

2 Chapter XX. There is an interesting anticipation of *Tom Sawyer* in this same chapter, when Harry is punished by his grandmother for Bill's misdemeanor. "Well, let it stand for something you did do, then; you do bad things enough that you ain't whipped for, any day."

3 See C. E. Stowe, *The Life of HBS*, pp. 320-23, and consider the possible references to Henry in the following poems: "The Crocus," " 'Only a Year,' " "Below," "Above."

4 *Our Charley and the Stories Told Him* (1858). See "RE," XVI.

5 Apparently, too, it is Charley that Elizabeth Stuart Phelps guardedly refers to in her comments on Mrs. Stowe's prowess in prayer, in *Chapters from a Life*, pp. 139-40.

6 As in her letter of February 4, 1881: "I protest with all the energy of my heart and soul against your joining the camp of the Unitarians, for altho there are many good soldiers and servants of Christ in it yet *as a whole*, it is a little band dissociated from the great body of Christ's church—Latin, Greek, Anglican and American.... Then the name covers every form of dissent and unbelief down to that of men like Savage who believe no more in Christ than a Jewish Rabbi."

7 Fred's spelling, in all his letters, is too precious to be altered.

8 *Saints, Sinners and Beechers*, facing p. 224.

Chapter V: THE FRIEND

1   See her eloquent denunciation of these barbarians in *Palmetto Leaves*, "RE," IV, 463-4.

2   Mary B. Claflin, *Under the Old Elms* (Crowell, 1895).

3   "RE," XIV.

4   She may have failed Delia Bacon in friendship. See Vivian C. Hopkins, *Prodigal Puritan: A Life of Delia Bacon* (HUP, 1959).

5   Cf. her letter to James T. Fields, Nov. 30, 1881 (Huntington): "I am come to those years where I may hope before long to join that circle of friends beyond the river that is every year growing larger and more inviting. All the companions of my early youth with but here and there an exception are there and some of my children. Of four sons but one is now living—living *here* I mean. I trust to find them all again."

6   On her rather amusing contacts and lack of contacts with Queen Victoria, too complicated to summarize here, see Forrest Wilson, *Crusader in Crinoline*, pp. 420-23.

7   Worthington C. Ford, ed., *Letters of Henry Adams, 1858-1891* (HM, 1930), p. 168.

8   See Ralph Milbanke, Earl of Lovelace, *Astarte*...New Edition...ed. by Mary Countess of Lovelace (London, Christophers, 1921), and cf. Samuel C. Chew, *Byron in England* (London, John Murray, 1924). In "Mark Twain and the Byron Scandal," *AL*, XXX (1959), 467-85, Paul Baender argues that Mark Twain wrote six editorials in the Buffalo *Express*, beginning August 24, 1869. The first declares: "Receiving the facts as she did, in the manner she did, from Lady Byron, it was her duty to make them public, especially since the publication of the memoir of Byron's most notorious mistress, with its impudent slander of his wife. But she ought to have presented them, and must yet give them, more fully and satisfactorily." The editorial argues further that the story is probably true: Lady Byron was a reliable witness and the act alleged perfectly credible in view of what was known about Byron. *"The True Story"* of Mrs. Stowe by "Outis" (1869) contends that Mrs. Stowe's story is to be read ironically. *The True Story of Mrs. Shakespeare's Life* (1869) burlesques Harriet's article elaborately, but since there are no real parallels between Shakespeare and Byron, or between Lady Byron and Mrs.

Shakespeare, it does not really make a point, though it is sometimes amusing.

9 M. A. DeWolfe Howe, ed., *New Letters of James Russell Lowell* (H, 1932), p. 147.

10 There are characteristic inaccuracies in Harriet's account of the circumstances preceding the publication of her article, which do not justify Forrest Wilson's somewhat melodramatic account in *Crusader in Crinoline*, Book VI. Charles H. Foster has already dealt with this matter admirably in *The Rungless Ladder*, Ch. IX, though his refutation is ignored by Richard D. Altick, in his rather naïve discussion in *The Art of Literary Research* (Norton, 1963), pp. 42-3.

11 They have not yet done so and probably never will. In *The Pilgrim of Eternity* (Doran, 1925), John Drinkwater devoted about 100 pages to the problem, concluding that no conclusion was possible. Even the latest word on the subject, Malcolm Elwin's *Lord Byron's Wife* (Harcourt, 1962), which very likely contains all the evidence we shall ever have, does not settle the controversy.

12 She quotes Tom Moore's suggestion to this effect but dismisses it without consideration. *Lady Byron Vindicated*, pp. 336-7.

CHAPTER VI: THE WOMAN

1 The clothes she wore for her readings were apparently an exception. "She looked beautifully," writes Gail Hamilton, "was richly dressed, in black satin Venice lace—hair in double rolls, arching her forehead, black lace draped about her shoulders."

2 Made in England, 1853. Now in WA.

3 W. D. Howells, *Literary Friends and Acquaintance* (H, 1900), p. 140.

4 *Mark Twain's Autobiography*, II, 243.

5 Patrick Braybrooke, *Great Children in Literature* (London, Alston Rivers, n.d.) shows that Eva is not to be summed up in a phrase: "her approach to life is a combination of the intellect with her emotions"; "she is never priggish"; "she is a practical Christian without being an unpractical dreamer," "one of those very rare people who induce in others a new point of view."

6 "Mrs. Marvyn had known all the story of her son's love, and to no other woman would she have been willing to resign him; but her love to Mary was so deep that she thought of his union with her

more as gaining a daughter than losing a son." *The Minister's Wooing*, Ch. XVII. I am sorry to find no suggestion that Harriet understood the horrifying implications of this selective "momism."

7   See, too, "The Yankee Girl," *Token and Atlantic Souvenir*, 1842, which glorifies a New Hampshire village girl as rose laurel, "whose root asks neither garden-bed nor gardener's care, but will take for itself stronghold where there is a handful of earth in the cleft of a rock, whose polished leaf shakes green and cheerful over the snows of the keenest winter." (English women are lilies, French "the ever bright and varying tulip," Spanish and Italian "the full moss rose: the richest and most voluptuous of flowers.") She does hard physical work but has the Yankee interest in learning and the pertness which often attracted her creator. She rejects the earl who offers for her while tending an injured companion, encourages a local swain to go to college and become a lawyer, waits for him, finally weds him and lives in Boston.

8   Harriet did have a certain sympathy for "cute" boys, matching her interest in pert girls; see James Benton in her first piece of writing of any consequence, "Uncle Lot," in "RE," XIV. Jim Fellows in *We and Our Neighbors* and Cap'n Kittredge of *The Pearl of Orr's Island* display similar characteristics; both are treated sympathetically.

9   *NR*, CXLVIII, June 29, 1963, pp. 20-21.

10   Edited by Ben Ames Williams (HM, 1950).

11   The best study of this aspect of slavery is in Severn Duvall, "*UTC*: The Sinister Side of the Patriarchy," *NEQ*, XXXVI (1963), 13-22.

12   "RE," XVI.

13   Ruth E. Finley, *The Lady of Godey's* (L, 1931).

14   On February 1, 1881, Harriet acknowledged a letter from "dear Lillie" about George Eliot's having "entered into light." "I am quite sure that tho *intellectually* mistaken and bewildered she was one of Christ's straying ones whom he has promised to look up—bring home. Her heart was right and when that is right it is easy to explain the mistakes of the head. Tried by every one of the beatitudes she was 'blessed'—and it is worthy of remark that it is to *dispositions* not to beliefs those blessings are promised. I have a favorite passage in the prophecies Ezekiel 34: 12-27 that I think relates to all bewildered sheep of Christ who have lost their way in the fog and mists that every once in a while envelop an era, such as that of scepticism in

our day." She goes on to say that she does not blame George Eliot for having married John Walter Cross and wonders whether Lillie knows whether there was ever "any form of marriage" between her and Lewes. "That they thought themselves rightfully married I have no doubt—that in all things she was to him a true and faithful wife, a mother to his children I doubt not—if you can shed any light on this one point, do." In a smaller way, Harriet met a similar test in her contacts with Mrs. Henry M. Field, who had been the Henriette Deluzy-Desportes of the Praslin murder case in Paris. She was, of course, not involved in the murder; whether she had, in any sense, sustained improper (or even indiscreet) relations with the Duke (who hacked his wife to death) is unknown and depends entirely upon how one interprets highly ambiguous evidence. Joseph Shearing's novel, *Forget-Me-Not* (1932), known in this country as *Lucile Cléry, A Woman of Intrigue* and later as *The Strange Case of Lucile Cléry*, is postulated on the hypothesis of guilt, Rachel Field's *All This and Heaven Too* (1938) on that of innocence. For a factual account, see William Roughead, *The Seamy Side* (Cassell, 1938); for Hawthorne's possible use of the case in *The Marble Faun*, see Edward Wagenknecht, *Cavalcade of the American Novel* (Ht, 1952), pp. 49-50, n. 23. Harriet loved Henriette, not only "as she charmed and amused and entertained me," but "as a woman of true courage and principle, a woman of high honor, who not only saw the right clearly, but had courage to do it under most difficult circumstances." This is from a long letter written after Henriette's death, included in the book which gives the fullest account of her: *Home Sketches in France and Other Papers*, by the late Mrs. Henry M. Field, with Some Notices of Her Life and Character (Putnam, 1875). But Harriet can hardly have taken any credit to herself for courage in this connection, for the possibility that Henriette was guilty seems never to have occurred to her, and it is only fair to Mrs. Field to add that it seems hardly to have occurred to any other of her American friends either.

15 I must add, however, that Mrs. Stowe was not shockingly liberal when, in the winter of 1878-79, her son Charley wanted to marry Susan Munroe at once, instead of waiting until May, when Harriet and others could attend the wedding. "Having waited three years you can wait three months more and get married in a respectable and sensible way with all your friends around you.... No no Charlie —learn to labor and to wait. Go on with your work and by May I

trust there will be some harvest—but just now give your whole heart to the work."

16 In 1870, in the office of the New York *Tribune*, Daniel McFarland shot and fatally wounded Albert D. Richardson, with whom his divorced wife had been having an affair. Mrs. McFarland married Richardson on his deathbed, and Henry Ward Beecher performed the ceremony. To *CU*, I (1870), 385-6, Harriet contributed an article called "Christ and Woman," in which, says Forrest Wilson, "she justified Mrs. McFarland's adulterous life, or at least excused it...." This is exactly what she did not do; she simply treated her with sympathetic Christian charity, denouncing the cruel publicity to which she had been subjected and contrasting it to Christ's delicacy toward the woman taken in adultery. Mrs. McFarland "lamentably erred in good judgment." But the worst she can have done is that "harassed by the insults and provocations and sufferings which beset the wife of a drunkard, she...fled to the protection of another man and allowed her heart too freely to go out in love to him." Many years later, as Abby Sage Richardson, the lady dramatized Mark Twain's *The Prince and the Pauper* for production by David Belasco.

17 In addition to Delilah, she uses in this book Salome, the Woman of Samaria, and Mary Magdalene. She does nothing with Salome and very little with the Woman of Samaria, but her treatment of Mary Magdalene is very curious. Identifying her with the woman who anointed Jesus in the house of Simon the Pharisee, she equates demoniacal possession with a sinful life, and thus perpetuates the quite unbiblical legend of her wantonness. She also has Mary of Bethany anoint Jesus after the raising of Lazarus, for which she is rebuked by Judas.

18 In *The Minister's Wooing* she comes close to extending this to betrothal, and Mary Scudder would have married the Doctor, even after the return of the man she loved, if the Doctor had not voluntarily relinquished her. Harriet finds it necessary to explain her quixotism but it is clear that she admires it.

CHAPTER VII: THE AESTHETE

1 *Biography and the Human Heart* (HM, 1932), p. 97.

2 As in the early story, "The Dancing School," *N-YE*, XIV (1843), 53, 57, where dancing is disapproved of because of the asso-

ciations to which it leads. The reasoning is not indefensible, but the case is weakened by absurd overstatement. Isabella, having attended dancing school, becomes indifferent to religion, takes a chill leaving a ball, and dies!

3 "At Sea," *CU*, XIV (1876), 510, contains a vivid description of a terrible three-day gale aboard *SS City of Atlanta*, bound for Charleston. A little dog died in the course of the voyage. "We heard of it in the morning and thought he had altogether the best of it in his escape." Who was President or who was Republican or Democrat was no longer important to anybody on board. She does not quite go the length of saying that it made no difference who was a Christian, but she comes close to it!

4 "Our Wood Lot in Winter" is in Vol. XIV "RE"; "The Snow Siege" is in *Ind*, Feb. 26, 1855.

5 All in *Queer Little People*, "RE," Vol. XIV. A letter of July 5, 1864, contains a delightful, detailed account of how Hum was rescued from a downpour and nursed back to life. See also, in WA, letter dated "Aug. or Sept. 1864."

6 There is an amusing letter to Mrs. Agassiz, June 7, 1869, (WA): "My husband came down in triumph the other night: he had caught upon his candle a kind of moth that he was quite convinced was not in your collection. The creature looked like an incipient humming bird with tail feathers about half grown and appeared stone dead. Mr. Stowe was going to send it as a votive offering to you and we had a nice little box in which we were going to enshrine it all neatly pinned in with a fine cambric needle when lo just as we proceeded to put him in, my lord just gave a *flap* and a *whirr* and was no where in a minute." Harriet took this dereliction with mock solemnity. "Can you imagine such brutal insensibility on the part of that moth—such indecent trifling with the feelings of a grave professor? Does it not look seriously like total depravity?" She goes on to ask a question about slugs, and then she adds: "I have none of Prof Agassiz' charity for these creatures and think they have no business to enjoy themselves at our expense—my great object in studying natural history would be to find the best means of extermination of all moths, canker worms, cut worms, borers, and other pests of society, —to say nothing of fleas and mosquitoes and cockroaches. Let science teach us to destroy and I will go for science with both hands." In view of later scientific triumphs, this has an ominous ring.

7 For a fine example of Harriet's independence and common sense in art criticism see "What Pictures Shall I Hang on My Walls?" *Atlantic Almanac*, 1869, pp. 41, 43-4.

8 Cf. HBS to the twins, Feb. 6, 1866? (WA):

I saw *Faust* again but think it a failure. She [Clara Louise Kellogg] is not made for high tragedy—there was not reality and pathos enough in the acting to make the story sublime and supernatural as Goethe does. Instead of Margaret going to church meek and saintly we see her for the first time in the midst of a ballet, where poor ballet girls are making very unnecessary displays of homely legs. The church scene was omitted and the seduction scene made unnecessarily prominent and on the whole I was glad Papa was not there. I thought it quite a disagreeable ensemble and thought it a pity so fine a girl as Miss Kellogg should be in it.

9 "The 'mise en scene' was brilliant, the orchestral music and the singing lovely, the *acting* modern and German. I could but think how Mario and Grisi would have made it thrill and burn but I don't believe Germans can *act*." Oct. 29, 1877.

10 See Marvin Felheim, "Two Views of the Stage; or, The Theory and Practice of Henry Ward Beecher," *NEQ*, XXV (1952), 314-26, which is mostly about the dramatization of Henry's novel, *Norwood*.

11 *The Christian Slave*, A Drama, Founded on a Portion of *Uncle Tom's Cabin*. Dramatized by Harriet Beecher Stowe, Expressly for the Readings of Mrs. Mary E. Webb (Boston; Phillips, Sampson & Company, 1855). There are a number of letters about Mrs. Webb, the most interesting being that to Longfellow, dated "Andover, Aug. 4" and preserved at Bowdoin College. (From another source we learn that Mrs. Webb read *Hiawatha* to Longfellow and pleased him.) She was part Negro and part Moorish and "might easily pass for a Spanish lady" but refused to disown her mother's race. "I never saw a person in whom the fire of genius burned with a flame more decided and clear, in whom every graceful artistic instinct was more native." "Full of lofty and heroic impulses, sensitive as an aeolian harp—delicately appreciative of every shade of poetic feeling—proud yet tender, she is to me a new and beautiful revelation of what womanhood can be. *In her art* she is as all true artists are inspired. In her finest moods

she sweeps all before her." "Her Queen Katherine is a most touching most dignified and subduing thing. Her Spanish blood and pride, joined with a pathetic softness and sweetness all render it with a richness of tone like the brown of Murillo's coloring. When I look at her acting I think the brown of her complexion like that of old paintings preferable to all the lighter tints of the world." Yet "her comedy is for a light gracefulness and airy playfulness equally remarkable. Her Lady Teazle I never tire of hearing." The purpose of the letter to Longfellow was to try to make it possible for Mrs. Webb "to give a reading at some fashionable watering place where she might gain some notoriety which would be of service for her winter's career." There is much more about Mrs. Webb's background in letters in the Barrett Collection at the University of Virginia, in one of which her father is identified as Espartero. Charlotte Cushman and Fanny Davenport are named as patrons.

12   Arthur Hobson Quinn, *American Fiction, An Historical and Critical Survey* (AC, 1936), p. 162, says that Mrs. Stowe dramatized *Oldtown Folks* in 1869, "but I cannot find evidence of its production."

CHAPTER VIII: THE READER

1   Wilson says (*Patriotic Gore*, p. 47): "There is not, so far as I know, any other writer in English who has produced, in the form of fiction, such a chronicle of religious history." Foster (*The Rungless Ladder*, p. 105) finds that Chapter XXIII of *The Minister's Wooing* "illustrates her ability to speak the yes and no of her culture and by that token to prophesy the mature understanding of Puritanism mid-twentieth century scholars like Perry Miller are beginning to furnish us."

2   *Lady Byron Vindicated*, pp. 335-9; *Sunny Memories*, I, 165-6, 205-6.

3   This book contains, in whole or in part, *The Pilgrim's Progress*, *Robinson Crusoe*, *The Vicar of Wakefield*, *Gulliver's Travels*, *Paul and Virginia*, *Vathek*, *Undine*, Madame S. R. Cottin's *Elizabeth; or The Exiles of Siberia*, Joseph Xavier Boniface's *Picciola*, and three stories from *The Arabian Nights*—"Aladdin," "Sindbad," and "Ali Baba."

4   In *Godey's*, July 1842, appeared "The Fisherman Caught, A

Ballad, Translated from the German of Goethe, by Mrs. H. E. Beecher Stowe." She cannot have done more than versify a literal translation.

5   "RE," Vol. XV.

6   "Waiting by the River," *CU*, VII (1873), 2.

7   In an 1830 letter to Mary Dutton (Yale), Harriet reports that she has been reading *Rasselas* and writing in imitation of Johnson's style as an exercise in composition. As a result, she complains, she is unable to talk except in Johnsonese. "The man writes as if some Fairy has spell bound him and given him the task of putting every word in his great dictionary in his book as a means of release."

8   *CU*, VI (1872), 121-2.

9   "The Glory of Sin: Byron," in *Saints and Sinners* (HM, 1932).

10   *The Letters of Charles Dickens* (Nonesuch Press, 1938), II, 430-31.

11   Says Charles H. Foster, "Though we are right in designating Scott as 'historical romancer,' we might almost as appropriately call him a writer of the expanded tale of travel. His characters are always on the move. . . . In making *UTC* a panorama of mid-America, Harriet could easily have been influenced by Scott" (*The Rungless Ladder*, p. 16). Jay Hubbell has humorously suggested that, in view of Scott's influence on *UTC*, perhaps Mark Twain was right after all in suggesting that Scott caused the Civil War!

12   "Sir Walter was, to be sure, a high tory; and his political prejudices colored all he wrote. In his Puritan characters, the faults and absurdities stand in the foreground, and the other side of the picture is, perhaps, coldly done. But it must be remembered, that a man can only describe from what is in him; and Scott, though a most amiable and conscientious man, had no kind of experience of anything like devotional fervor, and without such an experience he could not rightly appreciate or describe such men as Sir Harry Vane, and others of the best class on the Puritan side of the question. There are many indications that he was sensible of the leaning of his mind toward the royalist side, and that he endeavored to do historic justice. In *Old Mortality*, he places his hero, Henry Morton, on the Puritan side, and does his best to make him interesting—he gives him all heroic qualities, and endows him with just the same sort of cool philosophic religion that he had himself; and the consequence is, that Henry Morton seems neither like a Puritan, nor like anything else. There is nothing distinc-

tive about him; and almost any reader of the work will confess that either Lord Evandale, or Balfour of Burley, are far more interesting, because far more decided characters. In Puritan characters drawn from low life, such as Davie and Jeanie Deans, Scott has been more successful." So Harriet wrote in *N-YE*, XIII (1842), 120. The article is devoted to Scott, Byron, Bulwer, and Marryat. The sins of Charles Dickens were such that he preempted the whole of the second article on "Literary Epidemics"—XIV (1843), 109—to himself.

13   "The Primitivism of Wordsworth," in *On Being Creative and Other Essays* (HM, 1932).

14   In a letter to George Eliot, April 4, 1869, Mrs. Stowe says that she likes English prose better than poetry—"our language is a hard one for poetry"—and that she wishes *The Spanish Gypsy* had been written as a romance and also that Mrs. Browning had written more prose. "Did you ever think of the rhythmical pattern of prose, how every writer when they get warm, fall into a certain swing and rhythm peculiar to themselves, the words all having their place and sentences their cadences. But in blank verse proper or any form of metrical rhyme, the flow of the idea has to be turned backward to suit the fetters." In an article "Can I Write?" in *HH*, I (1869), 40, she complains that many modern poets "have *not* thought of what they wanted to say, or, if they have, have not succeeded in saying it; so that we are really quite uncertain whether they mean this, that, or the other, or, in fact, anything at all."

15   "RE," X, 193, 205.

16   For a strong expression of these, see her letter to the Kingsleys dated "Leeds, Sept. 4," Illinois State Historical Library.

17   See Emerson Grant Sutcliffe, "*Uncle Tom* and Charles Reade," *AL*, XVII (1946), 334-47.

18   Some of Mrs. Stowe's letters to George Eliot are in C. E. Stowe, *Life of HBS;* others will be found in the Berg Collection. WA has a number of letters from George Eliot to HBS.

19   *The Letters of Charles Dickens*, II, 430-31; III, 744, 748.

20   See, further, Harry Stone, "Charles Dickens and HBS," *Nineteenth Century Fiction*, XII (1957), 188-202.

21   Some of Holmes's letters to Mrs. Stowe are published in John T. Morse, *Life and Letters of Oliver Wendell Holmes* (HM, 1896). There is another warm expression of her regard for him in a letter to J. L. and J. B. Gilder, Aug. 20, 1884, in the Morgan Library.

22   *The Rungless Ladder*, pp. 176-7.

23   WA has an incomplete draft of a very interesting letter to Parton, replying to his of Feb. 14, 1868. "I think a great deal of your powers of writing. It has struck me that you have to a great degree what some author calls the power of *putting things*. But then too, you it seems to me very often project your personality upon the character you represent, so that we do not see really the person as he is but the person thro a portion of your personality. I always read with a secret scepticism. You take a tough case and you plane and you smooth and you varnish and it comes out a very fine article and one cannot deny its identity, but it is unaccountably altered. I read with delight always but with a sort of half smile behind all, for, I think after all, tough old Butler is about what he was for all this, yet I cannot deny a thing nor put my finger anywhere." She also discusses his projected life of Voltaire. "Now it would be cheap and easy to write a partisan eulogy of Voltaire—to follow him with admiration, to throw his faults in a dark closet and to make him out one of the serene benefactors of mankind.... This is quite a simple thing to do, for by a judicious selection it can be done." But she is sure no study of Voltaire can be really adequate which does not see him as "an age" and "a moral crisis." "He formed the France of today more than any man."

24   Her letter about Harte to the Fieldses, Jan. 29, 1874, is one of the very few evidences of her interest in gossip. "Why was a constable after him as you related? Do tell me how it eventuated. Bret seems to me a Horace [*sic*] Skimpole."

25   October 10, 1893—Pennsylvania State University.

Chapter IX: THE WRITER

1   *The Rungless Ladder*, pp. 13-17. See also Adams, pp. 56-8; John H. Nelson, "A Note on the Genesis of Mrs. Stowe's *Dred*," *Univ. of Kansas Humanistic Studies*, Vol. VI, No. 4 (1940), pp. 59-64. Despite the parallels pointed out by Charles Nichols, "The Origins of *UTC*," *Phylon*, XIX (1958), 328-34, the influence of Richard Hildreth's *The Slave; or The Memoirs of Archy Moore* (1836) remains doubtful. In a letter to the editor of the *Brooklyn Magazine* in the Barrett Collection (University of Virginia) Harriet denies that any of the characters in *UTC* are portraits of originals. See James

Lane Allen's letter to Richard Watson Gilder, Oct. 1, 1886, in the same collection, for his fruitless attempt to run down originals.

2 See Foster, *The Rungless Ladder*, pp. 20-22. The most careful analysis of the Eliza material is in Russel B. Nye, "Eliza Crossing the Ice: A Reappraisal of Sources," *Bulletin of the Historical and Philosophical Society of Ohio*, VIII (1950), 105-12.

3 On June 11, 1856, Mrs. Stowe added the following postscript to her husband's letter to the publisher M. D. Phillips: "*Dred* is in reality the hero of the book—the Dismal Swamp the theatre and now when every body is in an excited state and craving excitement this name will *go*—I see it. Had things remained tranquil as they were when the book began, it might have been quite another book and another name would have done. But now we both are persuaded that this is the best." Cf. J. C. Derby, *Fifty Years Among Authors, Books, and Publishers:* "Mr. Phillips heard Mrs. Stowe say that when she was about in the middle of the book, the assault on Charles Sumner took place, and she was so indignant at the outrage, that instead of carrying out some of her characters and making them like little Eva, charming and tender, she introduced the spirit of revenge under the name of the negro Dred."

4 Foster, *The Rungless Ladder*, pp. 87-90.

5 John Raymond Howard quotes her on *My Wife and I:* "It is not possible to write a story as you would do other things—just to suit yourself. You think you are going to write one kind of thing, and behold! your pen travels off in an entirely different direction. Now I thought I would make this *Harry Henderson* a free-and-easy, chatty sort of story. But just as I began it, Mrs. Stanton and all those people began making their loud talk and unsettling attacks on marriage and its sacredness, setting up new and false notions. I couldn't stand that; and so you see this story has taken a deeper hold of me than I thought it would; and you will see, it will take a deeper hold elsewhere." She added that she did not wish to hear adverse criticism while the story was running its serial course. "Writing a story is like a spider spinning his web.... He has to spin from what he has in him, and he finds one point here, and another there. Along comes some matter-of-fact housewife, or thoughtless boy or quick wind, and dashes through the web—instantly it hangs quivering and shaking and is almost destroyed.... Criticism can't give me anything new; it only

destroys what I myself have, and my ability to produce it ... and the story must go its own way."

6 I must admit that I am frankly horrified by one passage in her sketch of Lincoln in *Men of Our Times:* "It is a curious fact that neither then [i.e., in early life] nor afterwards did he ever read a novel. He began *Ivanhoe* once, but was not interested enough to finish it." Though a professional novelist, she does not seem to blame him for this; instead she adds that "whenever he could read a *good* book [italics mine] he did." Yet I, who am not a novelist, could not but regard such a man as either a psychic cripple or one supremely unfortunate in his capacity for enjoyment.

7 Cf. a less familiar statement of the same point of view in a letter to Dr. Wardlaw in Scotland, December 14, 1852: "For myself I can claim no merit, in that work which has been the cause of this. It was an instinctive irresistible outburst and had no more merit in it than a mother's wailing for her first born. The success of the work so strange so utterly unexpected only astonishes me! I can only say that this bubble of my mind has risen on the mighty stream of a *Divine Purpose*—and even a bubble may go far on such a tide." But many years later she wrote Mr. Derby from Mandarin: "What Jewett says about Uncle Tom is false. I was not altogether such a fool as he represents; although I confess I *was* surprised at the *extent* of the success."

8 Chapters I-II.

9 "RE," VI, 112.

10 "RE," X, 227.

11 Many attempts have been made to show HBS as a precursor of later writers. Some have misfired. Kenneth S. Lynn's idea (*Mark Twain and Southwestern Humor*, Atlantic-Little, Brown, 1959) that the relationship between Huckleberry Finn and Nigger Jim was suggested or affected by that between Eva and Uncle Tom is not convincing, and Lillian Beatty, "The Natural Man versus the Puritan," *Personalist*, XL (1959), 22-30, exaggerates the resemblances between *The Minister's Wooing* and *The Last Puritan* by George Santayana, but Foster is very penetrating in pointing out Harriet's anticipations of Mark Twain, Howells, James, Faulkner, and others. She herself was as keenly aware as any twentieth-century writer that the feudal aspects of Southern civilization made it a good field for novelists. "First, in a merely artistic point of view, there is no ground, ancient

or modern, whose vivid lights, gloomy shadows, and grotesque group-
ings, afford the novelist so wide a scope for the exercise of his powers.
In the near vicinity of modern civilization of the most matter-of-fact
kind exist institutions which carry us back to the twilight of the feudal
ages, with all their existing possibilities of incident. Two nations, the
types of two exactly opposite styles of existence, are here struggling;
and from the intermingling of these two a third has arisen, and the
three are interlocked in wild and singular relations, that evolve every
possible combination of romance. Hence, if the writer's only object
had been the production of a work of art, she would have felt justified
in not turning aside from that mine whose inexhaustible stores have
but begun to be developed." While still engaged with *UTC*, she wrote
Dr. Gamaliel Bailey of how the great Dismal Swamp enthralled her:
"What a theme for romance!—what description! If I were only a man
I would go and explore it. Can I get any body to tell me about it
who has explored! could I get any body to go there and explore?"

   12   Modern readers must be careful to remember that though
nineteenth-century people got along on what seem to us starvation
incomes, they still enjoyed some comforts which we are denied. Harriet's *House and Home Papers* are much concerned with the trouble
caused by servants, but except in "The Lady Who Does Her Own
Work" little or no attention is paid to the possibility of getting on
without them. There is even one overwhelming reference in passing
to "young people who cannot expect by any reasonable possibility to
keep more than two or three servants." Harriet always had "h
and, like her father, she was always sure that the Lord would provide.
"Money, I suppose, is as plenty with Him now as it always has been,
and if He sees it is really best, He will doubtless help me." It is astonishing to see how often He did help them both, the money coming,
as it were, out of a clear sky. How many wives today, in much better
circumstances than Harriet was in Cincinnati, could manage to go
away for ten months to that nineteenth-century delusion and snare,
the water cure, not seeing husband or children during the whole
period? Moreover, she had no sooner got home than Calvin went off,
going her one better by staying fifteen months.

   13   She did not take the loss without protest. WA has a draft
of an undated letter to Jewett in which she remonstrates with him
for persuading her to accept the royalty, also an undated letter to
Edward Beecher which shows that there were negotiations in which

she tried to get the terms modified, which failing she considered herself "entirely at liberty to decline future connections" with Jewett. Though she had been "actuated ... as much by sincere friendship for him and a desire to lead to a clear and satisfactory result as by any other motive," his conduct made her "feel increasingly that he is not the man I wish to be in business relations with. He is positive, overbearing, uneasy if crossed and unwilling to have fair enquiries made."

14 In 1855 she stated that her average table numbered twelve. WA has a copy of a 22-page letter which she wrote, March 4, 1858, to Lyman's third wife, Lydia Jackson, enumerating what she had contributed to their support. "How after all this you can write me that your heart has been made sick with hope deferred in consequence of my failing to fulfil engagements which I had made to provide for father's old age I cannot see—it is to me a painful mystery." Together with other correspondence with Lydia, this letter shows considerable aptitude for finance; it also proves that, generous though she might be, Harriet had no intention of being made a fool of. She acknowledges her responsibility to provide for her father and his wife, but she declines all responsibility for the wife's children by a former marriage. Incidentally she reports her earnings from *UTC* at $30,000, which is not, of course, necessarily accurate.

15 A topic of special interest in connection with Harriet's finances is her handling of the money which English antislavery friends thrust upon her during her first visit to England. See C. E. Stowe, *Life of HBS*, p. 250; Forrest Wilson, *Crusader in Crinoline*, pp. 371-2. Wilson is a little hard on Mrs. Stowe for her unsystematic accounting, and it is difficult to follow his reasoning that "morally she had every right" to this money because "the total amount ... was but a fraction of the royalties stolen from her by British publishers." The real reason why she stood clear is given in her letter to the Earl of Carlisle and others of which there is a copy in the Boston Public Library. She did not accept the money without carefully stipulating "that if the offering was to have any value to me as an individual that it was to be with the understanding that it was to be strictly mine as much as any portion of my private property and that I should be subject to account to no one but to God and to my conscience." "We have always replied to any attempts to dictate to us the use we should make of the money or to enquire into what we had done with it that it was *strictly our own private affair* and

that we should acknowledge the right of no one to take any account of it." Having said this, she proceeds to give a fairly careful, though not complete, account of the sums dispersed for various aspects of antislavery work. See, further, the letter to Joseph Sturge and his wife in the Friends Historical Library at Swarthmore.

16 A month later she wrote again. The article is now in active preparation. "I think it will take 14 or 15 pages of the *Atlantic* and I shall ask for $100—my usual charge for an article of that length." She adds, "If I am to judge by the letters that have come to me since Mr. Stowe's death I think you will find call for a good edition of this no." In December she even suggested binding in pictures of Calvin in some copies and selling these at an advanced price.

Chapter X: THE REFORMER

1 *Fields of the* Atlantic Monthly: *Letters to an Editor, 1861-1870* (Huntington Library, 1953).

2 A different kind of smugness appears at the very end of her career in *Poganuc People:* "Such were our New England villages in the days when its people were of our own blood and race, and the pauper population of Europe had not as yet been landed on our shores."

3 See C. E. Stowe, *Life of HBS,* pp. 237-8. For contemporary criticisms of Harriet's attitude toward English poverty, see George Shepperson, "HBS and Scotland," *Scottish Historical Review,* XXXII (1953), 40-45.

4 In her paper on Henry Ward Beecher in *Men of Our Times* she writes, "In the controversy then arising through the land in relation to slavery, Mr. Beecher from the first took the ground and was willing to bear the name of an abolitionist." In her paper on Salmon P. Chase she praises the "vigorous, radical young men, headed by that brilliant, eccentric genius, Theodore D. Weld," who made "an antislavery fort" of Lane Theological Seminary, but she ignores the fact that they failed to carry Lyman Beecher with them and consequently blew up the fort. The closest she comes to admitting that her father, or any of the Beechers, were Johnny-come-latelys in the abolition camp is in her paper on Garrison, where she reports Lyman's having refused to join in Garrison's work on the ground that he had too many irons in the fire. Garrison replied, "Then you had better let

all the others go, and attend to this one alone." She comments: "The results of time have shown that the young printer saw further than the sages of his day." Professor Adams states that George, converted by Weld in 1836, was the first out-and-out abolitionist among the Beechers. "The next year he converted his brother William. The other children, one after another, gradually capitulated to northern public opinion, Henry Ward and Harriet the last of all."

5 "Mrs. Stowe's 'Uncle Tom' at Home in Kentucky," *Century*, XXXIV (1887), 852-67.

6 Reprinted in "RE," IV.

7 *Publications of the Southern History Association*, II (1898), 165-6.

8 "The Captain's Story," a ghost story published in *Our Continent* as late as 1883 (Vol. II, pp. 789-93), deals with slave-running and murder and sadism committed for its sake.

9 See, for example, "HBS's Reply," *Mississippi Valley Historical Review*, XIX (1932), 260.

10 See her letter to William Lloyd Garrison, December 12, 1853 (Boston Public Library), trying to make peace between him and Frederick Douglass. She acknowledges that Douglass is "much excited" and that "he makes appeals to prejudice which I consider unfair—yet my dear sir I cannot but consider this a case in which great delicacy should be used and great allowances made. We that are strong ought to *bear* the infirmities of the weak, and *not* to please ourselves. *We* are the strong race—he belongs to the weak, the oppressed, the feeble one. It is one of the things we have to calculate upon, that every victim which we draw up from the abyss of slavery will have in the depths of his soul a *morbid* spot—a deep bleeding wound. He never so wholly confides in our race that he is not subject to this old rankling disease." After an interview with Garrison she pleads for Douglass again on December 19, with special reference to Garrison's having called him an apostate. "Where is this work of excommunication to end?"

11 She was "far more warm-hearted than the great body of the Abolitionists," says Dumas Malone (*Saints in Action*, Abingdon Press, 1939). "No mere moralist but a born story-teller, she worked in a richer medium. She stands as an example of the Puritan spirit, inveterate in its reforming tendencies, but liberated and humanized in the West, and with a distinctive warmth and fire that was inborn. There

was about her an endearing lack of practicality and a certain rich luxuriance."

12   "Mrs. Stowe and Her Uncle Tom," *Bibliotheca Sacra*, LXVIII (1911), 674-83.

13   In 1858 Mrs. Stowe wrote a friend that she had ceased working in the antislavery cause, believing it to be approaching a crisis which nobody could greatly help or hinder. The Boston Public Library has an undated letter to Anne Weston which, I think, shows that, in the days of her fame, she served strictly on her own terms and supports my view that she was a woman of family and a writer before she was a reformer:

I thought I was sufficiently guarded in my offers of personal attendance at the Swiss table in your Anti Slavery fair. I said that I could not take the responsibility of attendance, but that I would appear at it occasionally and do what I could incidentally.

My family affairs, owing to my husband's accident and other causes are still more stringent than they have been so that I fear I shall be even less with you than I had hoped, and of my daughters one is in N York and the other so engaged in attending school so that they cannot do anything. I hope nevertheless to be with you a good part of the first day and shall try to be there at the opening.

In regard to the tract I very much wish Mrs. Follen would write it because it seems to me that I could not add any thing to what I have already said on this subject, and I think it be best to have another name than mine—so at least it strikes me—tho I am willing to do anything I can.

I am sorry that I have been so pressed by family duties that I have not been able to write the article I meant to for the Independent and Congregationalist, but it has really been out of my power. My family is a large one always and lately there have arisen in it claims which I could find none but myself able to satisfy.

I say this that there may be no dependence on me—and then I will try to do what I can.

14   I do not believe she had much interest in politics as such. In one of her magazine papers she declares that "*party* is the great Anti-Christ of a republican government, and the discipline of party has hitherto been so stringent that it really has been impossible to

determine the sentiment of a Christian man by his vote." She was for Frémont in 1856, and the American Antiquarian Society has a slip of paper dated Hartford, November 2, 1880, containing the words "Garfield & victory" and her signature. In 1884 she and Calvin evidently split with Henry Ward on the Blaine-Cleveland issue, since WA has a letter from Blaine in which he thanks them for their "kind words." "In the trials of a National Campaign there is nothing so grateful as the warm support of those whom we feel entitled to claim as personal friends." He expresses his regret and surprise at being opposed by "your gifted and eloquent brother." Harriet did not often express views on European affairs, but it should be credited to her insight that she had little confidence in Louis Napoleon even when he was being hailed as a deliverer.

15 She had spoken more favorably of Lincoln after emancipation, and she wrote of him with qualified admiration in the *Watchman and Reflector*, reprinted in *The Living Age*, No. 1027, Feb. 6, 1864. "Nobody could call him selfish or self-seeking. There have been times when we could have wished for a more brilliant leader. But Lincoln has been the safest." For her memorial tribute in the *Chimney Corner* papers, see "RE," VIII, 439, and cf. F. Lauriston Bullard, "Abraham Lincoln and HBS," *LH*, XLVIII, June 1946, pp. 11-14.

16 The only novels in which war and peace are discussed to any extent are *Dred* (especially Chapters XLVI, XLIX, L, LIV) and *The Pearl of Orr's Island* (especially Chapters XV, XVI, XX).

17 "Do tell me," she wrote Fields, "if our friend Hawthorne praises that arch traitor Pierce in his preface, and your loyal firm publishes it. I never read the preface, and have not yet seen the book, but they say so here, and I can scarcely believe it of you, if I can of him. I regret that I went to see him last summer. What! patronize such a traitor to our faces!" For a discussion of this matter and of Hawthorne's and Pierce's views on the Civil War, see Edward Wagenknecht, *Nathaniel Hawthorne, Man and Writer* (OUP, 1961), pp. 124-30.

18 *Chimes of Freedom and Union: A Collection of Poems for the Times*, by Various Authors (Boston: Benjamin B. Russell, 1861).

19 The following about Thomas K. Beecher, from Lyman Beecher Stowe's *Saints, Sinners and Beechers*, p. 381, is interesting as illustrating the characteristic Beecher moderation: "The sermon which has the most pertinence today is that on 'Prohibition'—preached in

1886 when he was sixty-one. Thomas K. Beecher's occasional glasses of beer not only did him no harm, he believed, but even did him good. Therefore he allowed himself this pleasure—wholesome pastimes were desirable for a clergyman as for any one else. After long years of observation of the effects of drink, however, he decided the number of persons who could use it in such moderation as to have it harmless, or even beneficial, were so negligible, while its injurious effects upon the great majority were so obvious, as to call for prohibition for the greatest good of the greatest number."

20   See her letter to her son Charley, April 28, 1880 (WA), occasioned by a controversy in his church, where the majority wished to use water! His mother finds this absurd, but urges him to yield, if necessary, in the spirit of Christian love, reminding him that the Moravians in Greenland used milk. Christ's "principle seemed to be to take two of the common articles of their usual feast and set them apart 'from a common to a sacramental use.' "

21   Once at least it didn't come "safe and sure." The University of Virginia has a letter from Calvin to "Mrs. Phillips," dated simply "July 15," about some wine which has been broken in transit. "When temperance men will get wine, they always get found out."

22   HM, 1920.

Chapter XI: THE DAUGHTER

1   For a more scholarly and scientific statement of the Calvinistic scheme, we cannot do better than turn to Perry Miller, *Jonathan Edwards* (William Sloane Associates, 1949): "Justification by faith ... [Calvin] said, is entirely a 'forensic' transaction; a sovereign God is pleased, for no other reason than that He is pleased, to accept the righteousness of Christ in place of the obedience which no man can achieve, and He 'imputes' Christ's perfections to a chosen few who in fact fall far short of perfection. These are saved 'as if' they were Christ Himself.... In the realm of objective fact, salvation was conceived by the Puritans as the transfer of a balance on the divine ledger, wherein God arbitrarily accepted another's payment for the debt which all men owed Him by the sin of Adam, and condemned those for whom the debt was not paid, though in life there might be little to distinguish one from another."

2   For her tribute to Mather and an expression of her conviction

that had his views prevailed much of the New England agony would have been spared, see Chapter XVIII of *Oldtown Folks,* especially Vol. IX, pp. 414-17 in "RE." For the fullest exposition of New England theology in any of her novels, see *The Minister's Wooing,* Chapter XXIII. Forrest Wilson remarks, "It is hard to realize today that *The Minister's Wooing* was almost as revolutionary in the religious life of the nation as was *UTC* in its political life."

3 Stowe, Beecher, Hooker, Seymour, Day Foundation *Bulletin,* Vol. I, No. 3, September 1961, pp. 10-12.

4 See Edward Wagenknecht, *Mark Twain, The Man and His Work,* Revised Edition (University of Oklahoma Press, 1961), pp. 198-201.

5 Cited in Foster, "The Genesis of HBS's *The Minister's Wooing,*" *NEQ,* XXI (1948), 493-517. See also the warm tribute in *Oldtown Folks,* Chapter I.

6 Her attitude toward the great revival movements of the nineteenth century was sympathetic but a little detached. Even her father had been wary of the emotionalism of revivals. Harriet was wary of Spugeon, though she had only read his sermons. The one revivalist who really seems to have been important to her was D. L. Moody, and few spiritually sensitive people seem to have been able to come into contact with that vital, great-hearted, and completely unselfish man without loving him, whatever they may have thought of his theology. According to Lyman Abbott, Moody, who, despite the fundamentalistic character of his own theology, was no heresy hunter, once proposed a joint tour to Henry Ward Beecher, who declined on the ground that "he believes the world is lost, and he is seeking to save from the wreck as many individuals as he can; I believe that this world is to be saved, and I am seeking to bring about the kingdom of God on this earth."

7 In 1879 she wrote Charley (WA): "It was with some fear, for myself and my faith that I began these OT studies, but by keeping a prayerful attitude, by suspending first judgment and laying every difficulty in a filial spirit at the feet of my Father, I found a sweetness, light and comfort in those studies not inferior to what I found in the N Testament... In all the history I think the character of the God of Abraham Isaac and Jacob is a lovely one. Tho armed with terrible power, and tho capable of a terrible severity, yet He seems to me to be Love.... He educates Jacob as Jesus educated his disciples leading

him gently thro a life's experience and teaching him also to aspire towards a good that shall be for all mankind."

8 In 1850 she wrote Isabella: "I begin to be a little afraid that the Bushnell movement may go too far, and to hold on to the old ground, that is to say when people are suddenly set loose from what they have considered old truths they are apt to push their freedom too far and too fast. We must try to keep a Bible to live and die by and to hold to strict accurate ideas of inspiration."

9 In "Atonement—A Historical Reverie," N-YE, XIX (1848), 205, early as it is, Harriet stakes out a fairly advanced position when she writes: "The Bible, as it always does, gives on this point not definitions or distinct outlines, but images—images which lose all their glory and beauty, if seized by harsh hands of metaphysical analysis; but inexpressibly affecting to the unlettered human heart, which softens in gazing on their mournful and mysterious beauty."

10 The Rungless Ladder, pp. 138 ff.

11 The quite exceptionally hostile view of spiritualism in My Wife and I, Chapter XLV, is, of course, due to Harriet's dislike of Victoria Woodhull. See Richard M. Dorson, Jonathan Draws the Long Bow (HUP, 1946), pp. 218-21.

12 According to Mrs. Browning (Hazel Harrod, "Correspondence of HBS and Elizabeth Barrett Browning," University of Texas Studies in English, 1948, pp. 28-34), Harriet in 1861 wrote to her of having heard from her dead son Henry five times "without any seeking on her part." The only instance described in detail is a communication reported to her by Henry's roommate, Heywood, a disbeliever in spiritualism, who had it from a girl medium to whom he was entirely unknown, and who, it seems, practically impersonated those from whom she brought messages. He talked with her for two hours "on all branches and particulars of most private confidential affairs in which they alone had been involved, and she spoke freely without hesitation with the most perfect knowledge of names, dates, and places and persons and with all of Henry's peculiar turns of thought and expression." Henry had not been happy immediately after death "and warned his friend that if he wished for immediate happiness after death he must live in some respects differently from what they either of them had done." The other four reports all agreed on this point, whether they came from Calvinists, "who believe in no state of progressive holiness after death" or from "those who have

no fixed belief in the spiritual world." Another testimonial to Harriet's interest in psychic matters is her correspondence with Robert Dale Owen, author of *Footfalls on the Boundary of Another World* and *The Debatable Land Between This World and the Next*. She could not accept all Owen's conclusions, but she defended him when he was criticized and quoted Goethe to him, that "it is just as absurd to deny the facts of spiritualism now as it was in the Middle Ages to ascribe them to the Devil." Once, with characteristic caution, she writes, "You will regard this letter, I trust, as between ourselves." In 1870 Harriet contributed three articles on "Spiritualism" to *CU*, N. S. II (1870), 129-30, 145-6, 177-8, and followed these with another on "St. Michael and All Angels," N. S. III (1870), 243, in which she deplores the loss of a sense of angelic presences but fears that if used as intercessors, they may become idols. See, too, "The Ministration of Our Departed Friends," "RE," XV. On July 15, 1844 she wrote Calvin about some experiments in mesmerism she had been making with Henry Ward. The letter is in WA.

13   The only novel in which the matter is considered is *My Wife and I*.

14   I would conjecture that Hattie, who never married, had been involved in an unhappy love affair, since there is another letter fragment in WA which is in much the same tone: "Why should you mourn an unrequited love, since it is a noble and beautiful feeling in you and by it you can understand and come near to that God whose love is so constantly unrequited, whose life consists in going without return?"

BIBLIOGRAPHY

In this bibliography an effort has been made to avoid repeating information given in the Notes. The two sections should, therefore, be
used together.

For abbreviations employed, see p. 221.

The "Riverside Edition" ("RE") of "The Writings of HBS" (HM,
1896) comprises:

Vols. I-II—Uncle Tom's Cabin; A Key to Uncle Tom's Cabin
(abridged)

Vols. III-IV—Dred; Anti-Slavery Tales and Papers; Life in Florida
After the War (Palmetto Leaves)

Vol. V—The Minister's Wooing

Vol. VI—The Pearl of Orr's Island

Vol. VII—Agnes of Sorrento

Vol. VIII—Household Papers and Stories (House and Home Papers;
The Chimney Corner, etc.)

Vols. IX-X—Oldtown Folks; Sam Lawson's Oldtown Fireside Stories

Vol. XI—Poganuc People; Pink and White Tyranny

Vol. XII—My Wife and I

Vol. XIII—We and Our Neighbors

Vol. XIV—Stories, Sketches, and Studies (includes Little Foxes)

Vol. XV—Religious Studies, Sketches, and Poems (includes Footsteps of the Master)

Vol. XVI—Stories and Sketches for the Young (Queer Little People,
Little Pussy Willow, A Dog's Mission, Our Charley, etc.)

Not included in the set are *Bible Heroines* (Fords, Howard, &

Hulbert, 1878); *First Geography for Children* (Phillips, Sampson, and Company, 1855); *Lady Byron Vindicated* (Fields, Osgood & Co., 1878); *Men of Our Times*... (Hartford Pub. Co., 1868), republished with the addition of a sketch of B. Gratz Brown, as *The Lives and Deeds of Our Self-Made Men* by Worthington, Dustin & Co.; *Stories About Our Dogs* (William P. Nimmo, n.d.); *Sunny Memories of Foreign Lands* (Phillips, Sampson, 1854); *Uncle Sam's Emancipation* (Willis P. Hazard, 1853). Since only an abridged version of the *Key* is included in "RE," I have also consulted *A Key to UTC; Presenting the Original Facts and Documents Upon Which the Story is Founded, Together with Corroborative Statements Verifying the Truth of the Work* (John P. Jewett & Co., 1853). HBS collaborated with her sister Catharine Beecher in *The American Woman's Home* (J. B. Ford and Company, 1869), a work published, with variations, under other titles and imprints. To *Our Famous Women* (A. D. Worthington & Co., 1886) she contributed sketches of Catharine Beecher and Mrs. A. D. T. Whitney, and Rose Terry Cooke contributed a sketch of her. She also had a hand in *Autobiography, Correspondence, etc. of Lyman Beecher, D.D.* (H, 1864).

HBS contributed introductions to Charles Beecher, *The Incarnation; or, Pictures of the Virgin and her Son* (H, 1849); Josiah Henson, *Autobiography* (B. B. Russell & Co., 1879); William C. Nell, *The Colored Patriots of the American Revolution* (Robert F. Wallcut, 1855); C. G. Parsons, *Inside View of Slavery: or A Tour Among the Planters* (Jewett, 1855); Mrs. T. B. H. Stenhouse, *"Tell It All": The Story of a Life's Experience in Mormonism* (Worthington, 1874); *The Works of Charlotte Elizabeth Tonna* (M. W. Dodd, 1844); *A Library of Famous Fiction* (Ford, 1873).

There is no collection of letters by HBS, but many are quoted in her biographies, especially those by C. E. Stowe and Annie Fields, and others may be found in the *Bulletin* of the Stowe, Beecher, Hooker, Seymour, Day Foundation, Hartford.

The fullest list of uncollected serial writing by HBS is in John R. Adams, *HBS* (Twayne, 1963), but only a few items are cited in my notes.

The authorized biography was Charles Edward Stowe, *Life of HBS, Compiled from Her Letters and Journals* (HM, 1889). This was reworked and enlarged by Annie Fields, *Life and Letters of HBS* (HM, 1897). In 1911 C. E. Stowe and his son Lyman Beecher Stowe celebrated the centenary with *HBS, The Story of Her Life* (HM), and in 1934 L. B. Stowe wrote the story of the whole Beecher clan in *Saints, Sinners and Beechers* (Bobbs-Merrill). Isabella Beecher Hooker's *A Brief Sketch of the Life of HBS,* a pamphlet, privately printed in 1896, is worthless.

HBS disliked Florine Thayer McCray, *The Life-Work of the Author of UTC* (Funk & Wagnalls, 1889), much of which is childish enough, but the volume still contains some important data. The most elaborate modern biography, and the best (though I dissent from some of its interpretations) is Forrest Wilson, *Crusader in Crinoline* (L, 1941). Catherine Gilbertson, *HBS* (AC, 1937) and Johanna Johnston, *Runaway to Heaven* (D, 1963) are good, sound popular biographies, making no pretense of original research. Martha Foote Crow, *HBS* (AC, 1913) and Phyllis W. Jackson, *Victorian Cinderella* (Holiday House, 1947) are intended for girls. Charles H. Foster, *The Rungless Ladder: HBS and New England Puritanism* (DUP, 1954) and John R. Adams, *HBS* (see above) are important critical studies. Special topics are treated by Grace Edith Maclean, *UTC in Germany* (AC, 1910) and Mary B. Graff, *Mandarin on the St. Johns* (University of Florida Press, 1953).

Of the many books containing sketches or brief accounts of HBS, the following are important: Gamaliel Bradford, *Portraits of American Women* (HM, 1919); Annie Fields, *Authors and Friends* (HM, 1897); Nassau W. Senior, *Essays on Fiction* (Longmans, 1864); W. P. Trent and John Erskine, *Great Writers of America* (Ht, n.d.); Perry D. Westbrook, *Acres of Flint: Writers of Rural New England, 1870-1900* (Scarecrow Press, 1951); Edmund Wilson, *Patriotic Gore: Studies in the Literature of the American Civil War* (OUP, 1962). She also figures, of course, in books about the American novel, among which may be mentioned John Erskine, *Leading American Novelists* (Ht, 1910); Alexander Cowie, *The Rise of the American Novel* (American Book Company, 1948); Arthur Hobson Quinn, *American Fiction...* (AC, 1936); Carl Van Doren, *The American Novel, 1789-1939* (M, 1940); Edward Wagenknecht, *Cavalcade of the American Novel* (Ht, 1952).

The following books contain references to HBS: *The Americanization of Edward Bok* (S, 1920); J. C. Derby, *Fifty Years Among Authors, Books, and Publishers* (G. W. Carleton, 1884); H. Augusta Dodge, ed., *Gail Hamilton's Life in Letters* (Lee and Shepard, 1901);

Jay B. Hubbell, *The South in American Literature, 1607-1900* (DUP, 1924); John Herbert Nelson, *The Negro Character in American Literature, University of Kansas Humanistic Studies,* Vol. IV, No. 1 (1926); Helen Waite Papashvily, *All the Happy Endings* (H, 1956); John B. Peaslee, *Thoughts and Experiences In and Out of School* (Curts & Jennings, 1900); Fred Lewis Pattee, *The Feminine Fifties* (AC, 1940).

Articles not cited elsewhere include Eleanor P. Allen, *Lippincott's Magazine,* XLVI (1890), 261-72; George Willis Cooke, *NEM,* N.S. XV (1896), 3-18; Andrew L. Drummond, "New England Puritanism in Fiction," *London Quarterly and Holborn Review,* CLXXI (1946), 19-33; G. D. Eaton, *AM,* X (1921), 449-59 (which has value only as an example of how, in the 'twenties, authors were stretched on the Mencken version of the bed of Procrustes); John R. Howard, *O,* LIV (1896), 138-42; Julia Ward Howe, *Reader,* V (1905), 613-17; Walter Jerrold, "The Author of *UTC:* Some Centenary Notes," *Bookman* (London), XL (1911), 241-5; Frank J. Klingberg, "HBS and Social Reform in England," *American Historical Review,* XLIII (1938), 542-52; Constance D'Arcy Mackay, "The HBS Centenary," *NEM,* XLIV (1911), 453-60; E. K. Maxfield, " 'Goody Goody' Literature and Mrs. Stowe," *AS,* IV (1929), 189-202 (a cheap, smart-alecky article, unworthy of the serious journal in which it appeared); "Personal Recollections," *O,* LIV (1896), 142-3; Grace Seiler, *College English,* XI (1949), 127-37; Joseph H. Twichell, "Mrs. HBS in Hartford," *Critic,* IX (1886), 301-2; Edmund Wilson, *NY,* XXXI, Sept. 10, 1955, pp. 137 ff.; Margaret Wyman, "HBS's Topical Novel on Woman Suffrage," *NEQ,* XXV (1952), 383-91. (Where the title of the article is merely "Harriet Beecher Stowe," it has been omitted.)

The rest of these notes concern *UTC.* First, as to bibliography. Consult "*UTC* 100th Anniversary Exhibit," *Chicago History,* II (1951), 353-64; Chester E. Jorgenson, *UTC as Book and Legend* (Friends of the Detroit Public Library, Inc., 1952); also the bibliographical section of the 1878 edition of *UTC* (Houghton, Osgood). See, also, the following: Ralph G. Newman, *LH,* XLVIII, June 1946, pp. 23-5; Ralph Pierson, "A Few Literary Highlights of 1851-52," *ABC,* II (1932), 156-65; David A. Randall and John T. Winterich, *Publishers' Weekly,* CXXXVII (1940), 1931-3; William Talbot, "*UTC,* First English Editions," *ABC,* III (1933), 292-7.

The Annotated UTC, ed. Philip Van Doren Stern (Paul S. Eriksson,

Inc., 1964) adds to the text a series of notes, mostly referring to sources and derived largely from the *Key*. Byron Gysin, *To Master— A Long Good Night* (Creative Age Press, 1946) is largely about Josiah Henson, alleged original of Uncle Tom.

The following articles, mostly in periodicals, deal with various phases of the novel and its influence: James Baldwin, "Everybody's Protest Novel," *Partisan Review*, XVI (1949), 578-85; David Dempsey, "Uncle Tom, Centenarian," *NYTM*, June 3, 1951, pp. 55-6; Severn Duvall, "W. G. Simms's Review of Mrs. Stowe," *AL*, XXX (1958), 107-17; Alex Haley, "In Uncle Tom Are Our Guilt and Hope," *NYTM*, March 1, 1964, pp. 23, 90; Benjamin F. Hudson, "Another View of Uncle Tom," *Phylon*, XXIV (1963), 79-87; Frederick H. Jackson, "*UTC* in Italy," *Symposium*, VII (1953), 323-32; Felix J. Koch, "Where Did Eliza Cross the Ohio?" *Ohio Archaeological and Historical Publications*, XXIV (1915), 588-90; Arthur B. Maurice, "Famous Novels and Their Contemporary Critics, I," *Bookman* (New York), XVII (1903), 23-30; George S. McDowell, "HBS at Cincinnati," *NEM*, N.S. XII (1895), 64-70; Tremaine McDowell, "The Use of Negro Dialect by HBS," *AS*, VI (1931), 322-6; R. Gerald McMurty, "The Influence of the Stowe Book on the Popular Music of the Pre-Civil War Period," *LH*, XLVIII, June 1946, pp. 38-9; Newton MacTavish, "The Original Uncle Tom," *Canadian Magazine*, XXX (1907), 25-9; Herbert G. Nicholas, "*UTC*, 1852-1952," *Georgia Review*, VIII (1954), 140-48; Charles Nichols, "The Origins of *UTC*," *Phylon*, XIX (1958), 328-34; William Lyon Phelps, *Howells, James, Bryant and Other Essays* (M, 1924); Joseph Ridgely, "*Woodcraft*: Simms's First Answer to *UTC*," *AL*, XXXI (1960), 421-33; Joseph P. Roppolo, "HBS and New Orleans: A Study in Hate," *NEQ*, XXX (1957), 346-62; Joseph Rossi, "*UTC* and Protestantism in Italy," *American Quarterly*, XI (1959), 416-24; Francis A. Shoup, "*UTC* Fifty Years After," *Sewanee Review*, II (1893), 88-104; Hugh Alfred Taylor, *NR*, CXLIX, July 13, 1963, p. 31; "Uncle Tom's Message: The Book of War and Freedom," *Times Literary Supplement*, Oct. 4, 1963, pp. 777-8; Edmund Wilson, " 'No! No! No! My Soul Ain't Yours, Mas'r!' " *NY*, XXIV, Nov. 27, 1948, pp. 134 ff.; John T. Winterich, *Books and the Man* (Greenberg, 1929). An anonymous article in *The Manhattan*, I (1883), 28-31, is important because it embodies the reminiscences of the publisher Jewett.

The George L. Aiken version of the play *UTC* is published by

Samuel French, n.d. As A. E. Thomas revised it in 1933, it may be read in *S.R.O.*, ed. Bennett Cerf and Van H. Cartmell (D, 1944). The most elaborate account of the history of the play is Harry Birdoff's *The World's Greatest Hit: UTC* (S. F. Vanni, 1947); there is an excellent brief account in Wesley Winans Stout, "Little Eva Is Seventy-Five," *Saturday Evening Post*, CC, Oct. 8, 1927, pp. 110-11 ff. Cordelia Howard Macdonald's "Memoirs of the Original Little Eva" appeared in *Educational Theatre Journal*, VIII (1956), 267-82. See, further, Frank S. Arnett, "Fifty Years of Uncle Tom," *McClure's Magazine*, XXVII (1902), 897-902; F. Lauriston Bullard, "Uncle Tom on the Stage," *LH*, XLVIII, June 1946, pp. 19-22; A. M. Drummond and Richard Moody, "The Hit of the Century: *UTC*, 1852-1952," *ETJ*, IV (1952), 315-22; Barnard Hewitt, "Uncle Tom and Uncle Sam: New Light from an Old Play," *Quarterly Journal of Speech*, XXXVII (1951), 63-70; "Last Days for Uncle Tom," *NYTM*, July 12, 1931, p. 18; Joe Laurie, Jr., "The Theatre's All-Time Hit," *AM*, LXI (1945), 469-72; Richard Moody, "Uncle Tom, the Theater, and Mrs. Stowe," *AH*, Vol. VI, No. 6, Oct. 1955, pp. 28-33, 102-3; Velona Pilcher, "The Variorum Stowe," *Theatre Arts Monthly*, X (1926), 226-39; Joseph P. Roppolo, "Uncle Tom in New Orleans: Three Lost Plays," *NEQ*, XXVII (1954), 213-26.

INDEX